The Shadow of a Crown

THE SHADOW
OF A CROWN

*The life story of
James II of England
and VII of Scotland*

Meriol Trevor

Constable · London

First published in Great Britain 1988
by Constable and Company Limited
10 Orange Street, London WC2H 7EG
Copyright © 1988 by Meriol Trevor
Set in Linotron Ehrhardt 11 pt by
Rowland Phototypesetting Limited
Bury St Edmunds, Suffolk
Printed in Great Britain by
St Edmundsbury Press Limited
Bury St Edmunds, Suffolk

British Library CIP data
Trevor, Meriol, 1919–
The shadow of a crown: the life story of
James II of England and VII of Scotland.
1. England, James II. King of England.
Biographies
I. Title
942.06′7′0924

ISBN 0 09 467850 2

To Mary O'Regan
in gratitude
for all her help and encouragement

Contents

I DUKE

II KING

Illustrations

Royal Portraits: Charles II, c.1680: By Edward Hawker (*National Portrait Gallery, London*)

Royal Portraits: James II, 1685: By Godfrey Kneller (*National Portrait Gallery, London*)

James as King, 1685: By Nicolas de Largillière (*National Maritime Museum, Greenwich*)

James in ordinary dress: By Anne Killigrew (*By gracious permission of Her Majesty the Queen*)

Catherine Sedley, Countess of Dorchester (*National Portrait Gallery, London*)

James FitzJames, Duke of Berwick (*The Earl of Rosebery and the Scottish National Portrait Gallery.*)

Prince James Francis Edward and Princess Louise Marie, children of James II and Maria of Modena, c.1695: By Nicolas de Largillière (*National Portrait Gallery, London*)

The Château of St Germain-en-Laye

James II and VII in his last exile at St Germains: By François de Troy (*Barrett-Lennard Collection: photo: the Courtauld Institute of Art*)

James Francis Edward in 1701 at the death of his father: By François de Troy (*Scottish National Portrait Gallery*)

Maria of Modena in widowhood: Artist unknown (*In the collection of The National Trust for Scotland and on display at the house of the Binns. Photo: Scottish National Portrait Gallery*)

Acknowledgement

I owe a special debt of gratitude to Helen Watson of the Scottish National Portrait Gallery for help in tracing many of the pictures used for illustrating this book.

I DUKE

February 1685

James Stuart, Duke of York, was dressing on the morning of Monday 2
February – Candlemas Day – when he was interrupted by the intrusion
of an agitated young man. Thomas Bruce (son and heir of the Earl of
Ailesbury) rushed into the Duke's Bedchamber to blurt out the
alarming news that the King had been seized with an apoplectic fit, just
as he was sitting down to be shaved. Bruce had caught him in his arms
as he fell.

The King had been put to bed and bled by a surgeon but he was
unconscious when Bruce left him. The Duke, completing his dressing
in haste, hurried off with him, one foot thrust into a shoe and the other
in a slipper, unnoticed in the stress of the moment.

To their great relief the King, when they stood each side of his bed,
showed signs of recovery; he was conscious again and tried to speak.
They began to hope that the fit would not after all prove fatal. In fact,
for a day or two, Charles seemed to improve and a bulletin was issued
pronouncing him out of danger. But then, perhaps as a result of the
severe measures taken by the physicians (purges, emetics and hot irons
applied to the head) he had a relapse and hope gradually faded that he
would recover.

The deathbed of King Charles II has been described by many who
were not present and by some who were, which makes for discrep-
ancies. One thing, however, is certain: Charles was reconciled to the
Catholic Church by Father Huddleston, an English Benedictine who
had helped to hide him from the victorious Parliamentarians after the
battle of Worcester in 1651.

It was James who, noticing that the King had not answered the suggestion of the Church of England bishops that he should take the sacrament, asked if he should send for a priest. 'To which the King immediately reply'd, For God's sake Brother doe, and pleas to lose no time; but then reflecting on the consequence added, But will you not expose yourself too much by doing it?' This account, taken from James's own memoirs, is given in the *Life* compiled in the early 1700s. 'Sir, though it cost me my life I will bring one to you,' was his answer.

The King's rooms were crowded with people but 'never a Catholick' among them; the Duke had to send a foreigner to fetch a priest and then had to clear the crowd away, though he asked two Protestant noblemen to stay, the Earl of Bath (son of the cavalier Sir Bevil Grenvile) and the Earl of Feversham (Louis Duras, a Huguenot nephew of Marshal Turenne, naturalized English after the Restoration). James thought it 'not fit he should be quite alone with his Majesty, considering the weak condition he was then in.'

Father Huddleston, wearing a surplice and wig like an Anglican cleric, came in; Charles made his confession and received absolution and communion, which he did with humility and thankfulness, repeating often, 'Mercy, sweet Jesus, mercy.' Bruce, when he next visited the King, not knowing the reason then, yet saw in him a serenity which had not been present before.

Charles died on the morning of Friday 6 February. He had asked for the curtains to be drawn back so that he might see the sunrise, and he was conscious to within an hour or two of his death, dying peacefully about noon.

His brother James was kneeling at the bedside in tears. All his life Charles had been there, the admired elder brother, and James, though he had sometimes had his differences with him, had always followed, served and obeyed him – except in one thing. He had refused to compromise in matters of conscience. After his conversion to the Catholic Church he had resisted every attempt to get him to conform, even superficially, to the established Church of England. Now, on his deathbed, Charles too had been reconciled, and he said to James, 'You have been a good brother to me.'

So the King died, in his fifty-fifth year.

James was the King.

A known Catholic he was to reign over a kingdom which had been Protestant for more than a century, where the Catholic religion was proscribed, mass illegal, priests liable to execution and laymen to heavy fines for refusing to attend the services of the Church of England. If King Charles had not dissolved Parliament in 1681 an Exclusion Bill might have been passed, cutting James out of the succession and banishing him from England for life. Yet Charles had remained true to the principle of heredity, refused to divorce his barren queen or to legitimize his favourite bastard son, the Duke of Monmouth, or to allow his brother's right to be set aside by Parliament.

So now James succeeded to the Crown of the three kingdoms of Great Britain and his accession to the throne, so problematic only a few years ago, went through without the least trouble or unrest in London or in the country.

1 King's Son

In the famous picture by Van Dyck of Charles I's three eldest children, the younger Charles dominates the scene, a big black-haired child in his golden satin suit, full of smiling self-confidence. Holding on to his arm is James, three years younger, still in his infant petticoats and with a baby's cap tied over his fair hair. Beside him stands Mary, like a neat pretty little woman; born in November 1631 she came between the two brothers.

James was born on 14 October 1633 in St James's Palace, to parents who loved each other, something rare in royal marriages at that period. It was not so at first; the serious fastidious young King and the lively little French Princess (youngest daughter of Henri IV) who was barely fourteen when they married in 1625, spent their first years together quarrelling. It was not till the magnificent Duke of Buckingham was assassinated in 1628 that Charles turned to Henrietta Maria and they became devoted to each other, as witnessed by the later letters of the King to his 'dear heart'.

After James came Elizabeth, born in 1635, then two little girls who died as infants. Henry was born in 1640; Henriette Anne, the last, in 1644 just as the tide of civil war turned against the King.

The children were established in St James's Palace, though much of their time was spent in the old palace at Richmond, rebuilt by Henry VII on the banks of the Thames. The princes were brought up with the murdered Buckingham's two sons, whom the King had almost adopted. George was a couple of years older than Charles, who grew up admiring his flamboyance and wit. No doubt they were at Whitehall on festive occasions and saw some of the famous masques devised by Inigo Jones in which the King and Queen took part – masques intended to display the ideals of monarchy. Charles's education was supervised by the Duke of Newcastle, master of the arts of horsemanship and chivalry. They learned religious faith and practice under the high Anglicanism of Archbishop Laud; the Queen was not allowed to influence their religous education. James was always trying to keep up with Charles; there is an engraving of him, aged seven or eight, playing tennis, with spectators watching round the court.

This ordered royal existence was suddenly interrupted when Charles was twelve and James not yet nine years old. The Prince of Wales was old enough to be sent to the House of Commons to plead for the Earl of Strafford's life; the bid failed and the King signed the act of attainder which sent his loyal minister to the scaffold. The King never forgave himself for that and his sons never forgot it.

In 1642 the King left London and took Charles with him when he escorted his Queen to Dover to take ship for Holland, where the Princess Mary already lived, married (at ten) to Prince William II of Orange. From Dover the King went north to York, taking his eldest son with him, but James, who had been taken to Hampton Court with the rest of the family in flight from the London mob, was sent back to St James's Palace, with his sister Elizabeth and the baby Henry, who was only two. He was not left there long. The King, fearing that his second son might be used as a hostage by Parliament, wrote to the Marquis of Hertford (Seymour) to bring the boy to him. Because Parliament had already forbidden the removal of the Duke of York, the flight had to be made secretly by night, the first of the many escapes of James's life. A few days after they joined the King the eight-year-old James was made a Knight of the Garter.

This was in April, and it was not until 22 August that the King actually raised his standard at Nottingham, though hostilities had really started long before, with Parliament taking measures against the King; the Earl of Essex had been made Captain General of the Parliamentary forces in July, with his headquarters at Northampton. Not until October did the two amateur armies face each other at Edgehill; James had passed his ninth birthday only a week or two before. He and Charles were allowed to ride with their father along the lines before battle, when the scarlet cornet (the royal standard) carried before the King, attracted artillery fire from the enemy.

When the infantry advanced, the King rode in the rear, his two sons still with him. But after the first encounters, when the King's standard bearer Sir Edmund Verney was killed and the standard itself captured, the King determined to go forward in person to rally his troops. He did not want to risk his sons' lives as well as his own but he found it impossible to persuade the proud noblemen to take them out of the battle. The Earl of Dorset swore he was not going to be called a coward for any king's sons in Christendom.

The King thereupon ordered a Guard of Gentlemen Pensioners armed with old-fashioned poleaxes, whose function was ceremonial rather than military, to take them up the hill. There they nearly ran into a troop of Parliamentarians. Charles shouted fiercely, 'I fear them not!' trying to turn his pony and draw his pistol. In this moment of danger an officer shot the man who was charging the Prince and he fell off his horse; whereupon a Gentleman Pensioner finished him off with his poleaxe. The others fled.

Charles and James were hustled to safety, ending up for the night at Edgecote, eight miles behind the lines. They did not see their father that night; he spent only a few hours resting in his coach. The battle decided nothing but the King's army remained in the field whereas Essex withdrew next day to Warwick. It had been a fine day; it was a cold night. More than a thousand Englishmen lay dead, killed by each other.

It was afterwards said that if the King had moved on directly to London he might have taken the city and ended the war at once. But he moved too slowly; Essex got back to London before him and he fell back on Oxford, which he decided to make his winter quarters. It was well into November when he made a splendid entry into the city, the men marching to pipe and drum, the two young princes once more riding with their father behind the royal standard, and the officers in their finest array. They were met and loyally greeted by the Mayor and some of the Heads of Houses (colleges) and the King took up residence in Christ Church.

Oxford was to be James's home for the rest of the war, which lasted longer than anybody had expected – four years. For a child the years between nine and thirteen are an age and by 1646 it must have seemed to James to have lasted for ever. He was supposed to continue his education and had four learned tutors besides those who taught him the military arts. He learned French and acquired a facility in writing which was to stand him in good stead as an indefatigable writer of letters and memoranda. He was musical and learned to play the guitar, now superseding the lute as the fashionable instrument.

Oxford was a strange place during the war, overrun with roistering cavaliers and too often with drunken fights and brawls. When the King was there the colleges were crammed with courtiers and their wives and daughters – the girls enjoying a much freer and more exciting life than they would have done in peace-time, turning the heads of the students with their pranks and antics.

The next spring James was allowed to accompany his father on the campaign to the west, when Prince Rupert took Bristol. But though Charles was then launched on an independent career in the southwest, James had to return to Oxford and pursue his studies. In July that year (1643) when he was approaching ten, his mother arrived with weapons from France. But she left Oxford in April 1644, pregnant with her last child, giving birth to Henriette Anne at Exeter in June; a month later she fled back to France.

By 1646 when the tide had turned against the King, James was twelve. The painter William Dobson was making a portrait of him, wearing his Garter sash, and George, but his face is still a child's, his large cloudy blue eyes looking wistfully out, lonely, left behind. The portrait was never finished because Oxford fell to the Parliamentary forces.

When that seemed inevitable the King took flight, riding out disguised as a servant, his long brown hair cut short and his neat beard hacked about. There had been talk of his taking James with him but in the end, to the boy's disappointment, he was left behind again.

The city of Oxford surrendered on 24 June to Sir Thomas Fairfax on terms which were not exorbitant. Prince Rupert and his brother Maurice were allowed to leave England and the English royalists were given the choice of going abroad or staying and compounding for their estates – paying a fine to Parliament. But there was no choice for James, Duke of York. He was a prisoner of state.

When the Parliament officers came to take charge of him they all, except Fairfax, kissed the Prince's hand, acknowledging his royalty. But only one, Lieutenant-General Oliver Cromwell, accorded him the full honour of kneeling to kiss his hand. This ironic fact James always remembered.

In spite of the ceremony, the boy was a prisoner and realized it when his Governor (Sir George Radcliffe) and household were dismissed, even the dwarf, of whom he was very fond. Nobody listened to his protests. However, his prison turned out to be his old home, St James's Palace, and his warder Algernon Percy, Earl of Northumberland, the actual Lord High Admiral of England, acting for James himself, who had been given that title at four years old. Percy, head of the most powerful family in the north, had sided with Parliament but he treated the royal children with courtesy and kindness, though they were not allowed to leave the confines of the palace and private garden.

At St James's were Elizabeth, the sister James had not seen for four years, and Henry, still a small child in petticoats. The three of them were painted with James, very much the growing boy now, his hair brown and his features developing towards their manhood cast, leaning against a pillar. Schemes were soon afoot to effect his escape but the first was discovered; he then fell ill of a 'long ague' which lasted into the spring of 1647.

At the beginning of summer King Charles, now a prisoner, was brought south and James was taken (under armed escort) to meet him at Maidenhead. Later the King was installed at Hampton Court and James was allowed to visit him frequently, two or three times a week, going and coming back always under armed guard. That autumn he reached the age of fourteen and in the portrait done of him at Hampton Court with the King, he looks like a young squire, with sword belt

[7]

and sword, as he hands a pen to his dark clad stiffly upright father.

James revered his father, so that these interviews at Hampton Court must have been fraught with emotion, even though he could not have foreseen that father's terrible end. But the King seemed to anticipate his own death, saying that it was not many steps from the prisons of kings to their graves – words James remembered all his life. The King adjured his second son to be faithful to his brother Charles and impressed upon him that it was his duty to escape from the hands of his Parliamentary captors, so that he could not be used by them against the King or in preference to his elder brother. The succession was fixed by God himself, strictly according to primogeniture.

The King himself escaped from Hampton Court that November but he was soon recaptured; it was only the beginning of further peregrinations and imprisonments, which were to end more than a year later with his trial and execution in January 1649.

In the winter of 1647–8 there was another abortive attempt to effect James's escape, which he seems to have partly organized himself, with the help of his barber Hill (appointed by Parliament). Unfortunately a letter James had written partly in cipher was found on Hill and there was a tremendous row. Commissioners came and interrogated the boy, threatened him with the Tower, but failed to get anything out of him. But he was made to promise not to receive any letters which had not first been seen by the Earl of Northumberland. He kept this promise, even refusing to take a secret letter from his mother, offered to him in the tennis court; Henrietta Maria was extremely annoyed to hear of it. But extra men had been employed to watch the young Duke, since the Earl had said he was no jailer and would not be held responsible if the boy escaped.

Nothing daunted, James began planning again; this time nothing was put in writing but his Master of Horse, George Howard, communicated with a certain Colonel Bamfield (or Bampfield) who was something of an adventurer but willing to undertake the dangerous task of smuggling the young Duke out of England. It all took so long that it was 20 April 1648 before the plan was put into effect. James himself had worked out how he might get away without being noticed. For a fortnight before the fixed date he organized games of hide-and-seek

[8]

with the Percy children in the hour of play they were allowed after their supper at seven. He knew all the corners and cupboards of the ancient rambling palace and was so good at hiding that often he was not found for more than half an hour and sometimes emerged triumphant when the seekers gave up in despair.

On the night of his escape James shut Elizabeth's little dog (which followed him everywhere) into her room, so that it would not give him away. Then, instead of hiding, he crept down the backstairs and into the garden. He had been given a key to the gate; it turned and he was able to slip outside, where Bamfield was waiting and a footman with a cloak and wig as a temporary disguise. It was dusk but not quite dark and they had to walk at an ordinary pace so as not to attract attention till they reached the hired hackney coach; then they drove to the Strand and walked down a narrow lane to the Ivy Bridge jetty and hired a boat to row them downstream to London Bridge.

They landed above the bridge and soon Mistress Anne Murray (daughter of a Provost of Eton who had once been a tutor to the King) was disguising James in girl's clothes. She had taken his measurements when visiting the palace and told him that the tailor said he had never known a woman so short with such a large waist. It made James laugh but he urged her, 'Quickly, quickly – dress me!' She declared he looked a pretty girl but tried to drill him in the necessary deportment. By then it was after ten and there was no time for the supper she had got him, so she gave him a 'Wood-street cake' which she knew he liked, to take with him. This is all from James's memoirs.

Bamfield took him down river by barge. Sitting in the little cabin, where there was a candle on the table, James, feeling his stockings were coming down, put his foot on the table to give them a most unmaidenly hitch. The next moment the bargemaster came in, suspicious and alarmed; he had looked through a chink and seen his passenger's unconventional behaviour. To Bamfield's horror James, who thought the man had an honest face, told him straight out that he was the Duke of York and was trying to escape abroad. He had guessed right; the bargemaster was a royalist at heart and not only agreed to take them on but put out all the lights so as to slide quietly past the guard-boats in the dark.

Thus they reached Tilbury safely and the 70-ton pink, a small sailing vessel, where three gentlemen were waiting for the Duke. Owen, the friendly bargemaster, decided to go with them to Holland. The ship sailed at dawn and in spite of a scare on the way made safe landfall at Middelburg. When they went to an inn for the night the hostess was shocked that the young woman, alone in a party of men, refused to allow any maids to come up and put her to bed. For a few more days James had to appear as a girl, sending Bamfield to the Hague with letters to his sister Mary and an urgent request for male attire.

Mary came herself to fetch him to the palace of Honslaerdyke. She had not seen James for years and Charles was always her favourite brother but all the children of the King were loyally fond of one another. So she welcomed James to the neat, clean and beautifully furnished Dutch Palace, now her home. He had escaped from beleaguered Britain; he was free.

2 Youth in Exile

When James, aged fourteen and dressed as a girl, arrived in Holland in the spring of 1648, he had no idea that it would be twelve years before he saw England again. During that time he grew from boyhood to manhood and entered the profession of arms as a volunteer in the French royal forces. For these formative years virtually everything must come from his own memoirs, incorporated in the first part of the *Life* compiled at St Germains after his death in 1701. Other remains of this period naturally concern his brother Charles. But the memoirs provide the first evidence for James's character and style, forthright, colloquial, with occasional touches of ironical humour.

Not long after James's arrival some English ships, their officers disaffected from Parliament, put into Dutch harbour and the youthful Duke, as Lord High Admiral, proudly went abòard *The Constant Reformation* to take possession. He was not left long in this first naval command for Charles, coming back from Paris, took charge himself. Charles was now eighteen, a dark young man with a moustache, keen for action. He sailed his ships out but there was renewed dissension and some deserted. After an autumnal bout of unaccustomed illness Charles turned over his little fleet to his Palatine cousins, Rupert and Maurice, and off they went, first to Ireland and then to years of buccaneering life in southern seas.

In the winter at the beginning of 1649 Queen Henrietta Maria summoned James to Paris and then had to send hastily to halt him at Cambrai because civil disorders had broken out in the French capital. Stranded and penniless, James was taken in by the Benedictine monks of Saint-Amand till a pass arrived which enabled him to complete his journey.

Only a few days after he reached his mother, who was then living in the palace of the Louvre, they received the dreadful news of the King's execution. The unbelievable had happened: a crowned and anointed king had been put to death by his own people.

Not all his people; the so-called trial had been a solemn farce, conducted by the remnant of a House of Commons, purged, picked and packed to condemn the King for making war on his own people – a court whose authority he refused to recognize. But Cromwell and the Army had decided the King must go and so he had walked out of the Banqueting House, scene of so many royal masques, to the death which, seen as a martyrdom, was to redeem the cause of kingship in the time to come.

But in the cold winter of 1649, to his fifteen-year-old son, it could only be tragedy, the ultimate loss. And now his brother Charles was King, king without a kingdom.

In the summer Charles came to Paris and planned to go to Ireland where the Earl of Ormonde was holding out for the royalists. But in August came the news that Ormonde had been defeated at Rathmines. Charles decided to go to Jersey, which had sheltered him before when he was escaping from England and he allowed his brother, who now had his own household again (with Sir George Radclyffe once more his Governor) to accompany him. From there they could go to Ireland if the situation improved. But the devastation after Cromwell's victories in that country made any such expedition impossible. Instead, Charles decided to take up an offer from Scotland and left Jersey in February of the next year, 1650.

James did not go with him. Apart from the fact that he was only just sixteen, he had vehemently opposed the Scottish scheme, unable to see how Charles could swear to the Covenant and thus repudiate everything their father had stood for. James stayed in Jersey (as nominal governor) till September, when a letter from his brother ordered him back to Paris. However, as he had no wish to stay under the tutelage of his mother, he was easily persuaded by Radclyffe to go to Brussels, hoping to get help from the Duke of Lorraine – not then part of France.

It was in Brussels, in the autumn of 1650, that James heard the sad news of the death of his sister Elizabeth, still a prisoner of Parliament. She was only fifteen and most of her short life had been spent separated from the people she loved best, culminating in the parting from her dearly loved father the day before his execution. Elizabeth was nearest to James in the family; they had shared nearly two years as prisoners of state and both, young as they were, had deep religious feeling. It was a great loss to James.

Bad news came too from Scotland. The forces fighting for the King had been defeated at Dunbar on 3 September by the all-conquering Cromwell.

Since the Duke of Lorraine, though he gave the young English prince some much-needed ready money, did not offer more permanent support, James wrote to his sister Mary requesting refuge in Holland, but she, prompted by their mother, who wanted James back in Paris, refused.

James was saved from an ignominious return to his mother by the receipt of a tenth of the prize money (as Lord Admiral) from the capture of some Parliament ships by frigates from Jersey. Then came the unexpectedly sudden death of Mary's husband and on 4 November the birth of her son, the third William of Orange. In mid-December James was lent his aunt's house at Rhenen in the provice of Utrecht – the exiled Elizabeth of Bohemia's property – where he spent Christmas. In January 1651 Henrietta Maria relented and James was allowed to join his widowed sister Mary at the Hague. But after some months a letter from Charles ordered him to Paris, where he obediently proceeded in June.

He was there in September when the news of the King's defeat at Worcester reached him and for six interminable weeks there was no news of Charles at all – nothing till he landed at Fécamp near Le Havre.

Overjoyed, James travelled to meet him at Magny, between Paris and Rouen, and went back with him to the French capital, and their mother.

Charles, brown-faced and with his black hair cropped short, was so glad to have escaped capture that in spite of his defeat he was in good spirits and enjoyed telling the tale of his peregrinations as a fugitive in his own land, with a price on his head – though he could not then give the names of the loyal people who had helped him, or of the houses where they had hidden him. Spies were everywhere, even in France, reporting back to Cromwell.

The winter that followed was a hard one for the exiles. All prospects for a restoration of the monarchy seemed at an end. Cromwell, backed by his invincible Ironsides, was supreme in the new republic, the Commonwealth. Across the channel few believed in a royal future for Charles II and Stuart stock fell very low.

Henrietta Maria's main idea was to make good French marriages for her sons. She worked hard to effect one for Charles with her niece, Mademoiselle d'Orléans, the greatest heiress in France – as the only child of Louis XIII's brother Gaston. But Mademoiselle, though not ill-disposed to her English cousin (younger than herself) had conceived a grander destiny – to marry her other cousin, the young King Louis XIV. As Louis was then only about thirteen (five years younger than James) this was somewhat premature, but to hope to be the consort of a reigning sovereign seemed a better prospect than to marry an exiled one with no visible means of regaining his throne.

As a second string to her bow Henrietta Maria tried to make a match for James with Marie, daughter of the Duc de Longueville and the next richest heiress in France after the royal Mademoiselle.

The Duke of York was now eighteen and had grown up to be a good-looking young man, tall and lean but much stronger in build than his boyhood had suggested. His rather long nose was balanced by a firm chin and a wide full-lipped mouth; his fine chestnut brown hair was thick and grew to his shoulders in cavalier style. He spoke French well, much better than Charles, and Mademoiselle, describing him in her memoirs, makes no mention of the stammer which, like his father's before him, was worse at some times than others.

James was by no means averse to marrying Mademoiselle de Longueville, nor she to him, but the French Queen Mother and her

[13]

minister Cardinal Mazarin had no intention of letting the second richest heiress in France pour her family's resources into the bottomless maw of the English royal exiles. They absolutely vetoed the marriage.

James at once decided that he could not spend his youth hanging about the French court and he soon succeeded in getting his brother's permission to volunteer for the King of France's army. France was now in the midst of civil war, of a different kind from the English since it was a quarrel between the Princes of the Blood and the government of Mazarin and the Queen Mother. It might be called the backlash from Cardinal Richelieu's policy of weakening the nobles to increase the power of the King's centralized government. The result was by no means a foregone conclusion in favour of the absolute monarchy which Louis XIV was to develop.

The commander of the royal forces was the Huguenot Henri de la Tour d'Auvergne, Vicomte de Turenne, and it was to him that the Duke of York was to offer his services. But first he had to equip himself and that cost money. In the exiled court, as James dryly remarked in the memoirs, 'Nothing was so rare as money.' In the end he borrowed 300 pistoles from a Gascon moneylender (which he scrupulously repaid later); even so, he was not able to afford an extra horse for himself. His personal equipment was carried on two mules and his household was reduced to Sir John Berkeley (who had replaced Sir George Radclyffe) and Colonel Worden, plus a few servants and grooms.

The French court was temporarily in exile itself, at Angers, and Paris was under the command of Duc d'Orléans, who had thrown in his lot with the Frondeurs against Mazarin. So James had to make his departure discreetly, going off with Charles to the castle of Saint-Germain, ostensibly for the hunting, and leaving from there towards the end of April 1652, for Charenton, at the confluence of the Marne and the Seine, where they spent the night.

Next day they travelled south for about twenty miles, intending to stop at Corbeil where there was a bridge across the Seine. But on the outskirts they ran into several companies of the King's Guards, who said that the gates had been shut against them, showing that Corbeil, professing to be neutral, was actually inclining towards the party of the princes.

The Duke of York, still only eighteen and not yet commissioned, immediately protested; Corbeil was so near Paris that Marshal Turenne would certainly need to take it when he advanced on the capital. James suggested that the Guards should wait while he attempted to gain entrance for his own party first. So they rode up to the gates and James, announcing his name and rank (brother to the King of England), requested an interview with the town's magistrates. After some discussion he was told he could enter if he came alone and on foot. In spite of horrified protest from Sir John Berkeley James insisted on going. Once inside he represented the danger the town would run when Marshal Turenne came and besieged it. The magistrates were persuaded, the gates were opened and the French Guards admitted as well as the Duke's English party.

The commanding officer sent a message to Mazarin, who was then about ten miles away at Melun, and he immediately moved the fugitive royal court to Corbeil, which was a stronger town. The Duke of York was rewarded for his mediation with another horse (badly needed), two mules and some money, which last was very necessary as he had scarcely 20 pistoles left of the 300 he had borrowed from Gautier the Gascon. It was a good start to his venture into his chosen career of arms.

James was a born soldier and eager to learn all he could from Turenne, for whom he felt an admiration which only increased with time. For his part, the Marshal took to the young Englishman at once, kept him close to himself and was soon calling him 'my eyes' – since his own were short-sighted. He was an active commander, personally spying out the land in advance of an engagement, laying his plans and leading his troops into action.

The whole summer of 1652 was spent in the country outside Paris, which was the key to success on either side. Small fortified towns were won and lost, armies marched about, sometimes at night. Turenne was a master of surprise – he needed to be, as the royal army was usually outnumbered by the enemy, since the Prince de Condé had called Spanish forces to his aid.

When autumn set in these Spanish troops withdrew to winter quarters, whereupon Turenne took the initiative, prolonging the campaign in spite of the worsening weather. Some frightful winter marches in freezing cold had to be endured before the campaign at last ended, fairly successfully, in the February of 1653, when the Duke of York went back to Paris on leave.

He did not have long to amuse himself there because in early spring he joined Turenne for the next campaign and did so well that in the following year (1654) the Marshal promoted him to the rank of Lieutenant-General, the youngest in the royal army. He was just twenty-one.

Although James himself described these campaigns in his memoirs the modern reader can follow them most easily under the guidance of Major Jock Haswell in his book *James II, Soldier and Sailor,* for he explains the methods of warfare and weapons used in the seventeenth century and, with sketch maps, the course of Turenne's campaigns. Being a soldier himself he brings out clearly these experiences of James's formative years, in which his character developed, forthright but not boastful, practical and cool-headed, not risking his men against odds but ready to seize an opportunity when it offered, always keeping in mind Turenne's objectives, so that on several occasions he was able to bring in his squadrons where they were most needed.

In 1654 Mazarin made a treaty with the *de facto* ruler of England, Oliver Cromwell, and as part of it the young King Charles had to leave France. His brother was not mentioned and continued his career in the French royalist army for a further campaign in 1655. In the winter he was back in Paris and in February 1656 he went to Cambrai to meet his sister, who was coming to visit their mother, then living at the Palais Royale. In Mary's train as a Maid of Honour came Anne Hyde, daughter of Charles's Chancellor in exile, Sir Edward Hyde. James recorded that this was the first time he met Anne, whom he was to marry. Evidently she made a strong impression on him; perhaps he did on her, a tall young prince, already a successful soldier.

Mazarin was anxious to retain the services of the Duke of York and the Irish regiments; so long as he did not go to the Flanders front (where Charles was now finding support from the Spaniards) he could keep his rank and salary and was offered a command in Savoy, where a French aunt was married to the ruling Duke. His mother approved; so did Turenne, but when James wrote to Charles for permission, his brother not only refused it but ordered him to join him at Bruges at once.

Disappointed, James nevertheless made haste to obey, partly because he had heard that 'strange stories' were being told about him to the King – for instance, how he was sending 'one Tuke' to England, to treat privately. James was indignant; he had never attempted secret negotiations on his own or even tried to get a share of the money sent by 'the well-affected' out of England for the King's needs. Charles had also suggested he left Sir John Berkeley in Paris to complete any outstanding business; James had cleared up everything already and was determined to take Sir John with him, knowing that the trouble made with the King arose from suspicions of Sir John nursed by Sir Henry Bennet, who though officially the Duke's Secretary, spent more time with the King.

It was a quarrel between factions among the exiles: Bennet was pro-Spanish, Berkeley pro-French. Bennet, a cavalier who wore a black patch on his nose where he had sustained a wound, as a reminder to all of his loyal gallantry, was to become, as Lord Arlington, one of Charles's principal ministers, but at this time he was of no greater importance than Sir John Berkeley, who had also fought in the Civil War. Berkeley was a friend of Lord Jermyn's, who managed Henrietta Maria's affairs and had managed the King's till he had been put aside in favour of Sir Edward Hyde. His nephew, Charles Berkeley, was one of James's best friends at this time and with Jermyn's nephew Harry (later Lord Dover) was ranged against Sir Henry Bennet and Harry Killigrew – all members of the Duke's household. James remarks that he had tried to keep out of these quarrels, which it was fairly easy to do while he was so often away on campaign, but now he was going to the centre of things, Charles's exiled court.

On the way to Bruges James records an incident at Clermont, where he intended to change horses. He was warned that Lockhart, Cromwell's Ambassador to France, was staying at the post house, the best inn in town. It would be improper to insult him on French territory but impossible to show respect to this representative of the rebels who had murdered his father. James therefore had his coach draw up at the gates in full view of Cromwell's ambassador who was standing in the window with his retinue. 'His hatt was off,' James recorded, 'and for that reason

[17]

all the rest of them stood uncover'd; tis probable he chuse to have it so, thereby to avoid the putting off on the one hand and to shun censure on the other, in case he should not uncover.' Hat etiquette was important in seventeenth-century Europe; nobody must keep on his hat (which otherwise was stuck to indoors as well as out) in the presence of royalty.

But James stayed only long enough 'to gett on his boots, which he had in the coach,' and then mounted his horse and rode straight on, avoiding confrontation but in a manner which conveyed his defiance of the present régime in England.

A few days later he reached Bruges, the King and the Duke of Gloucester coming out as far as Furnes to meet him. Henry, Duke of Gloucester, had been allowed to join his mother in France in 1653 (when he was thirteen) where she had tried to make him a Catholic and a cardinal. Charles had called on James to see that Henry remained a Protestant and James had succeeded. Eventually Henry had been allowed to join Charles; he was now sixteen.

James was at once caught up in the French–Spanish conflict among the exiles. Charles wanted him to take service with the Spaniards and the Prince de Condé; Lord Jermyn wrote from Paris to urge him not to do so. James thought this was only because Mazarin wished to keep the Irish regiments who would otherwise follow him to Flanders and decided to obey his King and forgo his French pension. In spite of this Sir John Berkeley's enemies persisted in demanding his dismissal, which James felt unjustified. When Princess Mary arrived at the end of November, on her way home from Paris, she took James's part in this domestic conflict.

Then on Christmas Eve Lord Muskerry told the Duke that an oath of loyalty to Spain was being demanded on enlistment. James was scandalized. Such an oath (not demanded of Condé and Lorraine) might prejudice his taking part in a future expedition to restore Charles to the throne. Meeting the Earl of Bristol (George Digby, born 1612) James mentioned the oath, whereupon Bristol 'flew into a high passion' against the traitor who had told him of it – he obviously thought it was Sir John Berkeley.

James recorded: 'The Earle of Bristol spoke so loud that his Majesty who was in the same room and at not great distance, heard all he said; and coming to the Duke, he took part with the Earle of Bristol,' and pressed him to name the culprit. James refused, since 'My lord Bristol had accused him of high treason', and he gave his word it was *not* Sir John. Bristol then apologized.

But next day Bristol came and told him the King had ordered Berkeley's dismissal. This put James in a fix; either he must disobey the King or disgrace an innocent man. His sister Mary, much distressed at the quarrel between her brothers, still supported James. Charles had suggested that Sir John might be sent off to Holland as if on a temporary holiday and James decided to appear to accept this solution but actually arranged to follow himself. So in January 1657 Berkeley left Bruges with orders to wait for the Duke at Flushing. Two or three days later James 'called up his brother the Duke of Gloucester to go out a shooting'. His sister caused him some alarm by sending to ask him to speak to her first. 'And had not the room been somewhat dark (she being in bed) she could not but have taken notice of the disorder in which he was when he first enter'd her chamber and by it have suspected his design.' But after all she only wanted him to intervene to prevent two of their servants fighting.

When he got to Sluys, James sent Henry back, saying he was going to meet someone from England and might be late returning. But in fact he went on to Flushing, picked up Sir John and proceeded to Middelburg. He was intending to go back to France by way of Germany, 'but it then happening to freeze very hard he was forced to take his way by Tervere.' There Sir John proposed to take a French ship but Charles Berkeley opposed it, from the danger of meeting English ships on the way. So they went on, making for Helvoet Sluys, the final stage by open boat – 'the last that ventur'd over, the water being then almost chock'd up with yce and the hazard was thought to be so great that all the people of the town came out and stood upon the shore to see them go.' But they made it, and reached Brill. Sir John was sent to the Hague to ask permission to stay privately in the country for a few days.

James, having demonstrated his independence, now decided to write to the King to try to effect a reconciliation, and while waiting for a reply he stayed in various castles of the House of Orange and went to see the festivities of a local wedding. Charles sent his errant brother a message by the Marquess of Ormonde. Sir John Berkeley must stay a month in Holland but after that he could return to his old post with the Duke.

[19]

'Things past should be forgotten.' So everything was satisfactorily settled.

When James heard how disrespectfully Killigrew had spoken of him in his absence, he dismissed him, and Sir Henry Bennet too. Charles soon afterwards sent Bennet as his envoy to Spain, a post much more congenial to him, since he spoke Spanish fluently and liked the country. James now had none in his household who 'were not absolutely his own' and the King even made Sir John a peer – Lord Berkeley of Stratton, the scene of one of his civil war successes.

The Princess Royal returned to Holland and the King and his court moved to Brussels, where James discovered that Don John, the Spanish commander, had said none of the things Lord Bristol had said he did. Bristol had flattered Don John (a royal bastard, like the more famous Don John of Austria in an earlier generation) and as he was 'somewhat curious in astrology' had 'cast his nativity and was talking perpetually to him of Crowns and Sceptors'.

But the oath stood. James believed that if any opposition had been made Don John would have dropped it, but as none was, it was insisted on. So James became a commander in the Spanish forces on the same side as the Prince de Condé and against his beloved Marshal de Turenne. This did not prevent his soon becoming acceptable to Don John and especially to Condé, who praised his courage above anyone's who had served with him. He also sympathized with James's dissatisfaction with the Spaniards, none of whom would act in even small operations without orders from Don John. Condé told James that he would see 'more and grosser faults committed by them before the end of that Campagne'.

Unlike Turenne, the Spanish commanders set out *after* their armies and 'as for Don John, he for the most part went directly to bed, how early so ever it were, when he came to his quarters; he likewise sup'd in bed and rose not till next morning.' James describes the Spanish generals, before the siege of Ardres, going up on a tower where they 'viewed the Town with a perspective glass' and decided on tactics without further information. The Prince de Condé and the Duke of York went out themselves to take a nearer view of the defences.

One day James was out on patrol before Dunkirk when a party of Frenchmen, as he says, 'fir'd at me with their fusils which they carryd on horseback before them'. But then they caught sight of 'a great greyhound' he had had with him in France and called out to know if the Duke of York was there. 'I turning about at the same time, they immediately cry'd out, *Sur parole*, desiring they might speak with me.' They all alighted and the French officers crowded round and stayed talking for an hour, till Turenne sent to recall them. It shows how popular James had been in the French army.

After this Reynolds, Cromwell's commander on the French side, sent to beg an interview, which Charles told his brother to grant. Reynolds called him 'your highness' and was so respectful that James said, 'I answered as obligingly as I could.' It was an indication that even Cromwell's men had hankerings after the monarchy.

James had to stay with the army, seeing them into winter quarters, till New Year's Day 1658. He made no longer stay in Brussels but went to his sister at Breda, where Henry was recovering from an ague caught while campaigning with his brother. In mid-February they 'went all three together to Antwerp, there to meet his Majesty'. Here the Earl of Bristol was busily intriguing as usual to the Duke's disadvantage, but James, by remaining passive and saying as little as possible, weathered the crisis, which was resolved by Condé and put an end to Bristol's credit with Don John, to the Duke's relief.

In the spring the campaign started badly with the Spaniards failing to fortify Dunkirk, which James was sure (rightly) would be the first object of the French and Cromwell. When they had drawn up their lines on the dunes James was the first of the generals to ride out at 5 a.m. to observe the enemy's camp. There he saw all the principal regiments, whose colours he knew well, marching out with horses and cannon, and the English contingent, recognizable by their red coats.

Turning for his own camp he met Don John who asked what he thought were the intentions of the French. James said positively that they were drawing out to give battle. 'Which he, seeming not to believe, said, their design was only to drive in our horse guards.' That was too much for James, who retorted that it was not the custom of the French to ride out in such force merely to drive off some horse guards.

At that moment the Prince de Condé came up and gave the same account; he then asked the young Duke of Gloucester if he had ever seen a battle. 'Who, telling him he had not: the Prince assured him that within half an hour he should behold one.' The point of this story (much embroidered down the ages) was that Condé endorsed James's view (dismissed by Don John) that the French intended battle, and very soon too.

In the course of the battle of the dunes James, with his own English-Irish regiment, had to charge the Cromwellian English. Typically, he is full of praise for their courage; to him English soldiers, whichever side they were fighting on, were quite simply the best. The Cromwellians fought so well they beat the royalists and James himself was nearly unhorsed, saving himself by giving his assailant 'a stroke with my sword over the face which layd him along upon the ground'. After several times reforming and charging again the Duke, finding the Spaniards routed, had to retire; by then he had only about twenty horse with him, which he says saved him, because they were enough to deal with small groups of the enemy but not so many as to tempt larger units to attack them. After the rout the Spanish forces fell back on Furnes and Turenne returned to the siege of Dunkirk which surrendered within a few days.

At Furnes the Duke of York played a crucial part in the council of war, for he was the only one who dared to question Don John's proposal to hold the line of the canal, which James felt was impossible. He suggested instead that the army should be divided up to hold various key towns, thus preventing Turenne from sweeping through the whole country. And this was the course followed. 'When coming from this Junto,' writes James, 'the Prince of Condé asked me why I would venture to contradict Don John, as I had done. To which I answer'd him, Because I had no desire to be forced to run again, as we had done so lately at Dunkirk.'

James was posted to Nieukirk with the Marquis of Caracena and the rest of the summer passed for him in small skirmishes of no importance. Then, suddenly in September, he heard 'the welcome news of Cromwell's death'. He had died on the third of that month, anniversary of his greatest victories.

James immediately got his release from Don John and went straight to Brussels. Because of the uncertainties of the King's affairs he could not get back to the army before it went into winter quarters, so that saw the end of his service with Spain. He went to his sister at Breda and stayed there some time.

Cromwell's son Richard succeeded him as Protector as easily as a prince of Wales a king, but he had not the character or personal authority to keep together the sects and factions of the Commonwealth or to control the army, and the government of England was soon in a state of disintegration. This gave the royalists their chance and a grand plot for concerted risings in different parts of the kingdom was laid by the secret organization called in the memoirs The Select Knot. The date was fixed for 1 August 1659 and by that time the King and the Duke were ready to cross the Channel. But then Sir Richard Willis sent notice that the date must be put off ten days. Willis was in fact a double agent and had changed the date to cause confusion, but unaware that Sir George Booth (made Baron Delamere in 1661) was leading the rising in Cheshire he had not told him, so Booth rose on 1 August, according to the original plan.

News of this came while James was paying a visit to his sister; he rushed back to Brussels to find Charles had already left for Calais, leaving a message for his brother to follow him. (The Duke of Gloucester was to stay in Brussels.) James 'made no longer stay than just to put on his disguise, in which he was resolved to go to England'. He took only Charles Berkeley and a trumpeter, and travelled day and night till he overtook the King at St Omers.

Charles sent him to Boulogne, went to Calais himself, heard that only Booth was rising and decided it was not convenient for them to venture overseas yet. He would go along the coast towards Dieppe and if he heard better news would cross to the West. The Duke of York was to 'hover' where he was till further orders.

So Charles went off on what turned into a secret journey to Spain where, at Fontarabie, a conference was in progress between the French and the Spanish with a view to a peace treaty. He never told James anything of his intentions which left him in a very awkward position, not knowing where the King was or what he ought to be doing himself.

Presently he paid a visit to Calais where he narrowly escaped capture; somebody recognized him and reported him to the Governor, who shut the gates and ordered a hunt for him. Although the gates were opened for an hour in the evening, James suspected a trap and decided to spend the night at an inn. Between twelve and one at night there was 'a hott alarm' at his lodging; he was

> waken'd with a great knocking and bouncing at the door of the Inne, and going to the window he heard, as he thought, the noise of Soldiers: neither was he mistaken in that opinion, for so they were: But their business was not to search for the Duke, it was only to bring home the master of the house, who was dead drunk and brought home betwixt four of them.

Next morning he got safely away to Boulogne where he heard that Turenne wanted to see the King about his affairs. A chase failed to catch up with Charles and so James decided to go to Turenne himself. The Marshal was at Amiens and he made a fantastic offer of men, arms, provisions and vessels to convey them to England. To finance this he would use his own credit and pawn his plate. And it was done, not at the orders of the Cardinal, who was at the conference, but simply out of his kindness for the Duke and his family.

James 'accepted this noble offer with great joy' and immediately began to make preparations and lay plans; he decided to land at Rye and even devised his initial strategy after landing. Turenne had given him a letter to the Governor of Boulogne to supply vessels, his nephews were to go with the Duke as volunteers, and everything was fixed for embarkation at Etapes when news came from England of Booth's defeat by General Lambert.

The Duke went at once to Turenne, who was now at Montreuil, but to his great disappointment the Marshal advised him not to go over to England now but wait for a more favourable opportunity. In vain James pressed him, saying the King might even now be in the West and in need of help, but Turenne remained firm. The Duke ought to return to Flanders and await developments. Then the good man, knowing that James as usual was in want of money, lent him 300 pistoles and gave him a pass.

So that was the end of the grand design for the return of the King and no one then knew that before a year was out he would be home again, not by force of arms but by invitation from the crumbling government of the Commonwealth.

3 Miraculous Restoration

It was in that disillusioned time towards the end of the year 1659 that James gave Anne Hyde a promise of marriage and their love was consummated in secret.

Anne was the eldest child and only daughter of Sir Edward Hyde; born in 1637 she was only twelve when she crossed the channel into exile with her parents. She was now twenty-two; James was just twenty-six. She was not considered a beauty, but her face, more heart-shaped than the fashionable oval, shows charm as well as a lively intelligence.

The account in the *Life*, taken from James's memoirs, relates: 'It happen'd that after some conversation together, the Duke fell in love with her, she having witt and other qualitys capable of surprising a heart less inclinable to the Sexe then (than) was that of his Royall Highness in the first warmth of his youth.' Conversation in those days implied social acquaintance and after he had to leave France James was always going to stay with his sister Mary; Anne may have been the reason for those frequent visits.

Unlike Charles, James was not credited with known mistresses in his youth, so that until he met Anne it is probable that he only had casual sexual encounters with women, who would have been of a different social class. Although Anne Hyde was not considered an equal for a royal prince, she was certainly an equal for James in terms of culture, education and manners; and throughout their eleven-year marriage he was to treat her as one, consulting her on political and religious issues. Anne was sincerely religious, brought up in the same high Caroline tradition of the Church of England as James; it is unlikely that she would have consented to be his mistress without the solemn promise of marriage.

Because the Restoration took them by surprise only a few months later, this promise appeared to outsiders as an ambitious trick on her part and on James's a foolish yielding to persuasion on the promptings

[25]

of desire. But at the time there must have seemed little reason why they should not marry. Now that the rising had failed and the French and Spanish were in the process of making peace, it did not look as if there was any chance of the Stuarts getting back to England. James was making a successful career for himself as a soldier of fortune and just after Christmas he received a dazzling offer from the Spaniards of a military command in their war against Portugal, as their High Admiral, with the title of Principe del Mar, rarely conferred on any but members of the royal house of Spain, with a right to a fifth of all prizes.

Charles, who had returned from his unsuccessful secret journey to the peace conference with little hope of a return to England, gave his permission and James planned to take up his new command in the spring. He could perfectly well have taken Anne to Spain as his wife. It was just about this time, in January 1660, that she conceived their first child.

And then, suddenly, General Monck's negotiations began for the restoration of the monarchy and in a few months the whole future had changed, for James as well as for his brother. 'And when the motion was once begun,' the memoirs relate, 'it went on so fast, that his Majesty was almost in his own country, before those abroad, especially the Spaniards, would beleeve there was any Revolution towards it.' James illustrates this by telling how the Marquis of Caracena urged Charles to come back to Brussels to meet some 'important persons from England'. James, sent to investigate, 'found it was only Col. Bampfield who was come over with some ayry propositions from Scott and some of that party'. (Bamfield continued to be a minor nuisance for years to come.) James hurried back to Breda and all the bustle of embarkation.

Here he came for the first time within the view of Samuel Pepys, whose diary gives such a vivid picture of life in the sixteen-sixties. Pepys, born in February 1633, was only six months older than James. As a boy he had been among the London crowd at the execution of Charles I and had even cheered that revolutionary event. But like so many other English people he was now heartily sick of the Commonwealth and the Rump Parliament. 'Boys do now cry "Kiss my Parliament!" instead of "Kiss my arse!"' he had noted in February, 'so great and general a contempt is the Rump come to among all men, good and bad.'

[26]

Pepys's patron was Edward Mountagu (Montagu), a relative higher up the social scale, who had been a Cromwellian general and was now a senior Admiral; and while Pepys held a post as a clerk in the Exchequer, he was also Mountagu's secretary and as such accompanied him to Holland to fetch the King home.

The Duke of York came on board the *Naseby* to salutes of guns, with his brother the Duke of Gloucester; both seemed very fine gentlemen to Pepys, who characteristically noticed that York was in yellow trimmings, Gloucester in grey and red. This was the time of that fussy fashion of decorating the open-kneed breeches, like long shorts, with multiple loops of ribbons round the waistband and in knots at the sides of the knees; similar ribbons bedizened the sleeves of the short doublet. Luckily this ugly fashion was shortlived; presumably it expressed the younger generation's determination to break free of the earnest and idealistic attitudes of their fathers.

Pepys recorded that 'upon the Quarter Deck table under the awning the Duke of Yorke and my Lord (Mountagu), Mr Coventry and I spent an hour at allotting to every ship their service in their return to England.' James, as Lord High Admiral, was determined to make that office a real one. A first necessity was to change the name of the ship; *Naseby*, commemorating the greatest royalist defeat, was rechristened the *Royal Charles*, and some lesser vessels were discreetly royalized too.

When the King came on board Pepys was amazed at the way he went 'walking here and there, up and down (quite contrary to what I thought him to have been) very active and stirring.' Commonwealth propaganda had presented the exiled King as a lazy profligate. Meanwhile, the Duke of York, when he met Pepys again, not only remembered his name but promised him future favour, thus inaugurating a lifetime's cooperation in the service of the Royal Navy.

It was on his thirtieth birthday, 29 May 1660, that the King and his two brothers rode through the City of London to the palace of Whitehall. This triumphal procession was watched by John Evelyn, the other great diarist of the age, thirteen years older than Pepys and a very different sort of man, though they became friends and fellow members of the Royal Society. Because Evelyn outlived everybody and kept his diary till the end (whereas Pepys had to give up his in 1669) his journalizing is indispensable to the history of his times.

[27]

'This day came in his Majestie *Charles* the 2d to London,' Evelyn recorded,

> after a sad and long Exile and Calamitous Suffering, both of the King and the Church . . . with a Triumph of above 20,000 horse and foote, brandishing their swords and shouting with unexpressable joy: The wayes straw'd with flowers, the bells ringing, the streetes hung with Tapissary, fountaines running with wine: the Major (Mayor), Aldermen, all the Companies in their liveries, Chaines of Gold, banners; Lords and Nobles, Cloth of Silver, gold and vellvet every body clad in, the windoes and balconies all set with Ladys, Trumpets, Musick, and myriads of people flocking the streets . . . I stood in the strand and beheld it, and blessed God. . . .

.   The excitement continued for days. Evelyn recorded on 4 June the infinite concourse of people at Whitehall, and the King gave free access to all. Whitehall Palace was a rambling collection of buildings alongside the Thames, with a road running through the middle; it was the seat of government as well as the King's main residence and all the ministers and court officials had lodgings there – sets of rooms in one building or another. The public were freely admitted to the galleries to gaze at pictures and passing celebrities, and at the King himself, for they could go into the great dining hall, lean on the balustrade at one end and watch the King dine in public (hat on) served by noblemen on bended knee. There were guards stationed at the entrances but everyone was free to come and go, provided they behaved decently.

Evelyn, who had met the royal brothers in Paris when travelling abroad, was received graciously at court. On 5 July he records 'I saw his Majestie go with as much pompe and splendor as any Earthly prince could do to the great Citty feast: (The first they invited him to since his returne) but the exceeding raine which fell all that day, much eclips'd its luster. . . .' English weather for the English monarchy restored.

It was nine years since Charles had fled after Worcester battle – and his hiding in the oak tree at Boscobel soon became part of national mythology and was worked into innumerable pieces of embroidery and stumpwork boxes. It was twelve years since James had slipped out of the garden gate at St James's Palace and gone down the river in the dark to

Tilbury. The world had changed immeasurably since that time and yet London and Whitehall seemed much the same, except that many of their father's famous collection of pictures were gone from his galleries.

Gone too, it was soon apparent, was his style of kingship: remote, dignified, paternally autocratic. The second Charles won the hearts of his people by being almost the opposite of his father – informal, friendly, talking to everyone, promising to hand over all important decisions to the new Parliament, which would be elected after the coronation, whenever that would be. For the regalia and the crown itself had to be made anew; Cromwell had sold off the jewels. Anyone, in the public galleries or in the park, could come up to the King with a petition, and so many did that sometimes Charles could only say, 'God bless you!' and walk on, with his long rapid stride.

James had his part in that triumphant summer, always with his brother – they even rowed up the river together to bathe and swim with the more energetic of the courtiers; they played tennis, they raced their yachts, they danced. Londoners were charmed; the King and the Duke were real young men, not dignified dummies.

Then in the midst of all this jubilation James was forced to introduce a discordant note. He had to confess to his brother that he had promised to marry Anne Hyde. Anne could not much longer conceal her pregnancy; the baby was due in October and it was now August.

James's own account is that Charles at first positively refused his consent

> and used many arguments to dissuad the Duke from that resolution: and not only his Majesty but many of the Duke's friends and most especially some of his meniall servants, with a violent Zeal opposed the match. However, (the Duke still continuing in his resolution to be true to his word, and chusing rather to undergo the censure of being fraile in promising, then of being unjust in breaking his promise) the King at last, after much importunity, consented to the marriage; and it may well be supposed that My Lord Chancellor did his part, but with great caution and circumspection, to soften the King in that matter, which in every respect seem'd so much to his own advantage.

[29]

Sir Edward Hyde, now made Baron Hyde and the King's chief minister, was well aware he would be accused of overweening ambition and made a great outcry at his daughter's behaviour – she ought to be sent to the Tower, he would rather she were the Duke's whore than his wife, etc. Meanwhile he shut Anne up in Worcester House in the Strand, where the Hydes were living in some style. But Charles could not fail to realize how awkward it would be to humiliate the indispensable Chancellor; besides, he would soon be marrying himself, and with several illegitimate children already it would be improbable that his brother would long remain his heir.

James's reference to his 'meniall servants' is to the gentlemen of his household and a tall story of their efforts to disengage the Duke is told by Anthony Hamilton, a cousin of the Marquess of Ormonde, in his *Memoirs of Count Grammont*, a Frenchman who was to marry his sister. Since this dynastic crisis took place two years before Grammont came to the English court and when Hamilton himself was only fourteen, the tale is the merest gossip, yet by constant repetition has acquired almost the status of fact. Charles Berkeley, Harry Jermyn and Dick Talbot (afterwards Earl of Tyrconnel) are supposed to have invented shocking stories of Anne's freedom with her favours to them, to give James the excuse to get out of the marriage. Even so, the story ends rather lamely with the Duke coming out from a long interview with the King and presenting them to his Duchess – the King had told his brother he must stick to his promise. This is almost the reverse of what James says, and indeed sticking to his word is more characteristic of James, and diplomatic evasion of Charles.

James and Anne were married privately at Worcester House on 3 September 1660 by Dr Crowther, the Duke's chaplain. Since her father refused to take any part, she was given away by Lord Ossory, Ormonde's son. The witness was Anne's maid.

The royal family were all extremely angry about the marriage. The Princess Royal, coming over from Holland, was particularly annoyed that her Maid of Honour, a mere gentlewoman, should marry her brother. Henry Duke of Gloucester was said to be very scornful, remarking that Anne 'smelt of the green bag' – referring to her father's professional origins as a lawyer.

Only a week or two later Gloucester was struck down by small pox and died within a few days. His death was a severe shock to the family, for he was only twenty but already showed great promise.

Henrietta Maria, who was also coming over to England, wrote that she was hoping 'to marry her son the King and to unmarry the other'. But she arrived too late to unmarry James and was persuaded by the cunning Mazarin to make it up with her old enemy Hyde, who was now in a position to secure her pension and pay off her debts.

James himself went to Dover to meet his mother and sister Henriette, at the end of October, and escorted them to London. By that time his first child, a son, was born and in December the marriage was publicly owned and people came to Worcester House to kiss the hand of the Duchess of York – though many of them, especially those more nobly born than Anne Hyde, found it a strange business.

Then, just before Christmas, Princess Mary fell sick of the small pox and died. It was a great grief to all the family, but especially to Charles and James, whom she had helped all through the years of exile. Just when they could make her some return, she was taken away.

Her son William was left an orphan at ten years old. Charles offered to bring him up in England, since the Dutch had already refused to allow him the title of Stadholder, which they said was not hereditary and not royal, as Holland was a republic. But as Prince of Orange he inherited vast estates and palaces scattered over the Netherlands, as well as his tiny titular province in France, valued for conferring the rank of (non-royal) prince. And so in the end he was brought up in Holland by his Dutch grandmother and became entirely Dutch in feeling and outlook.

Henrietta Maria, terrified that her other daughter would succumb to the fatal disease, hurried her away back to France early in January 1661, where she was soon afterwards married to King Louis' brother Philippe, the effeminate Duke of Orléans. The newly restored royal family in England was reduced to the King and the Duke of York, with his English wife and child. The baby had been christened Charles (by permission) on New Year's Day but he was to die next May, seven months old.

Charles gave his brother St James's Palace, so familiar from childhood, and he settled there with great content, though he kept his lodging at Whitehall, a splendid suite of rooms looking out on the river

[31]

Thames. And he had a yacht built at Woolwich which he named the *Anne*.

Anne, who had spent her formative years at the Princess Royal's court, was quite capable of filling the role of royal duchess; some people thought she became altogether too royal and knew too much of affairs of state, influencing the Duke. Perhaps she did, for she was a strong-minded, intelligent woman. She built up a court circle at St James's, patronized the painter Peter Lely, shared the Duke's liking for music and plays, and backed him up in the power game which soon began to entangle him.

Charles announced his coronation for St George's day, 23 April 1661, and made his Chancellor Earl of Clarendon. While the King was down at Portsmouth, seeing his mother and sister off to France, an incident occurred in London which showed that not all the extreme elements liberated by the experimental English republic had disappeared. Indisposed at the time, James had stayed in Whitehall, and one morning was woken up by General Monck, soon to be made Earl of Albemarle, who had a lodging at the Cockpit, a building on the site of an earlier cock-fighting centre, which is now part of the Downing Street complex. Monck reported that a man called Venner, of the Fifth Monarchy sect, was marching through London with thirty armed men all shouting 'Live, King Jesus!' and calling everyone to join them. Jesus, not Charles, was to be King of England.

Monck was worried that there were scarcely any Guards to deal with them, because it was part of the negotiations for the Restoration that no standing army should be kept by the King, and the Cromwellian army was being rapidly disbanded. So 'the Duke and the Generall immediatly took horse' but by the time they reached Leadenhill Street the Militia had cornered the rebels and killed most of them; Venner himself was so badly wounded he scarcely lived to be hanged.

'And so ended this mad attempt of furious Zeal,' James wrote in the memoirs, 'which seem'd in a manner designed by Providence to convince the King and his Ministers, of the necessity of providing better for the safety of his person, and the Security of the Government, then hitherto they had done, by letting them see what dangerous spirits lay still scatter'd about in the body of the Kingdom; nor indeed could it well be otherwise, since so very lately the Government of the Nation was in the hands of phanaticks, and that men of the same temper were still in being, tho not in power.'

A Council was called at once and on James's advice they wrote to the King to halt the disbanding of the General's troop of horse guards and the regiment of foot, which were to have been paid off that very day. Charles concurred, and gave orders for more regiments of horse guards to be raised. This was the foundation of the brigade of guards as a permanent institution and the nucleus of the future British army.

James wondered that Lord Chancellor Hyde and the Earl of Southampton, who had been eye-witnesses of the great rebellion in the time of his father, had not advised the King better on security. He also observed that those two elder statesmen were 'the great opposers in the House of Lords of the King's inclination and intention to grant, according to his promises given at Breda, a Toleration to Dissenters so limited as not to disturb the public peace of the Kingdom.' But by opposing toleration and neglecting the King's security, 'the consequence unavoidable of their Counsels was to irritate an Enemy and not to arm against him.'

This shrewd judgement must date to a later time, for the religious settlement was not made till 1662, when the revised Prayer Book was imposed and a large number of Presbyterian and independent ministers resigned from the Church of England, to swell the ranks of dissenters, who henceforth had no legal standing in the nation. In a series of measures, known as the Clarendon Code after the Chancellor, who promoted them in Parliament, all dissenters were penalized, conformity enforced and fines imposed for non-attendance at church on Sundays. The stage was set for the imprisonment of Quakers and nonconformists like Bunyan through the whole of Charles's reign, against his personal wishes.

But none of that was settled when Charles was crowned on St George's day in April 1661. It was a two-day event, with the traditional procession from the Tower to Whitehall on the twenty-second, with the creation of new peers at the Banqueting House, and the coronation itself in Westminster Abbey next day. In the procession from the Tower the Duke of York rode ahead of the King with his guards; General Monck followed him, bareheaded and leading a spare horse.

Pepys was well-placed to observe it, in a room upstairs in Cornhill, 'with wine and good cakes and saw the show very well'. The ladies, leaning out of windows hung with carpets, added to his delight 'and made good sport among us . . . Both the King and the Duke of York took notice of us as he saw us at the window.'

Evelyn was near the Temple Bar, where the Lord Mayor was received by the bailiff of Westminster, 'The fountaines running wine, bells ringing, and speeches made at the severall Triumphal Arches. . . .' Evelyn spent the evening inspecting the Arches, which were to stand for a year, and which he thought of good invention – high praise from a virtuoso, or connoisseur, as Evelyn undoubtedly was. He was present next day at Westminster Abbey and witnessed the whole ceremony; after it Charles 'went on foote upon blew cloth, which was spread and reachd from the West dore of the Abby to Westminster Stayres where he took Water in a Triumphal barge to Whitehall, where was extraordinary feasting'.

Needless to say Pepys, who had also been at the Abbey (though unable to see the actual ceremony), contrived to get in at the feast, which was held in Westminster Hall. Through Lord Sandwich (his patron Mountagu) he even got 'four rabbits and a pullet' and some bread, 'and so we at a stall eat it, as everybody else did what they could get. I took a great deal of pleasure to go up and down and look upon the ladies – and to hear the musique of all sorts: but above all the twenty four violins.' This string band was an innovation, copied from the French court. Afterwards Pepys got into a private party drinking the King's health till 'if ever I was foxed it was now'. In spite of waking up next morning 'wet with my spewing', Pepys concluded, 'Thus did the day end, with joy everywhere.'

On 8 May the King rode in state to open the new Parliament and in the evening announced that he was to marry the Infanta of Portugal, Catherine of Braganza. The marriage was arranged then but did not take place till the next year, when the Duke of York was sent to meet the Princess at sea and escort her into Portsmouth.

That was in May 1662. On 30 April James's eldest (surviving) child had been born, and she was christened Mary, after the sister he had lost.

4 Public and Private Affairs

In the Parliament the King opened in May 1661, the Duke of York took his seat in the reconstructed House of Lords which was then in fact as well as in theory more powerful than the Commons. The King's senior ministers were all peers, though many were men he himself had raised to the peerage, able and ambitious men who were political careerists and more or less of an age with the King. One reason for Clarendon's unpopularity was that, as a man of the older generation, his policy was determined by his experience of the civil war and seemed to his juniors out of date.

Clarendon was the Duke's father-in-law and James, while he had reservations about the Chancellor's views on Toleration, the army and the settling of the royal revenue, which was inadequate for carrying on the government and dependent on the vote of Parliament, respected him as a faithful royalist and was considered to be his political supporter. From the start James was recognized as the backer of the ex-cavaliers, the Church-and-King men, who later became known as Tories. He was suspicious of the ex-Parliamentarians whom Charles advanced in an effort to unite the divided nation behind the restored monarchy. This political orientation is the key to the opposition to James, first as Duke and then as King. But while Charles was still expected to have legitimate children it did not manifest itself strongly.

In the early sixties James established himself as his brother's right-hand man, more or less in charge of the military forces, certainly of the navy, a royal watchdog in the House of Lords, with a seat on the King's Council, which then acted more or less as a cabinet, and on the various committees, such as that for foreign affairs, organized within it. He was always with the King, each patron of a new theatre where women performed for the first time, of the new trading companies being formed, of the Royal Society, concerned with all the arts and sciences, and other enterprises which were to encourage the development of the nation and its increasing prosperity in this second half of the century.

[35]

James made it his business to encourage overseas trade and set up a new company for 'Guiny' (West Africa) which he says in the memoirs 'was absolutely necessary for the support of the Foreign Plantations and for hindering the Dutch from being absolute masters of the whole Guiny trade.' Some rather sharp practice went on when English merchants 'got the secret which the Dutch had of dying the Sayes of such a coulour as the Blacks liked, and of giving them the smell in packing them up, like that which was used at Leyden, from which place formerly all the sayes were brought that were sent into Guiny.' All's fair in the trade war, in fact. Thus was begun the Royal African Company and the Duke sent Sir Robert Holmes, a tough and ambitious naval commander, to seize Cap de Vert and the Castle of Cormentin from the Dutch and plant 'factories' (trading stations) along the coast.

On the other side of the Atlantic more moves were made against the Dutch. According to James, Long Island 'had always belonged to the Crown but the Dutch encroached during the Rebellion', trying to secure the beaver trade to themselves. (The pelts were much in demand for hats.) The King gave the Duke a patent for Long Island and he sent two men-of-war under the command of Colonel Richard Nicholls, an old officer of his, with 300 men to take possession, 'which the Dutch gave up upon composition without stricking a strok'. Most of the Dutch remained there, with 'the old English inhabitants and some other Nations who had first planted there with the English'. They called the place New York after the Duke, and the fort up the river, Albany. (Albany was the Duke's Scottish title.) Incidentally James ordered the Governor to allow liberty of conscience there from the start.

The English and the Dutch, both maritime nations, were bound to be rivals in this century of expansion beyond Europe, and at the beginning of Charles's reign the Dutch, in the minds of most Englishmen, were the chief enemy. France, so long engaged in the internal wars of the Fronde, did not then appear the threat it was soon to become, under the strong and aggressive government of the young Louis XIV. So to make war on the Dutch was popular and Parliament voted the funds for it with enthusiasm. Charles, though he frequently made rude remarks about Dutchmen, was not over-anxious to start a war; nor was Lord Chancellor Clarendon, though he unfairly got the blame for it later. As for James, he was determined to command the fleet if it did come to war, and tremendous preparations were made.

The two fleets were out late in 1664 but did not meet in battle owing to the accidents of the weather. At the beginning of December the Duke left the fleet under the Earl of Sandwich (Pepys's patron) and went back to Whitehall for Christmas.

The real campaign began in the spring of 1665. James was at the Gunfleet (on the Blackwater estuary) by 23 March, but then was faced with four or five weeks' delay before the fleet was ready to put to sea. However,

> he employ'd his time to the best advantage he could, by ordering all the Flag officers to meet every morning on Bord him, and there to agree upon the orders of Battel and Rancke; for tho in the late Fights in Cromwell's time, the English behaved themselves bravely, yet they minded not any set order, and their Victories were still more owing to their valour, than method; so that this war, begun now under the conduct of his RH was the first wherein fighting in a Line and a regular Form of Battell was observ'd.

James always recorded his campaigns and battles in detail; he gives the numbers and rates of vessels, the names of the admirals in command of the three squadrons, Red, White and Blue, and their vice-admirals and captains. He himself led the Red in the *Royal Charles* (once *Naseby*) flying the Royal Standard from the masthead. Prince Rupert led the White, flying the Union Flag. (Rupert had given up his place in the Palatine succession to be naturalized English; Pepys calls him Prince Robert and was irritated by his gruff scorn of committees.) The Blue was commanded by the Earl of Sandwich.

They put to sea at the beginning of May but it did not come to a battle till the 3 June 1665.

The battle and sea manoeuvres can best be read today in Jock Haswell's book (*James II, Soldier and Sailor*) for he explains the nature of seventeenth-century warfare at sea as clearly as he deals with that on land. For instance why, with all those broadsides being fired off, ships were so rarely holed and sunk. The reason was partly the low velocity of the heavy roundshot, partly the quality and thickness (nine to twelve

[37]

inches thick) of the ship timbers. The damage done by a broadside was not to the hull but to the rigging and to the men on deck. Ships could be disabled by bringing down masts and sails; they could then be more easily boarded, when the fight was hand to hand with cutlass and sword. A much favoured (and dreaded) trick was the employment of fireships sent in to set light to the men-of-war. Fire, and especially fire among the stocks of gunpowder, was the really fatal weapon at sea.

To follow a naval battle of those days it is essential to understand the significance of wind direction and strength; getting to windward of the enemy often took hours. On this June day the fleet sailed at 3 a.m. but the close engagement did not begin till 10 o'clock. From then on the fight was fierce and not least round the *Royal Charles*.

It was at this hardpressed time that a cannon ball killed at one shot three of James's friends who were standing by him on the quarter deck, so close that he was splashed with their blood. Charles Berkeley and Lord Muskerry were old companions in exile; young Richard Boyle, second son of the Earl of Burlington, was a volunteer of eighteen. James mourned Berkeley most; although he had been made Earl of Falmouth he had served the King so disinterestedly that he had virtually nothing to leave his wife and baby daughter, 'so that if the King and the Duke had not provided for them, they must have starved', James records and adds 'such an Example is hardly to be found amongst those who enjoy their Prince's favour.' Most people were out for what they could get.

In spite of this tragic incident the fight was going against the Dutch and about two in the afternoon the Duke ordered his Master Gunner to fire his guns in succession as they passed Opdam's flagship; the third shot must have hit the powder store for the great ship blew up, the Admiral was killed and his whole fleet, disheartened, began to draw off. The English sailed in pursuit and did more damage with fireships, so that the sea was soon full of Dutch sailors. The Duke ordered out boats to pick them up.

The pursuit of the fleeing Dutch went on all the evening, the *Royal Charles*, which was a fast sailer, in the lead. When it was quite dark James left orders to sail on ahead and went below to lie down fully clothed and sleep the sleep of exhaustion. While he was asleep Mr Brouncker, one of his Grooms of the Bedchamber, took it upon himself to tell the Captain the Duke had ordered him to shorten sail, which he did, letting the rest of the Dutch fleet get away in the night. Because at daybreak sail was put on again before James came on deck, he did not know what had happened till much later – two years later, in fact, when trouble was made over his 'failing to pursue the enemy'. They were now within sight of the coast of Holland but as the Dutch ships had got into Texel harbour the Duke had to lead his fleet back to the Buoy of the Nore to refit.

On 16 June Pepys (who ordered himself a new suit to celebrate the victory) got a message that the Duke was back, 'So after dinner and doing some business at the office I to Whitehall where the Court is full of the Duke and his courtiers returned from sea, all fat and lusty and ruddy by being in the sun.'

Evelyn noted, 'I also waited on his R. Highness now come triumphant from the fleete; goten in to repaire.' On 23 June he was there again: 'The Duke of Yorke told us that his dog sought out absolutely the very securest place of all the vessel, when they were in fight.' No Stuart was ever without dogs, even at sea.

Towards the end of June, James records, the King sent for him and for Rupert to make their report. Then he told them he had decided neither of them should return to sea. James tried hard but failed to change his mind; Charles said his brother's life must not be risked further. At this time James had three children living and the second was a boy, James, Duke of Cambridge, born 12 July 1663; the baby was Anne, born 6 February 1665. But the Queen, who had had a miscarriage, had not yet given up hope of a child. Some people at court thought Charles was jealous of his brother's success and popularity but, as James remarked in another context, it was not in Charles's nature to be jealous.

On 1 July the King went down to the Buoy of the Nore to review the fleet. Evelyn was there too and after dining with Lord Sandwich aboard the *Prince* (in spite of the pasting she had received, still afloat) went on board the *Royal Charles* and heard the King's decision that 'his R. Highnesse should adventure himself no more this summer . . . and so came away late, having seene the most glorious fleete that ever spread saile.'

The King now left London because of the plague and stayed at

Hampton Court before moving further into the country. He sent James to the north in case the Dutch should attempt a landing there; probably this was an excuse to soften the blow of enforced retirement. In York the Duke was received with great rejoicing. That summer the King held a Parliament at Oxford which voted a large sum of money to the Duke for his victorious service. It was this great victory at sea which really made James known to the people of England in his own right; he became immensely popular, greeted everywhere with cheers; plates were decorated with his portrait, medals issued in classical style to commemorate his victory. From now on he was a person to be reckoned with in public affairs.

The court returned to Hampton Court in January 1666, where John Evelyn received the King's thanks for his service in charge of the Dutch prisoners 'in a time of great danger, when every body fled their Employments . . . Then the Duke came towards me and embrac'd me with much kindnesse and told me, if he had but thought my danger would have been so greate he would not have sufferd his Majestie to employ me in that Station.' Soon after, at the beginning of February, the King being now back at Whitehall, Evelyn went to lay before him his project for an Infirmary (the beginning of the Chelsea Hospital) which the King heard 'with great approbation, recommending it to his R. Highnesse'. In fact it was to be James who completed the project.

In June there was another great sea-battle, known as the Four Days Fight, which although it was at first greeted as a victory was, as Evelyn recorded, 'rather a deliverance than a triumph', for the English losses had been heavy. On 25 July (St James's Day) there was another sea-battle in which the English reckoned they had the victory.

It was really impossible for a war between the two naval nations to come to any definite conclusion; something which does not seem to have occurred to the leaders on either side. Who lost most men-of-war and whether the rich merchant ships were captured or got home safely, were the only measures of who was winning. So the war dragged on, becoming more and more unpopular with the Parliament which had at first been so much in favour of it.

On 2 September 1666, 'this fatal night about ten, began that deplorable fire, near Fish-streete in London,' wrote Evelyn. His description, less well-known than Pepys's, is equally vivid.

All the skie were of a fiery aspect, like the top of a burning Oven, and the light seene above 40 miles around for many nights: God grant mine eyes may never behold the like, who now saw above ten thousand houses all in one flame, the noise and crackling and thunder of the impetuous flames, the shreeking of Women and children, the hurry of people, the fall of towers, houses and churches was like an hideous storme, and the aire all about so hot and inflam'd that at last one was not able to approach it . . . Thus I left it this afternoone burning, a resemblance of Sodome, or the last day.

Pepys was more closely involved, since he was then living at the Navy Office, in danger from the spreading fire. It was Pepys who brought the first news of the fire to the King who was with the Duke at Sunday service in the Chapel Royal. Both came out to hear the tale of the disaster. 'They seemed much troubled and the King commanded me to go to my Lord Mayor and command him to spare no houses but pull down before the fire every way. The Duke of York bid me tell him that if he would have any more soldiers, he shall.'

The Lord Mayor proved a broken reed. 'He cried like a fainting woman, Lord, what can I do? I am spent! People will not obey me. I have been pulling down houses. But the fire overtakes us faster than we can do it.'

Pepys now had to take steps to save both his own goods and the Navy Office records; at 4 a.m. he was taking money and plate to Bethnal Green, 'riding myself in my night gown in the cart'. (Night gown was what we should call dressing gown.) He went back on foot and spent the whole day packing and saving things. 'The Duke of Yorke come this day by the office and spoke to us, and did ride with his guard up and down the City to keep all quiet (he being now Generall, and having the care of all).'

Both the King and the Duke had been taking part in the fire-fighting as Evelyn recorded, 'even labouring in person and being present to command, order, reward and encourage the Workemen'. The Duke supervised the pulling down of houses which eventually stopped the fire from spreading further. It was stopped short of the Navy Office and Pepys was able to bring all his goods back again, with great thankfulness.

Evelyn immediately made a survey of the ruins of London and 'a Plot for a new Citty' which he showed the King as soon as 11 September. Charles had called him into the Queen's Bedchamber (her suite of apartments) where, with only the Queen and the Duke present, they discussed the plan for nearly an hour. Evelyn added that the Queen 'was now in her Cavaliers riding habit, hat and feather and horseman's Coate, going to take the aire'.

The fire became the King's excuse to introduce a reform of dress, supposed to be economical, when he brought into fashion the long coat or vest, which was to become the principal garment of a gentleman's suit for more than a century to come. At first it had quite short wide sleeves, the shirt sleeve showing almost from the elbow, but the sleeves were soon lengthened, made with huge turn-back cuffs, allowing a ruffle of fine linen or lace to fall over the wrist. The breeches at the same time became less baggy and were gathered into bands at the knee. The new line was certainly an improvement on the short doublet and ribboned petticoat breeches but as to economy the price of lace was such that cravats and ruffles must have run away with most of the savings on ribbons.

On 13 October 1666 Pepys recorded, 'To Whitehall, and there the Duke of York (who is gone over to all his pleasures again, and leaves off care of business, what with his woman, my lady Denham, and his hunting three times a week) was just come in from hunting. So I stood and saw him dress himself and try on his vest which is the King's new fashion, and will be in it for good and all, on Monday next, the whole court.' As he went on to say that as soon as the Duke was ready he chaired a committee on Tangier, business can't have been so neglected after all.

The King had already brought in the fashion of wearing wigs, perhaps because, as Pepys noticed, he was already 'mighty grey'. In February 1664 Pepys had seen the Duke of York put on a periwig for the first time. 'But methought his hair, cut short in order thereto, did look very prettily of itself before he put on his periwigg.' Needless to say, Pepys was soon ordering one for himself.

The mention of Lady Denham provides a context for some account of James's private life, which he did not include in the memoirs, though when he was writing advice for his son in 1692 he confessed to having lived irregularly, indulging 'the forbidden love of women' for almost the whole course of his life. In repenting this sin he detailed the troubles consequent on it for princes, whose mistresses were generally out for what they could get, for themselves and their bastards, and rarely had any genuine love for their royal lovers. He used his brother's trials as illustration (since by then Charles was dead) but in describing the difficulties of gaining the object of desire, only to find that soon one 'wanted a change' he seems to be speaking of his own experience.

The Restoration court was a young man's scene; at thirty the King was among the most mature and others, like him, had grown up either in exile or under a hostile régime. Charles's view was that God would not damn a man for taking a little pleasure on the side; the worse sin was malignity, of which he felt he was not guilty. James did not justify his pursuit of pleasure in this way; he knew adultery was forbidden by the Lord but could not resist the temptation. In the early sixties, when both brothers were in their thirties, the licence of the restored court soon became common gossip, shocking men like Evelyn and Clarendon, who could compare it with the prevailing tone of married virtue under Charles I.

Most of the stories of James's affairs come from Anthony Hamilton's gossip-column *Memoirs of Count Grammont*, hardly trustworthy. Some relate laughable frustrations, like his unsuccessful pursuit of Frances Jennings, a fair pretty girl, one of Duchess Anne's Maids of Honour. Both the Duchess and the Queen had Ladies of the Bedchamber, who were the wives of peers; the Maids of Honour were daughters of gentlemen, usually somewhat impoverished, who received a salary and were expected by their families to make good marriages. To some the advantages of being a royal mistress outweighed those of a respectable marriage but Frances Jennings was not one of these. When the Duke slipped a *billet doux* into her muff, she shook it out on the floor for all to see. James's friend Dick Talbot was also in love with Frances Jennings but at the time he had little money (he was the youngest of a large Irish family) so she prudently married Sir George Hamilton and went abroad with him on embassy; Talbot married someone else. Years later, when both spouses were dead, Frances and Talbot married each other and so she ended up Duchess of Tyrconnel. Her younger sister Sarah was to become the Duchess of Marlborough.

Duchess Anne does not seem to have worried unduly about the

Duke's pursuit of her Maids of Honour, but she was sufficiently annoyed by his infatuation with Lady Chesterfield to complain to the King. Lady Chesterfield was a Butler, daughter of the loyal Marquess of Ormonde (now a Duke); she had married Philip Stanhope, the Earl of Chesterfield, who had been the first lover of Barbara Villiers, before she married Roger Palmer and became the King's most famous mistress, as Lady Castlemaine. Although notorious for his own love affairs, Chesterfield was furiously jealous of his wife when he suspected her of yielding to the Duke of York and carried her off to the country. As she died soon afterwards, there were rumours that he had poisoned her. Hamilton tells a ridiculous tale of green stockings allegedly admired by the Duke and considered proof of his having enjoyed the lady who wore them – probably mere gossip.

These ladies apart, James undoubtedly did succeed in bedding some of the women he pursued, but the affair with Lady Denham proved a turning point in his life. She had started her career as Margaret Brooke, one of the Duchess's Maids of Honour. She had already attracted the attention of the Duke when she married an eccentric middle-aged man, Sir John Denham, the King's Surveyor, to establish herself socially before yielding to the Duke. But she was said to have declared that she was not going up and down the privy backstairs, like Mistress Price. The backstairs led to the King's private apartments, where he could meet people informally – respectable people as well as favourite actresses – and they were presided over by Mr Chiffinch, Page or Groom of the Backstairs, who also ran the King's Secret Service, such as it was.

Lady Denham, however, aspired to be an acknowledged or public mistress, as Lady Castlemaine was to the King. The Duke must come openly, with his gentlemen, to her morning toilette, as the King visited Barbara Castlemaine. And James gave in and did as she desired. He was infatuated, as Pepys noted in September 1666, relating how

the Duke of York was taking her aside and talking to her in the sight of all the world, all alone, which was strange and what I did not like. Here I met with good Mr Eveling (Evelyn) who cries against it and calls it bichering, for the Duke of York talks a little to her, and then she goes away, and then he follows her again, like a dog.

[44]

Sir John Denham was so enraged that he was thought by some to have gone mad; he certainly wrote some virtriolic verses, attacking the Duke and his friends. When his wife fell ill in November 1666 some thought he had poisoned her. She recovered then but died very suddenly in January 1667. Her death came as a great shock to James; he was deeply distressed and was heard to vow he would never again have a public mistress. Although he kept this vow, it did not prevent him from having private mistresses. Evidently he felt that to flaunt his adultery was openly to mock the law of God; sins committed privately carried only personal guilt.

Needless to say gossips maintained that Duchess Anne had poisoned Lady Denham. Anne had certainly resented her ex-Maid of Honour's flaunting her power over the Duke and establishing herself as a rival at court, but she would never have attempted so wicked a crime; like all her family Anne was a devout Anglican and a regular communicant.

It was some time before the Lady Denham episode that Anne herself was suspected of having a love affair with Henry Sidney, who was Master of Horse in the York household. He was the youngest child of the Earl of Leicester and had been partly brought up by his eldest sister Dorothy (hymned by the poet Edmund Waller as Sacharissa), whose husband William Spencer, first Earl of Sunderland, had been killed at the battle of Newbury. Their son Robert was almost of an age with his uncle Henry Sidney and they remained close friends all their lives and worked together to bring in William of Orange in 1688.

When James discovered Sidney was paying attentions to Anne, he dismissed him. It seems unlikely that Anne had gone further than appreciating the compliments of handsome young Mr Sidney, but people who censure James for refusing his wife the extra-marital adventures he so freely indulged in himself, should remember that the royal succession was involved. Any child of Anne's would be in line for the throne, whereas James could father any number of children outside marriage without disturbing the succession. Such is the unfairness of patriarchal heredity.

However, James and Anne made things up after these ruptures, for they not only went on producing children but were often seen together in public, at the theatre ('leaning against each other' once, to Pepys's disgust) or dining out with friends, and in private discussing politics

[45]

and religion. Anne had eight children by James altogether; in the spring of 1667 four were alive: Mary, five years old; James, Duke of Cambridge who was nearly four and was already made a Knight of the Garter; Anne, who was two, and the baby, Charles, Duke of Kendal, born 4 July 1666. A portrait exists of the infant James, showing a charming little face, rather like his father's in childhood, but smiling, not wistful.

James was very fond of his children. Pepys noticed him carrying Mary round on his arm, playing with her 'like an ordinary father' and even keeping her on his knee during a meeting on naval affairs, when she was only two or three. Then in May 1667 both boys fell ill. Anne was nearly distracted, running from one to the other, and she was carrying another baby at the time.

Pepys records the King walking across the Park to see how 'Cambridge and Kendal' were doing. The baby, his namesake, died on 22 May but the older boy seemed to be recovering; then he had a relapse and died on 20 June, to the terrible grief of his parents.

Another boy was born on 14 September 1667 and christened with the unusual name of Edgar, apparently because (according to the Marquis of Worcester) the Saxon King Edgar was 'the first King that had dominion of the seas'. But this Edgar was always delicate, though he too lived to be nearly four, dying in June 1671, about three months after his mother. The last two of the York children were both girls, Henrietta and Catherine, and each lived only for about ten months.

Later, some suggested that James's children died because he had venereal disease. But not only did the older boys die of fever but at the time the last little girls were born James was fathering healthy illegitimate offspring, including the son who became the Duke of Berwick and a famous Marshal of France in the early eighteenth century. Infant mortality was horribly high in the late seventeenth century and not just in royal families. John Evelyn (that highly moral man) lost most of his nine children before they grew up and two daughters as very young women. William Penn the Quaker lost his first three babies by his wife Guglielma.

The year 1667 was a bad one for James altogether. It began with the death of Lady Denham, then there was the tragic loss of his sons; in public affairs came the Dutch raid up the Medway, when they towed away the *Royal Charles* in triumph, and this was used by the Chancellor's enemies to bring about his fall in the autumn of the same year.

The humiliating naval disaster was due to the King's having been persuaded to lay up the great ships, a course the Duke had argued against in vain. In his view this would encourage the Dutch to build up their fleet again, and what might be saved by it 'would be spent in maintaining the Militia and other necessary forces for the security of our Coasts and Ports; and that we should suffer, not only in our interest, but in our honour, by permitting the Dutch to ride masters of the Seas, just under our noses.'

Nobody listened; but James was proved right by the shameful incident in the Medway. And that led directly to a peace being made; the war had not really achieved anything for either side and at home had merely opened the way for a new faction to rise to power in opposition to the old monarchists, as represented by Clarendon, whom they destroyed by reviving the old Parliamentary weapon of impeachment.

The honeymoon period of the Restoration was now definitely over.

5 The Scene Changes

The fall of Lord Chancellor Clarendon was to affect the Duke of York mainly through the politicians who organized his removal and came into power themselves in consequence. The chief movers were the Duke of Buckingham and Lord Arlington, with Anthony Ashley Cooper (Lord Ashley) a much cleverer man, coming up behind. Buckingham, handsome, witty but utterly unreliable, and Arlington (Henry Bennet) both had the friendship of the King, who by this time was tired of his old mentor's assumption of authority and annoyed at his moral censorship of Barbara, Lady Castlemaine. She hated the Chancellor and did her best to turn the King against him. At this time he was still infatuated with her, although with her tantrums, greed for riches and her roving eye for other lovers, she led him a tempestuous

[47]

life. But she was still in her twenties and her beauty and vitality held him enthralled.

In the memoirs James records that he 'was very much put to it how to behave himself in that whole affair'. When the King took the Seal of Office from the Chancellor, leaving him open to impeachment in Parliament, James was torn between his duty to the King, who was determined to drop Clarendon, and his duty to his father-in-law who had acted in the best interest of the monarchy, as he saw it. Now he would have to vote for or against Clarendon in the House of Lords. He did not know what he would have done 'had it not pleas'd God in the heat of the prosecution to visit him with the small pox; so that before he was able to come abroad, this great business was over, the Earle having by privat intimation of the King, to avoid further storm, withdrawn himself out of England; whereupon there issued an Act of Parliament to banish him out of England during his life.'

Although James's attack of small pox let him off the hook over Clarendon's impeachment, it was of course a dangerous illness. It struck in November 1667 and James shut himself up in his rooms at Whitehall, attended only by servants who had had the sickness before, sending the rest of his household to St James's and keeping all others out, as Pepys discovered when he called on business. James weathered the attack and on 11 December Pepys was able to see him, noting, 'blessed be God, he is not at all the worse for the smallpox, but is only a little weak yet. We did much business with him.'

When he had recovered the Duke 'gave his reasons in the House for his voting against the Banishment as a thing unprecedented, there being no proof of any of those Crimes layd to his charge'. James was convinced that Charles had made a fatal mistake in allowing Parliament to proceed against the Chancellor by reviving the process of impeachment, which gave it so much power against the ministers of the monarchy; it also meant that men became wary of serving the King when they knew he might at any time throw them over to their enemies.

The new government became known as the Cabal, from the initial letters of the principal ministers' names: Clifford, Arlington, Buckingham, Ashley and Lauderdale; but they were not a cabal in the sense of a tight-knit group – merely a bunch of ambitious rivals, who had no sooner got rid of the old Chancellor than they began to intrigue against

[48]

each other. Arlington had been made a lord at the coronation and an earl in 1665, and had acquired considerable lands and wealth; he had only a daughter to inherit, to whom Charles would marry his illegitimate son Henry, Duke of Grafton, astutely grafting him into the English nobility. Arlington's stately manner, said to have been learned in Spain, made him slightly ridiculous among the younger courtiers and was the exact opposite of Buckingham's which was careless and farouche in the extreme.

'One thing there was', James recorded in the memoirs, 'which they, and all the stickers for the removall of the Lord Chancellor agreed in, which was, To lessen as much as they could the Duke's interest with the King,' for fear he might prevail on the King to bring Clarendon back; this was the reason behind the bill of banishment, which they succeeded in carrying. Clarendon had to leave his newly built house in Piccadilly (model of the new classical style) and flee to France, where he lived sadly in exile writing his book on the Great Rebellion, till he died in 1674.

James's speaking in the House against Clarendon's banishment 'made the King colder than usually to his RH, which imbolden'd the Faction to venture one step farther, and under pretence of Duty and Zeal represent to the King, That the great power and credit of the Duke in the Nation was look'd upon as a lessening to his Majesty, and that in the present circumstances of affaires, it might be unsafe to have the entire command of the Sea, with a great part of the Land Forces wholly at the Duke's disposal; considering ... the influence which (Clarendon's) party and especially the Dutchess his daughter, may have upon his RH to excite his ressentment.'

From which it is clear that the hostility of the Parliamentary faction to the Duke of York antedated by several years his conversion to the Catholic Church, which was always afterwards made to bear the blame for it. The opposition to the Duke had originally nothing to do with religion; it was political, and it was strong because he was strong. With his integrity, his industry and popularity with the people, the Duke was a formidable obstacle to those who wanted to increase the power of Parliament and lessen that of the King.

During the time that Buckingham and Arlington were in the ascendant (even though feuding with each other), James was isolated at

Council, not listened to and when possible overridden, even in naval matters. The ministers systematically got rid of the Chancellor's men and put their own into official posts. Buckingham imposed as Treasurer to the Navy Sir Thomas Osborne, a wealthy landowner from Yorkshire, tall, thin and fair, who was soon to become better known as Lord Danby. The appointment of the Duke's nominee for a post as Commissioner of the Navy was obstructed for some time because he was a 'tarpaulin' or old professional sailor and not a gentleman amateur – the very reason why James thought him 'the fittest man in England for that employment'.

Pepys recorded that the Duke once told him his policy was simply to sit out the opposition and carry on as far as he could without disobedience to the King. They could not get rid of him, after all, as they got rid of other rivals.

But it was a difficult time for James. Not content with banishing the Chancellor 'they' also contrived to get Ormonde out of his post as Lord Deputy in Ireland, and Ormonde's only defender was the Duke of York, 'who thought it very scandalous that one who had allways been so loyall, should be prosecuted and run down by men who had most of them been downright Rebells or little better'.

Lord Ashley had been a downright rebel. Born in 1621, the son of a wealthy baronet landowner in Dorset, he had taken an active part in the Civil War, first for the King and then in 1644 changing to the Parliament side. He supported Cromwell at first but turned against him in his dictatorial years and then helped Monck to engineer the King's return, for which he was raised to the peerage. Basically he remained a Parliamentarian, but in the sixteen-sixties he evidently thought the King could be managed in that interest.

James thought Buckingham's Civil War record poor, for he had

renounced the King his master to gain favour of Cromwell, whose daughter he would have married. But that usurper had at least so much of honour in him as to say, He would never give his daughter to one who could be so very ungrateful to his King. Having fail'd there, he with much ado and great submission gott to marry with the Lord Fairfax's daughter, who had been General also of the Parliament army.

[50]

And when Buckingham tried to get the Duke on his side in his efforts to oust Arlington, James repulsed him, saying he was resolved to serve the King his own way.

It was Buckingham – with Bristol, who was still around, though not a minister – who first brought before the King the project of a divorce. 'Many at court enter'd into the project and there wanted not lawyers and some Divines, that wrott papers to show the lawfullness and reasonableness of it,' wrote James scornfully in the memoirs. Bristol even went to Italy to inspect the daughter of the Duke of Parma, as a suitable substitute for the barren Catherine.

James recorded that Buckingham and Bristol were heard to say, of the proposed divorce, 'That if the Duke could be persuaded to consent to it, he would make himself to be laught at and dispis'd by all the world; and, if he oppos'd it, it would ruine him with the King.' Charles took an interest in Lord Roos's divorce, carried by two votes in Parliament and held up as a precedent, but he also quipped 'That had he a conscience which would permit him to be divorced, it would not stick at taking a quicker and surer way (not unknown in history) of marrying again without giving Parliament any trouble about it.' (With Henry VIII in mind, presumably.)

About this time Buckingham was going about saying that the Duke of York intended to have him murdered, and 'went out in Town with two Musketoons in his coach and many horsemen well armed'. But when this came to the King's ears he 'laught at the folly of that Duke's suspicions and spar'd not to tell him how ridiculous he made himself thereby'. And James adds, with some satisfaction, 'His Majesty's eyes were open'd every day more and more to convince him that the Duke of Buckingham was not cut out for a Minister of State, who, though very agreable in his person and conversation, and full of flashy witt, had nothing of steady or solid in him.'

But Buckingham, in spite of his scandalous behaviour, somehow always managed to get round the King and keep his popularity with a certain section of the House of Commons and those dissenters whose dissent was more political than religious. He was still the principal figure on the political stage as the decade ended but he was too unstable to exercise any real power and even the King left him out of the secret negotiations with France which were his first personal essay in political

[51]

action abroad, now that he was free of his tiresome old mentor, Lord Clarendon.

The aftermath of Clarendon's fall involved not only the Duke of York but the entire Navy Board and particularly Pepys, who had to defend its activities first before the Committee set up to inquire into the Miscarriages in the conduct of the war, and later (on 5 March 1668) before the House of Commons, where his speech was a tremendous success and brought congratulations from all sides but especially from the King and the Duke of York. A further committee was appointed to look into the accounts, an even more tricky brief for Pepys, which did not come to a head till 1669; in between Pepys composed an epoch-making report for the Duke, who adopted it as his own and was therefore able to put through a thorough-going reform of the naval administration.

It was from this time that the Duke became Pepys's principal patron and Pepys the principal civil servant for naval affairs; he and James were both thirty-five in 1668. Pepys's modern editor has listed three to four hundred entries in the diary concerned with the Duke's naval administration, on finance, reforms, appointments, discipline, the design of ships, visiting and inspecting them, fortifications of docks, marine regiments, signals, regulations and innumerable meetings of the Navy Board and the Tangier committee; and this is only in the sixties, before Pepys's bad sight forced him to give up his diary in 1669.

On 22 April 1668 Pepys was on his way by boat from Whitehall to Westminster Hall, 'and taking water, the King and the Duke of York were in the new buildings; and the Duke of York called to me whither I was going and I answered aloud, "To wait on our maisters at Westminster;" at which he and all the company laughed; but I was sorry and troubled for it afterward, for fear any Parliament-man should have been there. . . .' He knew the party divisions were becoming more marked all the time – and the hostility.

Pepys's relations with James were now very easy. On 29 June after meeting the Duke at Whitehall on Navy business, he recorded, 'Thence to the Chapel, it being St Peter's day, and did hear anthem of Silas Taylor's making – a dull old-fashion thing of six or seven parts that nobody could understand; and the Duke of York, when he came

out, told me that he was a better store-keeper than anthem-maker –
and that was bad enough too.'

The entry for 10 February 1669 reads: 'To Whitehall, where I stayed
till the Duke of York came from hunting ... and when dressed did
come out to dinner and there I waited and he did tell me that tomorrow
was to be the great day that the business of the Navy would be
discoursed of before the King and his Caball; and that he must stand on
his guard.' But this did not spoil his dinner for he

did mightily magnify his sawce which he did then eat with everything,
and said it was the best universal sauce in the world – it being taught
him by the Spanish Imbassador – made of some parsley and a dry
toast, beat in a mortar together with vinegar, salt and a little pepper.
He eats it with flesh or fowl or fish. And then he did now mightily
commend some new sort of wine lately found out, called Navarr
wine; which I tasted, and is I think good wine; but I did like better the
notion of the sawce and by and by did taste it, and liked it mightily.

On 4 March Pepys walked to Deptford to the Treasurer's new house
to find the Duke of York, who was dining there with his Duchess and a
number of ladies of the court, including Lady Castlemaine.

I did find the Duke of York and Duchess with all the great ladies,
sitting upon a carpet on the ground, there being no chairs, playing at
'I love my love with an A because he is so and so; and I hate him with
an A because of this and that'; and some of them, but particularly the
Duchess herself and my Lady Castlemaine, were very witty.

But by May Pepys was finding his eyes so troublesome that he feared
he was going blind and wrote to the Duke for leave to go abroad. On 19
May on his way in his own coach, he saw the Duke conducting exercises
of his troops in Hyde Park with the Duke of Monmouth looking 'mighty
fine' – Monmouth was now about twenty. At Whitehall Pepys watched
the King and Queen at dinner in the Queen's lodgings, 'she being in
her white pinner and apern, like a woman with child; and she seemed
handsomer, plain so, then dressed.' (Catherine was once more pregnant, but shortly afterwards miscarried.) Still waiting for the Duke, he

[53]

was taken to Mr Chiffinch's lodging about four in the afternoon and given a dish of cold chicken and good wine – 'and I dined like a prince, being before very hungry and empty'.

> By and by the Duke of York comes, and readily took me to his closet and received my petition, and discoursed it about my eyes and pitied me, and approved my proposition to go into Holland and observe things there of the Navy, but would first ask the King's leave, which anon he did, and did tell me that the King would be 'a good maister to me' (these were his words about my eyes). . . .

So on the last day of May 1669 Pepys closed his diary, sadly foreseeing nothing but blindness and an early grave. In fact he did not go blind, though he had to get most of his writing done by clerks. The wife he had loved and quarrelled with died soon after their return from abroad but Pepys himself was to live a long and active life; he did not die till 1703, two years after James, who was always 'a good maister' to him.

6 The Truth of Conversion

'It was about this time, in the beginning of the year 1669, that his RH (who had it long in his thoughts that the Church of England was the only true Church) was more sensibly touched in conscience and began to think seriously of his salvation.' Thus begins the account in the *Life* of James's crucial conversion.

> Accordingly he sent for one Father Simons a Jesuite, who had the reputation of a very learned man, to discourse with him on that subject. And when he came, he told him the good intentions he had of being a Catholick, and treated with him about his being reconcil'd to the Church.

From this it is evident that James had already done quite a lot of thinking about the faith of the Church and we can discover something

[54]

of it from the précis of what he wrote some ten years later in answer to friends who were trying to get him to return to the Church of England – 'to let them see it was not done hastely nor was it the effect of a Childish Imagination, or the fruite of perswasion when he lived in Catholick Countrys.'

In this account from 1680 James says that the first origin of his doubts proceeded from a treatise which

a learned Bishopp of the Church of England writ and desired him to read while he was in Flanders; the drift of which was to clear the Church of England from the guilt of schisme by separating from the Church of Rome, which being the first writing he had ever read of that kind, instead of confirming him in that belief had quite the contrary effect, especially after he had seen the answer to it, which that Bishopp likewise recommended to him: this made him more inquisitive after the grounds and manner of the Reformation, so he read all the Historys he could relateing to that subject, and though at that time he confess'd he lived not so regularly as he ought, yet he had some good intervals which he employ'd that way; that after his return to England, Dr Heylin's History of the Reformation and the Preface to Hooker's Ecclesiastical Polity thoroughly convinced him that neither the Church of England, nor Calvin, nor any of the Reformers, had power to do what they did, and he was confident, he sayd, that whosoever reads those two books with attention and without prejudice, would be of the same opinion.

When Duchess Anne read them, she began to think the same. Her brother Henry Hyde, Lord Cornbury, lent her a Protestant history which like the treatise given to James in Flanders had the contrary effect to that intended. She concluded that Henry VIII and Queen Elizabeth had no right to make themselves heads or governors of the Church in England and repudiate the authority of the Apostolic See of Rome.

James and Anne both started from the high Caroline position (Anglo-Catholic as it was to be called in the nineteenth century) that the Church of England professed the true Catholic faith, reformed from medieval Roman corruption. It was from their reading of history that they became convinced that it had been separated from Catholic communion for reasons political as much as religious and partly corrupted by heretical opinions which increased the rift as the generations passed.

Because James's path to the Catholic Church was an historical one it has been called intellectual, or if the critics subscribe to the idea that James was stupid, at least theoretical, the mere conclusion of an argument, not engaging the emotions. They point to several contemporaries who said that James maintained such an impassive front that they could not guess what he was thinking. They were wrong: James rarely concealed his *thoughts* – his outspokenness got him into trouble over and over again – but he did keep tight control over his *feelings*, in this more like Englishmen of a later period. His deepest feelings were involved in his conversion but they only showed themselves in his subsequent actions.

His historical reading in the works of Anglicans introduced him to the Catholic doctrine of the unity of the Church – one, holy and apostolic – and he came to accept this as the truth. The Church was a single universal communion united by the spirit of Christ, existing from the time of the apostles, the bishops being their successors as teachers, the final authority resting with the successor of St Peter, the Bishop of Rome. Once James had recognized this it became a duty of conscience to join it, however difficult this might prove for a member of the English royal family and the heir presumptive to the throne.

When he discussed it with Fr Simons, however, he found that he could not be received 'unless he would quitt the Communion of the Church of England'. Until then James had believed, along with 'the Church of England Doctors' that dispensations were easily granted for secret receptions. To make sure he wrote to the Pope himself and got a reply which confirmed Fr Simons' judgement, that it was 'an unalterable doctrine of the Catholick Church, Not to do ill that good might follow'. This made James 'think it high time to use all the endeavours he could, to be at liberty to declare himself and not live in so unsafe and uneasy a condition'.

It therefore seemed providential when he discovered that Charles was 'of the same mind' and had already discussed the subject with a Catholic peer, Lord Arundel of Wardour, and with Lord Arlington and

[56]

Sir Thomas Clifford (soon to be Lord Clifford) who were both inclined towards Catholicism. The King then arranged for a meeting with these three to be held in the Duke's closet on 25 January, 'the day in which the Church celebrates the Conversion of St Paul', as James recorded in the memoirs.

There the King 'declar'd his mind . . . and repeated what he had newly before sayd to the Duke, How uneasy it was to him not to profess the Faith he beleev'd and that he had called them together to have their advice about the ways and methods fittest to be taken for the settling of the Catholick Religion in his Kingdoms, and to consider of the time most proper to declare himself.' He foresaw the difficulties but felt it should be undertaken now 'when he and his Brother were in their full strength and able to undergo any fatigue . . . This he spake with great earnestness and even with tears in his eyes.'

The consultation lasted long and eventually they decided that the project could only be achieved in conjunction with France, and so the secret was to be entrusted to Monsieur de Croissy Colbert, the present French Ambassador, so that he could negotiate between the two Kings.

This was the beginning of what was to become the now famous Secret Treaty of Dover, which was not finalized till the May of the next year. To eighteenth-century Whigs it seemed an infamous sell-out of a free England to the hated enemy, the absolute monarchy of France. But in 1669 the situation had not hardened into its later lines. In the recent Dutch War France had joined in on the Dutch side; in the past France had often been the ally of Holland against Spain. But Louis XIV was about to alter all that and launch an attack on Holland (now allied to Spain through the Spanish Netherlands) and thought it worthwhile to engage the English on his side. (They had after all been fighting the Dutch all through the middle of the century, under Cromwell as well as under Charles II.) In return, Louis was prepared to finance Charles to make him independent of Parliament while he carried through his change of religion.

As to this, Charles did not intend to make the state church Roman Catholic; both he and James knew that after a century of Protestantism this was impossible. The intention was to introduce the liberty of conscience promised at Breda in 1660 and to release Catholics from the severe penalties imposed by Queen Elizabeth's settlement. With

[57]

the King a Catholic the religious situation would be a sort of mini-version of the Empire, where the Catholic Emperor had many Protestant princes and their subjects under his rule.

If it is hard to see how the worldly-wise Charles could have contemplated such a programme, it should be remembered that in the sixteen-sixties there was a good deal of feeling in favour of religious toleration, with Ashley (later Lord Shaftesbury) himself in favour of it. Nor had Louis XIV at that time established himself as the most powerful monarch in Europe; the Dutch were still regarded as the main enemy. Charles, of course, had always been pro-French in his personal tastes, and his affection for his French sister Henriette Anne, Duchess of Orléans, now led to her becoming involved in the secret negotiations. In May 1670 she at last got her husband, Louis' brother Philippe, to consent to her coming to England, on condition she went no further than Dover; as King Louis was then in Flanders visiting his recent conquests, it was easy for her to cross the channel.

As it happened, Parliament had just passed a new act against conventicles (meetings of dissenters) and the King left the Duke in London to prevent any disorder this might occasion, so that Madame arrived several days before James could get to Dover.

In which time she so prevail'd with the King that when the Duke got there he found all the former measures broken, and the resolution taken to begin out of hand with the war with Holland; and it was no little surprise to his RH, that both Lord Arlington and Sir Thomas Clifford, being gain'd by Madame had concurr'd in it. They met the Duke as soon as he arrived, before he had seen the King, and told him the changed priorities.

James said,

he was very sorry for it, for he was sure it would quite defeat the Catholick design; because when once his Majesty was engaged in such an expensive war as that would be, and was not absolute master of affaires at home, he unavoidably would run in debt and must then be at the mercy of his Parliament, which, as matters had been order'd were not likely to be in a very good humour; and therefore, though

[58]

they had given very large supplys for the former Dutch War, in all probability they would not do the same now, since that war was of their own proposall, whereas this is undertaken without their advice and in conjunction with France; for which reason alone they would not approve of it, and besides it would give them a jealousy and suspicion of what was further intended.

James was certainly right about the expense and reactions of Parliament, but though he tried hard to change Charles's mind 'he could not prevaile to get that fatal Dutch War put off'.

Madame also got Buckingham restored to favour with the King, 'and when his RH found fault with her for so doing, she ingenuously told him, she did it to make her court to the King, who she saw had a mind to be press'd to do it.' James sourly commented that because of the King's great tenderness for her, 'she could have persuaded him to have done almost anything she had a mind to.'

The days spent at Dover Castle were ostensibly employed in feasting and entertainments; the court went to May dances in the country round about – weather permitting, for it rained a lot. Duchess Anne was there too; it was probably on this working holiday that she conceived her last child.

Charles was reluctant to part with his beloved younger sister and he was never to see her again, for soon after her return to France she was suddenly taken ill and died – so suddenly that there were the usual rumours of poison, administered by one of Monsieur's male favourites. Indeed, in the first shock of hearing the news Charles himself blamed Philippe, but the post-mortem (always made in France at royal deaths) revealed no trace of poison.

Queen Henrietta Maria had died less than a year before her youngest daughter, at the end of August 1669. Charles and James had heard this news in September, when they were hunting in the New Forest. So in 1670 they were the last of the family of Charles I left alive; Charles was forty, James thirty-seven.

Soon after the death of his sister James 'fell ill of a great cold, to that degree that it was fear'd it would turn to a consumption, so that he was oblig'd to go to Richmont(d) for a change of air, to get well of it; nor did he perfectly recover till almost the end of the summer.'

But he did recover, whereas Anne, who had also begun to be ill, grew steadily worse. She had grown very large (a family failing) and people who disliked the Hyde connexion gossipped about her greed, but she continued to live her usual life almost to the end, going out to dinner with the Duke only a few days before her final collapse. Her 'great indisposition' was in fact cancer, starting with cancer of the breast.

Only one thing she had given up: receiving the Sacrament every month, and so regular had she been that this omission was soon noticed. The King remarked on it to the Duke 'who owned the truth to him, That she was resolved to be a Catholick, and soon to be reconcil'd.' The King charged his brother to keep it secret, which he did till she died.

Anne was reconciled to the Catholic Church in August 1670 by Fr Hunt, a Franciscan, and besides the Duke no one was present but Lady Cranmore and James's faithful valet Dupuy.

In February 1671 Anne gave birth to a daughter, Catherine, named after the Queen, who lived only till the end of that year. (The baby Henrietta, born in January 1669, had died in November of the same year.) Edgar was still alive, a delicate three-year-old. Mary was nearly nine, Anne just six.

As she was dying Anne asked James to see she was not disturbed by controversy. So when her younger brother Laurence Hyde brought Dr Blandford to visit her, 'the Duke, meeting the Bishop in the drawing-room, told him what the Dutchess had charg'd him with.' The Bishop's reply was that 'he made no doubt but that she would do well (that was his expression) since she was fully convinced and did it not out of any worldly end; and afterwards went into the room to her and made her a short Christian exhortation suitable to the condition she was in, and then departed.' James adds, 'Her brother, the Lord Cornbury (Henry) a violent Church of England man, came not near her when she was so ill because he suspected she was become a Catholick.'

Anne received all the last sacraments of the Church. 'She dyed with great devotion and resignation, and the morning before her death, finding herself so very ill that she could no longer hold out, she desir'd the Duke not to stir from her till she was dead.' And so James stayed with her till the end; in those days unusual among royal persons. She died on 31 March 1671.

James himself, though convinced of the truth of Catholicism, was still waiting for Charles to pursue the great design, but now that the war was to come first the likelihood of its ever happening receded. But it was not till preparations were in hand for the war, in which James (though still against it) had obtained from the King permission to command the fleet at sea, that he felt he could wait no longer. Parliament was not sitting when the King, early in 1672, brought out a Declaration of Indulgence, giving a limited toleration to all nonconformists and allowing Catholics to celebrate mass in private. It was therefore not illegal for James, as a private person, to become a Catholic.

In his explanatory letter, written from Edinburgh in 1680, James wrote that 'in the year 1672, before he went to Sea, he withdrew from the Communion of the Church of England, yet for some time continued to wait upon the King to Chappel.' James does not actually say he was reconciled then but the implication is there; the reason he did not declare it was surely in obedience to the King, since it was not in James's nature to keep such a thing secret, and indeed it was not to be a secret long. But now he would go into battle fortified by the rites of the Holy Catholic and Apostolic Church, which he believed to be the one true Church founded by Jesus Christ.

7 Tests

Although he had not wanted England to join France in war against Holland, James was active in fitting out and manning the fleet; he alone of the Council, when it was proposed to stop the outward-bound merchant ships and take their crews to man the navy, successfully opposed it, because it would have hindered trade and reduced the customs revenue essential to the Crown's finances. He promised to find the men elsewhere, and did so.

War was declared in March 1672 after what was virtually an act of piracy against the Dutch Smyrna fleet in the Channel, conducted (and bungled) by Sir Robert Holmes. An English land contingent was sent to join the French under the command of the Duke of Monmouth, then a handsome young man of twenty-three. His contemporary, John Churchill, who was later that year to fight with Monmouth against the Dutch, began his war service with Holmes and then joined his patron the Duke of York aboard his flagship the *Prince*.

The naval war began with the usual complex manoeuvres, bedevilled by sudden summer fogs, and late in May, the Dutch having retired to their coast, the English fleet put into Southwold Bay, known as Solebay, to take on fresh victuals, water and ballast. While the wind was in the west (offshore) the Duke was not in fear of an attack but he gave orders that if it were to change to east the ships must stand further out to sea and anchor in order of battle. But when the wind did change his captains assured him there was no danger, because a packet boat had reported seeing the Dutch ships taking in provisions. So he allowed another day.

Thus the fleet was caught on a lee shore (the wind blowing towards it) when the first news of the Dutch approach came at about 2 a.m. on 28 May 1672. They made haste to get to sea but with 'a leeward tide and east wind, few were in line when the engagement began'. This was at dawn. 'As soon as it was day we perceived the Enemy just to windward, bearing right down upon us.' Of the Red and Blue squadrons 'there were not above twenty ships in all that bore the brunt of De Ruyter's and Van Ghent's squadrons.' (The French – the White – were engaged southward with the Zealand squadron and scarcely played any part in the main battle.)

De Ruyter made a dead set at the Duke's flagship, sending in the dreaded fireships which, however, were disabled before they had come near enough to do any damage. But in the course of this preliminary skirmish James's flag-captain (who had persuaded him to stay in the bay) was killed.

The Duke was so plyed by de Ruyter and his seconds that his ship the *Prince* had before eleven of the clock her main top mast shot by the bord, her fore topsayl, her starbord main shrowdes, and all the rest of her rigging and fighting sails shot and torn to pieces and above 200 of her men kill'd and wounded; so that his RH finding his ship unable to work any longer, was forced to leave her, after having

[62]

privately order'd his Captain to tow out of the line and endeavour to refitt, or at least save her from the Enemies fireships; And to avoid noise and surprise, he went down between decks, as it were to order something there, and then slipping into his Boat, he took with him only Lord Feversham (Turenne's nephew Louis Duras), Mr Henry Savile, Mr Ashton, Dupuy and his Cheife Pilot.

The ship he made for was the *St Michael*, commanded by Sir Robert Holmes. He had taken his flag with him and put it up as soon as he got on board.

The rest of his ships were not in line till the afternoon but the Duke managed to keep the fight going even when he had the enemy on both sides of him. Perhaps it was now that a shot grazed his cheek and burnt off one side of his wig.

Soon after a gentle gale sprang up at East, and being got clear of the smoke he could look a little about him. The first thing he saw was the Earl of Sandwich's Blew flag some distance on head of him, appearing above the smoke, which was so great about that place that one could not see any hulls.

Sandwich was engaged in a desperate fight with Van Ghent's flagship. The Dutch Admiral was slain by a shot but it was too late to save Sandwich, for a fireship had set the *Royal James* on fire and she burnt to the waterline and then sank. She did not blow up because virtually all her ammunition was already spent.

This the Duke beheld with Sorrow, but could not help, he being to leeward of her, though he past close by her and saw the Sea all covered with her men, some sinking, some swimming and others buoying themselves up upon what they could next catch hold of. Hereupon he order'd the *Dartmouth*, which was just coming up to him, to ly by and save all she possibly could. She and others picked up two or three hundred.

But not the Earl of Sandwich; he was drowned. His body was found later and given a state funeral, buried in Henry VII's chapel in Westminster Abbey.

[63]

The battle went on and on. *St Michael* was holed and though the leaks were at first stopped, later she began taking in water again. At about 5 p.m. Sir Robert Holmes reported that he was no longer able to sail her and the Duke decided to go on board the *London*, commanded by Sir Edward Spragge. Before leaving he ordered Holmes 'not to strike the standard nor bear away till he saw the Standard flying on board the *London*, least the disappearing of it for any time should discourage his own fleet.'

It was lucky he thought of this ruse because, as the *London* was ahead of the *St Michael*, it took three-quarters of an hour to reach her. And when the Duke got on board 'he found her also much disabled, especially in her head sails.' But still the fight went on till about 7 p.m. when de Ruyter bore away to join his Zealand squadron, which gave an opportunity for twenty-five or thirty men-of-war to join the Duke's battered remnant.

Thus ended this memorable day, in which the Dutch, with all the advantage they could desire, of surprise, of wind, and of number of ships that engaged, were far from Victory over the English as their being first to leave the Sea and retreat into their harbours, will hereafter more fully appear.

That was after a night spent refitting and a day of further manoeuvres, when James was once more on board his own ship, the *Prince*, now refitted and recruited from the crews of two fireships. But finally fog hid the Dutch retreat and the English fleet retired to the Buoy of the Nore to refit.

Thus a kind of victory was snatched out of a near defeat, largely due to James's persevering leadership in action, which must have made it the more frustrating when at the end of June 'the King came down, with some of the Committee for Foreign Affairs' – among them Ashley, now made Earl of Shaftesbury, and Sir Thomas Clifford, now Lord Clifford – and the Duke's advice was overruled. He wanted to sail straight for the Weelings and attack the Dutch in their own waters. But Shaftesbury pressed the King to use the navy to intercept the Dutch East India fleet which was sailing home round the north of Scotland. Hope of gain warped the King's usually sound naval judgement and 'the Duke and the Sea Officers were overruled by the King and the Cabinet Council.'

So in July they cruised as ordered but the weather turned so foul that the Duke 'was obliged to anchor a whole forthnight with his yards and topmasts down' and the East India fleet got by and safe home to Holland. The English fleet returned to shore at Burlington Bay in August. Three thousand men were sick, mostly of the scurvy, which James put down to the heat below decks when battened down; most of them recovered ashore but not soon enough to join their ships before the fleet sailed and so 'some had hardly hands enough to get up their anchors.'

At the beginning of September they lay at anchor 'off Laistoff' – Lowestoft. Now, when the right time had passed, the King who, with Prince Rupert and Lord Shaftesbury, met the Duke at the Buoy of the Nore, wanted him to go across to fight de Ruyter. James this time had 'made sure the old commanders came as well as the Flag men' and they backed him up, Sir Jeremy Smith telling of dire dangers faced in Cromwell's time on the continental coast at this season. The King was convinced, overruled Rupert and Shaftesbury and sent the great ships to Chatham to refit.

'And so ended this Summer Campagne at Sea,' James finished his account. It was to be his last with the English fleet, though he did not then know it. For before next summer he was to face a more severe test than even the test of battle at sea.

It began at Christmas when the King sent Lord Arundel and Lord Clifford (both Catholics) to persuade the Duke to receive the Sacrament with him in the Chapel Royal. James replied that he would attend the service but if he received communion it would only give people 'an ill opinion of his Christianity, by receiving in one Church and being of another, which would make him despised of all good men.'

Then in February 1673 Charles needed a supply for the war and had to recall Parliament. In his opening speech he asserted that he would stand by his Declaration of Indulgence. But the debates showed that the majority disliked the war in alliance with France (as James had forecast) and disliked the Indulgence quite as much. Those who favoured some toleration for dissenters did not like its being done by the King rather than by Parliament, nor the inclusion of Catholics.

[65]

Anglican royalists, while theoretically supporting the King's prerogatives, were determined not to allow dissenters or papists any legal
establishment. In the end the Commons voted to reject the Declaration, recording a resolution 'that penal statutes in matters ecclesiastical
cannot be suspended but by an act of Parliament.' The Commons'
right to make such a judgement was doubtful; what would Henry VIII
have said, after making himself Head of the Church of England?

The Commons then brought in bills, which became the first Test
Act, imposing on all taking office an oath of allegiance which included a
repudiation of the Pope and the Catholic doctrine of transubstantiation
in the mass, and also an obligation to receive the Sacrament in the
Church of England. In March, in order to get his supply, Charles was
forced to withdraw his Declaration and break the Seal on it, though he
did not admit the validity of the Parliamentary resolution. And he gave
his assent to the Test Act.

Easter Day fell on 30 March that year, 1673. John Evelyn went to the
Chapel Royal especially to

> see whither (according to custome) the Duke of York did receive the
> Communion, with the King, but he did not, to the amazement of
> everybody; this being the second year he had foreborn and put it off,
> and this being within a day of the Parliament's sitting, who had lately
> made so severe an Act against the increase of Poperie, gave exceed-
> ing griefe and scandal to the whole Nation: that the heyre of it, and
> the sonn of a martyr for the Protestant Religion, should apostatize;
> What the consequence of this will be God only knows and wise men
> dread.

Evelyn was exaggerating when he said scandal was given to the whole
nation; what he meant was to the gentlemen at Whitehall and possibly
the citizens of London. Even they did not take in the implications of the
Duke's negative act till June, when he decided that he could no longer
hold the office of Lord High Admiral because he could not in
conscience take the new oath.

This was undoubtedly the greatest sacrifice that James could make
for conscience' sake. He had made the office peculiarly his own, the
navy had become the work of his life and the way in which he knew he

[66]

could best serve King and country. Because Parliament had passed this grossly unjust statute he had to give it all up – or give up his faith. But he could not deny the truth according to his conscience.

So he resigned and Prince Rupert commanded the fleet that summer, though the engagements were not decisive either way. But now people did begin to realize that the Duke of York, the heir presumptive, had become a papist.

8 An Italian Bride

In the autumn of 1671 Charles had told James that he must marry again. By this time Catherine was about thirty-five and hope of a living child had been abandoned. Charles's conscience would not allow him to divorce her or to legitimize the Duke of Monmouth. So his brother must make a state marriage and produce the son and heir for the next generation. The proposed bride was a Habsburg princess and everything had been arranged when the Empress suddenly died and the Emperor decided to marry his cousin himself. By then the Duke was fully occupied with the naval war and the project was not taken up again till 1673, 'the King being now sensible of the necessity there was of his RH being married out of hand,' as the memoirs record.

This may have been because James had rashly proposed marriage to a young widow known as Lady Susan Bellasys, a Protestant who had been married to the son of an old Catholic peer. Charles is said to have forbidden James to make a fool of himself a second time and Lady Susan agreed not to take up the rash offer on condition that she kept the letter in which it was made. Instead she married a Page in the Duke's household (pages were not all boys) but was made a baroness in her own right, remaining always Lady Bellasys. As such she became a Lady of the Bedchamber to the new Duchess of York and a good friend and correspondent to her.

Outside marriage James's mistress at this time was Arabella Churchill, the sister of John. They were the children of a west-country knight, Sir Winston Churchill, and his wife, one of the ramifying Villiers clan. Arabella was one of Duchess Anne's Maids of Honour in the later sixties and because she was discreet and never set up to be a rival, Anne seems to have tolerated her. It was Arabella who got her brother John taken into the Duke's household, at first as a Page; later he was given a commission in the Duke's regiment and started on the military career which was one day to make him world famous as the Duke of Marlborough.

Hamilton tells one of his gossipy tales of Arabella taking riding lessons from the Duke when he was in the north in 1665, falling off her horse and exposing her beautiful white legs (allegedly more handsome than her pale face) so that the Duke, hurrying to pick her up, was instantly infatuated. However that might be, Arabella had four children attributed to James, two boys and two girls, and after the Duchess's death she lived in a house in St James's Square which was kept by her aunt, Mrs Godfrey, who also had charge of the King's children by Barbara (Villiers) Castlemaine. James FitzJames, afterwards Duke of Berwick, was born in 1670 in France where Arabella, ever discreet, had gone for her confinement. (In 1677 she married her cousin Colonel Godfrey and had two daughters in respectable matrimony.) In her portrait, fashionably plump and attractive, she looks pleased with herself. After all, she and her brother had done pretty well out of her liaison with the Duke of York.

The King, in the early seventies, was becoming tired of Barbara's tantrums and bent his energies on winning a new mistress, Louise de Keroualle, whom he had met as his sister's Maid of Honour at Dover. He succeeded in getting her to come to the English court as a Maid of Honour to the Queen. Louise came of a noble but impoverished Breton family, of which she was inordinately proud. She resisted King Charles's advances for a whole year but in the autumn of 1671 he successfully bedded her at Euston Hall, Arlington's seat, conveniently near Newmarket for the races. There was a kind of mock wedding (so John Evelyn, who was staying there, heard – and disapproved) and Louise certainly behaved as if she were a morganatic wife, especially after the birth of her son in 1672 (made Duke of Richmond while still an infant) and unlike Barbara she did not take other lovers. Louise had taste and her apartments at Whitehall, where the King spent much of his time, were splendid far beyond the Queen's and furnished in the latest French style.

In 1673 the man chosen to find a bride for the Duke of York was Henry Mordaunt, Earl of Peterborough, an old cavalier of about fifty, long attached to the Duke's household, who had fought with him at Solebay. He left an account of his adventures abroad which has amused all the biographers of Mary of Modena from Agnes Strickland to Carola Oman. His brief was to inspect several German princesses, one of whom, rather fat and dull, was piqued not to be chosen and in consequence when later she became the third wife of the Emperor she was suspected of turning him against James.

Another (charming) German princess had been chosen when Peterborough received orders that he was to go to Italy and secure the hand of Maria Beatrice d'Este, daughter of Alphonso, Duke of Modena and Laura Martinozzi, one of Cardinal Mazarin's beautiful nieces, so much admired by the youthful Stuart brothers in their days of exile; she was in fact much the same age as James. Her daughter was not yet fifteen and her son Francis two years younger. The father had died when they were infants and Duchess Laura not only brought them up but ran the state of Modena (admittedly not very large) as Regent for her son. Modena was the birthplace of the poet Tasso and the painter Correggio and the Este family had been much greater in the past when they had ruled in Ferrara as well.

Lord Peterborough quite fell in love with Maria himself; she was tall for her age and slim, white-skinned and blackhaired, and with large luminous dark eyes. Maria however was not at all delighted with the marriage proposal. 'She was so innocently bred', is written in the *Life*, 'that till then she had never heard of such a place as England nor of such a person as the Duke of York.' Her great desire at that time was to become a nun; her beloved governess had entered the local Convent of the Visitation, an order founded quite recently by the French bishop St François de Sales. Maria cried and cried, swore she would never marry the English Duke and thought he should rather marry her aunt, who was about thirty – nearer his age.

Peterborough thought no such thing; he was determined to win this lovely young creature for his master and so he did, in spite of difficulties with the Pope because James had not yet declared himself a Catholic.

Because King Louis had offered to advance the dowry, Duchess Laura pressed on and a private ceremony was performed by an exiled English priest on 30 September, a few days before Maria's fifteenth birthday, with Peterborough standing as proxy for the Duke of York. Maria had consented on condition her mother accompanied her to the unknown country in the north. She was to blame herself for this in after years, as by the time Duchess Laura got back to Modena the reins of government had been seized by another (male) member of the family.

When the news of the proxy match came to James he is said to have exclaimed, 'Then I am a married man,' and told his daughters (then living at Richmond) that he was bringing them a playfellow. Indeed Mary was only four years younger than her stepmother. Although the Italian bride was called Mary in England – Queen Mary in due time – I shall call her Maria; that was how she signed letters later in France and it prevents confusion with James's daughter, who also became Queen Mary.

James wrote in the memoirs:

> The noise of the Match coming to the ears of the House of Commons, who at that time were mightily heated against that which they called Popery, *as they usually are when discontented with the Government*, entered into a hot debate about it and at last resolved upon an Address to the King to break the Match, because the Princess was a Roman Catholick and that it was promoted by France. (Italics mine for James's ironic comment.)

Arlington was sufficiently alarmed to advise that the new Duchess of York should be stopped in France, but the King would have none of it. The marriage was made and must stand. But 'the court was so affrighted, few or none accompanied the Duke down to Dover, when he went to meet his new Dutchess.'

James was on the beach and jumped Maria out of the boat into his arms. The poor girl burst into tears but James passed off this awkward moment with compliments in French and escorted his bride and her mother to Dover Castle.

After a brief rest there was a second marriage ceremony, or rather a ratification of the proxy marriage, conducted by Dr Nathaniel Crewe, a

Church of England clergyman who had continued friendly to the Duke after his conversion; he was now Bishop of Oxford and was soon to be translated to the princely see of Durham. Supper followed, attended by all the company.

Carola Oman says there is a pocket book of James's at Windsor containing the dates of the births and deaths of his children, which states that his bride was 'wedded and bedded' on 21 November. They stayed three nights in Dover, 'as much for the consummation of the marriage as the need for repose after the sea-passage,' wrote Duchess Laura's secretary, Guglielmo Codebo. It was important that consummation should not be delayed, since so many people wanted the marriage undone. James was delighted with his bride and though she was not immediately delighted with him, as she soon loved him 'passionately' (her own description) he must have been from the start a kind husband to her, as people in those days expressed it.

They entered London by water and the King came down the river to meet them. Years later Maria told the nuns at Chaillot that Charles 'was always kind to me, and was so truly aimiable and good-natured that I loved him very much, even before I became attached to my lord the Duke of York.'

Parliament being now prorogued, London received the Catholic princess without rioting; the court received her with rejoicing. Codebo and Prince Rinaldo d'Este (a youthful uncle of eighteen) were impressed by the maritime might of England. Rinaldo admired the Duke too and his offhand way of dismissing the efforts of the dreaded Parliament to prevent his marriage. All the same it was thought better that the foreign visitors should leave in January before the new session.

Maria wept again when her mother left but was soon writing to the Reverend Mother of the Visitation Convent at Modena, 'the Lord Duke is a very good man. He has a holy fear of God and is very kind to me, and would do anything to show it.'

James's way of showing kindness to his young bride was to shower her with presents, especially of beautifully set jewels, and take her to all kinds of entertainments, from the first Italian opera to be performed in England, to the magnificent court balls which almost anybody seemed able to witness; Pepys and Evelyn both did. There were concerts of music and some informal music-making in St James's Palace: Maria could play the harp, James the guitar and one of his physicians the theorbo. There were visits to places like Cambridge, where she was greeted with poems and declamations. She very quickly picked up the English language and learned to read and write it fluently; because the nuns at Chaillot kept her papers and letters much more is available from this time on James's domestic life.

In the summer (1674) the King and court removed to Windsor. Charles had had splendid new apartments designed for the Castle; his mistress Louise, now Duchess of Portsmouth, had an elegant suite of her own. Summer life at Windsor was pleasant and relatively informal. The next year (1675) Maria wrote to Lady Bellasys, 'we go every night either by water or by land, a walking or a fishing, or sometimes to country gentlemen's houses, where we dance and play at little plays, and carry our own supper and sup in the garden or in the fields.'

In the first summer (1674) the Duke indulged in rather a large play; he and the Duke of Monmouth got up a mock siege of Maastricht. Monmouth had just returned from the real thing, where he and Churchill had distinguished themselves, fighting for King Louis against the Spanish and Dutch. Fifteen-year-old Maria sat on the terrace with the King and Queen to watch this spectacle, which went on into the night by the light of torches.

Evelyn and Pepys were spectators too, Evelyn recording,

Greate Gunns fir'd on both sides, Grenadoes shot, mines sprung, parties sent out, attempts of raising the seige, prisoners taken, Parlies, and in short all the Circumstances of a formal seige to appearance, and what is most strange, all without disorder or ill accident, but to the greate satisfaction of a thousand spectators.

He and Pepys did not get back to London till three in the morning.

In September that year Evelyn noted the loss by fire of Lord Arlington's London house; he also lost his place as Secretary of State, which he had held for twelve years. But Charles kept him at hand as Lord Chamberlain and continued to consult him till the end of his reign. Arlington had hankered for the position of Lord Treasurer but he was quite unfitted for it. Charles gave it to Buckingham's protégé, the Treasurer of the Navy, Sir Thomas Osborne, and created him Earl of Danby. He proved the best manager Charles had yet had. Clifford (whom James always praises as the best minister) had resigned rather than take the Test, thus showing himself a committed Catholic; he then retired to the country and died – some suspected by his own hand.

Buckingham too was out. His extravagant behaviour over the Countess of Shrewsbury had as much to do with his fall as his alleged misdemeanours in foreign policy, for which he had been called to answer at the bar of the House of Commons. The Earl of Shrewsbury, wounded in a duel with Buckingham, died after it; his unfaithful wife lived openly with her lover (his duchess being forced to go back to the Fairfax parental home) and bore him a son. When the baby died Buckingham had him buried in Westminster Abbey under the title of Earl of Coventry. It was this act that shocked the Lords most; burying bastards in the Abbey as infant Earls – what next?

The Countess (a Catholic) retired to a convent in France and Buckingham to his northern estates. Charles, having dismissed him from his court offices, bought the most valuable (£20,000) for his own bastard son the Duke of Monmouth, who now became the King's Master of Horse and took over Buckingham's Whitehall lodgings at the Cockpit, by then a splendid residence, thoroughly modernized.

Finally, Shaftesbury had not only left the government but moved into opposition. Charles had made him his Lord Chancellor in 1672 and he had got Parliament to vote money for the war, making a famous speech in which he echoed the Roman denunciation of the rival power of Carthage: *Delenda est Carthago* – Carthage must be destroyed! But since then he had, as James put it, 'changed sides again' and the King suspected him of intriguing with Dutch agents in England. He therefore sent Henry Coventry to demand the Seals from Shaftesbury, who is said to have declared, 'It is only laying down my gown and girding on my sword!' His sword was the weapon of political cunning. He became the founder of the Whig party and the first systematic organizer of electioneering, political pamphleteering and mob manipulation. And James, Duke of York was to be his principal target.

9 Schemes and Diversions

For the five years between James's resignation as Admiral and the public frenzy over the Popish Plot he kept his place on the Council and his seat in the House of Lords, so that although his replacement at the Navy Board by a commission of gentlemen amateurs caused havoc in the navy (to Pepys's disgust) the Duke was still a formidable obstacle to the Parliamentary faction, which it is now convenient to call Whig. The Test oath, while it removed him from office, could not demote him from his hereditary position as the King's heir, and though nobody expected Charles to die soon, as he enjoyed such magnificent health, James as heir and father of the future sovereign was believed to exert considerable influence in court circles and over the traditionalists in Parliament and country, soon to be known as Tories. In Parliament Lord Danby (Osborne) became the Tory political leader, organizing them by a judicious use of places, called bribery by the Whigs. James, although he considered himself above parties, was generally regarded as the property of the Tories because of his belief in the traditional monarchy, with the King in control. Thus, in contrast with the euphoric sixties, the seventies saw the revival under new forms of the old struggle between monarchy and Parliament for supremacy.

But at first this was not apparent; the court was still brilliant, lascivious and lavish. There was a revival of court masques and Charles ordered one to be played in December 1674, just before Maria's first child was due. The subject was the classical story of Callisto (a nymph seduced by Jupiter) hastily revised by the poet Crowne so that Callisto preserved her chastity – as the Lady Mary was cast in the part, he could hardly do less.

Mary was twelve that year, a pretty graceful girl, dark-haired and very emotional; she was carrying on a secret romance with an older girl, Frances Apsley, daughter of the Duke's Treasurer, Sir Allen Apsley, writing passionate ill-spelt letters to her 'husband' Aurelia and signing herself Clorine, in the style of the poetic plays then in fashion. Anne was ten, rather too plump but with her father's auburn hair and a musical voice which the King was having trained in speaking by one of his actress mistresses.

All the principal parts in the masque were played by girls, Jupiter by Henrietta Wentworth, then only fourteen, who was to become Monmouth's last mistress. Monmouth himself was in the cast but only to dance, at which he excelled. Juno was played by Barbara's eldest daughter Anne (unsuccessfully claimed as his by her husband Roger Palmer) and already married, at thirteen, and the Countess of Sussex. The part of Mercury was appropriately taken by Sarah Jennings who, at fourteen and Maid of Honour in the Richmond household, was already beginning to exercise a strong fascination on the little princess Anne.

The goddess Diana was played by Margaret Blagge, a Maid of Honour to Duchess Anne in 1665 but a more virtuous one than Arabella Churchill. At the Duchess's death the Duke had got her a place among the Queen's Maids but she found the King's court unbearably frivolous and immoral. But while there she had met Mr Evelyn and they formed a 'spiritual' friendship, meeting together alone for prayer and meditation. It was a nasty shock for Evelyn when he discovered that his saintly paragon had made a secret marriage with Sidney Godolphin, the younger son of an old Cornish family, still making his way at court. However, at the time of *Callisto* this secret marriage was not yet made and Evelyn went to watch his 'deare friend' in the masque and recorded that to her consternation she had lost a jewel worth eighty pounds, lent her by the Countess of Suffolk. But the Duke of York generously paid over the sum and all was well.

The Duke's daughters were playing cards with their young step-mother just before the birth of her first child in January 1675, and they became godmothers to Catherine Laura. Maria had committed a political blunder by having her baby baptized by her Catholic chaplain, but when King Charles came to see her he ignored this illicit act, insisting on a christening conducted in the Chapel Royal by an Anglican bishop. James then explained to Maria that if he did not allow his children to be brought up Protestants they would be removed altogether from his care.

Maria's baby lived through the summer of picnics at Windsor but died in October. The following winter was very cold and snowy; out with the Duke in the garden at St James's, Maria, excited by the northern snow, suddenly threw a snowball at her mighty husband and then fled along the paths into the palace, with James in hot pursuit, up the stairs and into her own room, where she slammed and locked the door against him. And though he beat on it, she would not let him in. This little episode illustrates what Maria meant when she said she soon came to love the Duke passionately. No more than James's first marriage was this a conventional passionless relationship, but while Maria was falling in love for life, James was treating her as a lovely child, to be petted and shown off, but not confided in or consulted, as he had consulted Anne. But then he could hardly confide in a beautiful Italian not much older than his eldest daughter.

Maria's second child was born in August 1676, when she was nearly eighteen; it was another girl, christened Isabella, and destined to live into her fifth year. She was a fair, pretty child and James had her portrait done, just as he had with Mary and Anne – another little daughter to carry about on his arm. But of course he wanted a son. The third child was due in November 1677; just at the time when James's daughter Mary was to be married to her first cousin, William of Orange.

William had grown up entirely Dutch and with the conviction that he ought to be Stadholder (military leader) as his forebears had been. But the republican oligarchy had thought his posthumous birth a good chance to break a tradition which looked like becoming hereditary, if not monarchic. William proved himself when he was only twenty-two as the leader of the resistance to Louis XIV's invasion in 1672 and, on a wave of popular enthusiasm, was appointed Stadholder on his own merits. But although the French had to retreat from Holland, defeated by the flooding of the flat country, they continued their campaign in Flanders, where Louis laid claim to some of the towns (which have now long been a part of France). In William's eyes, however, the Spanish Netherlands (now Belgium) were an indispensable barrier against France. Thus the three-cornered situation was the exact reverse of what it had been in the previous century, with Spain and Holland now allied against France. As the Spanish Netherlands were predominantly Catholic the war was in no sense religious; it was national.

England had made peace in 1674, promising neutrality, but Orange made an alliance with the Emperor and some of the German states and was determined to drive the French out of their recent conquests. In the spring of 1675 William fell dangerously ill of the small pox; he felt he owed his recovery to his friend Willem Bentinck, who volunteered to share his bed, since the doctors said the heat of another body would bring out the rash and abate the fever. It also gave Bentinck the small pox; he too was very ill but recovered and remained ever afterwards William's trusted right-hand man. The war dragged on, unsatisfactorily for the young Stadholder, in three summer seasons; in 1677 he was defeated. He then sent Bentinck over to England to try to get Charles into the war on his side, but all Charles offered were talks about peace and an invitation for an autumn visit.

By this time William had been convinced by Sir William Temple (the English Ambassador) that a marriage with the Lady Mary would be popular with the Protestant English and not (as he feared) alienate the Parliamentary party by seeming to ally himself with the court. By it he might win English support against France; his aim was more political than dynastic.

The King had prevented Parliament's sitting for over a year, by constantly proroguing it to a date a few months ahead and then proroguing again, so that a session was always expected but never actually took place. This infuriated Shaftesbury and his party, as they could do nothing when Parliament was not sitting. At last in the autumn of 1677 Charles allowed a brief session in which there were furious debates culminating in a lively scene when Shaftesbury, Buckingham, Salisbury and Wharton were sent to the Tower for maintaining that Parliament (which ought to sit every year) could dissolve itself if the King 'illegally' prorogued it, and refusing to beg the King's pardon. Needless to say, they were not there for long.

The session over, Charles went off to Newmarket and James, who went with him, sent royal yachts to Holland to fetch William, who landed at Harwich and drove straight to Newmarket, ignoring all local attempts to entertain him. He then annoyed his uncles by refusing to discuss peace terms till his marriage to Mary had been arranged; what was more, he refused to make a formal offer till he had seen her. They thought him badly brought up but Charles consented to go back to

Whitehall, where James lodged William in his own fine apartments overlooking the river.

Mary was at St James's Palace and thither William went for the introduction. He was satisfied with Mary's appearance and manners and afterwards embraced Sir William Temple, who had done so much to forward the match. But it was Lord Danby who persuaded the King that this Protestant marriage would be popular in the country and allay suspicions that he was secretly in collusion with France. In fact, he had signed another secret treaty with Louis, in which each king promised not to join forces with the other's enemies, and Charles, in return for a subsidy, would dissolve the (anti-French) Parliament. When he did not dissolve but merely prorogued it, Louis showed signs of withholding the money, but was eventually persuaded to pay it in quarterly instalments. It was not enough to make the King solvent but staved off his worst difficulties while Danby reorganized customs and excise and the financing of loans with far greater efficiency than any earlier minister. Danby was a firm Protestant; it was he who had persuaded Charles to reaffirm his allegiance to the Church of England and allow the new anti-Catholic laws to be enforced.

When the Prince of Orange applied to the Duke of York for his daughter James had insisted on peace talks first, marriage plans afterwards. But on going to his brother he found that Charles had given the Prince leave to apply. James retorted that he wished he had known that. 'At which the King broke off short and said, He would speak of it another time.'

Charles knew that James hoped his daughter might marry the Dauphin and one day be Queen of France. He had also promised James that Mary should not be given away without his consent. But Charles was the King and James was his subject. 'Oddsfish, he must consent!' Charles is reported to have said.

James did not record this. His account is that the King, sitting in Council, summoned the Duke and announced the marriage.

> The Duke then publicly consented and said he hoped he had given sufficient testimony of his right intention for the publick good and that people would no more say, he design'd the altering the Government in Church and State, for whatever his opinion in Religion

might be, all that he desired was that men might not be molested meerly for conscience sake.

Thus he took the opportunity to enunciate his own principles before the King's Council.

After that James had to tell his daughter, now fifteen, that she was to marry her cousin William and go to live in Holland. The princesses' chaplain, Dr Lake, recorded that Mary cried 'all the afternoon and all the following day'.

William might be pleased with Mary but Mary was not so pleased with William. He was twenty-seven and his unsmiling taciturnity made him seem older. Mary had not yet reached her full height, not much under six feet, but William had certainly reached his, which was not more than five foot six. His head, big for his small slight body, was quite impressive, with a strong hooked nose and dark eyes; he wore his own brown hair still, thick and long. But he was so serious and humourless and spoke English with a Dutch accent; Mary, emotional and rather frivolous, seems to have wept most at the foreignness of the match. When Queen Catherine tried to cheer her by saying that when she came to England it was to marry a man she had never seen, Mary replied petulantly, 'But you were coming to England, madam, and I am going from it.'

This retort and King Charles's joky remarks at the wedding were recorded by Dr Lake. It took place privately at nine o'clock in the evening of 4 November, William's birthday. Though James was present it was Charles who gave the bride away; he seems to have overdone the pleasantries, perhaps to repress the consciousness that he had forced his brother's and his niece's consent to a marriage made for his own convenience.

Mary was ceremonially undressed and put to bed by Queen Catherine, Duchess Maria and the Duchess of Monmouth (Anna Scott, heiress of Buccleugh) while the few guests took refreshments in the next room. Then William was brought in to get into bed beside her and there they sat, receiving congratulations from courtiers and diplomats. Finally Charles drew the bed curtains with a last maddening joke: 'Now, nephew, to your work! Hey! St George for England!'

Anne was not at the wedding; she had gone down with small pox.

[79]

James visited her every day but did not tell her when Mary was leaving, for fear distress at parting with her sister might retard her recovery.

One of Charles's jokes at the wedding had been to tell the Bishop of London (Henry Compton, who had confirmed Mary and made sure her religion was strictly Protestant) to hurry, lest the Duchess of York be delivered of a son and 'the marriage be disappointed'.

On 7 November Maria did just that; her first-born son arrived 'just a quarter before ten at night' as James noted in his pocket book. Dr Lake recorded that the baby was 'little but sprightly and likely to live'. The French ambassador thought this event 'moderated the joy felt at the marriage of the Prince of Orange' among the Londoners, who had lit bonfires to celebrate the Protestant royal wedding. But a son for James did not at this stage mean 'a Catholic heir' as some modern writers have put it. The very next day he was christened (Charles) according to the rites of the Church of England, in which he would have been brought up so long as King Charles lived. For Charles had realized by now that if he became a Catholic he would lose his throne.

William was one of the sponsors but he was eager now to get back to Holland and irritated at everything which delayed him, including the weather. They started on 19 November but had to go ashore when the wind changed and stay at Canterbury, William refusing James's invitation to return to Whitehall. In his letter James said that if the French did not agree to the peace terms 'the King ought to lett the King of France know that unless hee would forebear any further conquests in Flanders, hee could not hinder England from coming into the war.'

James had been converted to William's view that the Spanish Netherlands must remain a barrier to French aggression. Letters went off every week by packet boat to Holland, addressed to 'my sonne the Prince of Orange' and as William kept them all, there they still are, written in James's blunt colloquial style but always assuming shared family interests. But one of the first brought the sad news that the baby Charles had caught the small pox and died, just one month old, on 12 December. 'I wish you may never have the like cause of trouble, nor know what it is to lose a son.' Dr Lake thought the Duke had never grieved so much for the loss of any other child.

The Lady Anne was recovering; she had been allowed to kiss her new little brother on 3 December and some people thought that was what had given him the dread disease. Anne did not miss Mary as much as her father had feared. She moved into Mary's apartments and became the most important princess.

10 The War that Never Was

The year 1678 began with James in constant correspondence with William of Orange about the war, which seemed about to involve England, since King Louis did refuse the terms worked out in November between Charles and William. The Duke was busy raising troops and arranging their transport to Flanders, and even contemplated taking up a command himself.

Parliament was now in session and surprised James by obstructing the grant of funds for the war with France which they had been so zealous for before. On 2 February he told William, 'now that his Majesty has done all they desired in their former address, how they chicane and fly off from what they have formerly said; attack the prerogative, and would impose upon his Majesty such things as cannot subsist with monarchy and was never before pretended by a house of commons.'

If James could have read the despatches the new French Ambassador, Paul de Barillon, sent back to King Louis (printed with translations by Dalrymple in 1773) he would have discovered the explanation of Parliament's obstructive ways.

Barillon had first been approached by some of the opposition in November 1677, soon after he arrived in England; in January he turned these tricky negotiations over to M de Rouvigny, a former ambassador who was a Huguenot. On 14 March he wrote a 'mémoire' in which he reported that Rouvigny had convinced Lord Russell (heir to the Earl of Bedford and Whig leader in the Commons) that it was not in the King of France's interest 'to make the King of England absolute master in his kingdom'. So France was willing to pay members to obstruct the raising of money and troops for the proposed war. Russell agreed to the scheme, though disclaiming any interest in money, but others not so rich were not above bribery to do something so congenial as thwarting the King, even in the projected war they had promoted; Barillon soon had quite a number on his payroll – a nasty shock for the Whig Dalrymple when he discovered it!

Rouvigny found Lord Hollis 'so embittered against the court and the ministry' that he dared not say anything of King Charles's desire for peace, for fear Hollis should immediately become a partisan for the war. Russell told Rouvigny that he was resolved 'to support the affair against the treasurer (Danby) and even attack the Duke of York and all the Catholics'. So the campaign against the Duke was planned months before the Popish Plot was heard of. Barillon assured King Louis he was doing all he could to fortify the party opposed to the court but added, 'It is not easy to succeed when the King of England conforms himself to all that his subjects prescribe to him, even though the most contrary to his interest.'

From these accounts it is clear that the opposition cared not a fig for William of Orange or the aggressions of France; all they cared about was to reduce the power of the King and increase that of Parliament, or rather, of their party.

In April a new element appeared, the fears of 'the heads of the cabal' (Russell, Hollis, Shaftesbury and Buckingham) that the King intended to use the new army to subject England, spurred on by the Duke of York who was in command of it. On 18 April Barillon summed up his impressions of the Duke, saying that he 'believes himself lost as to his religion, if the present opportunity does not serve to bring England into subjection . . . he thinks that by declaring strongly against France, he will diminish the animosity against himself. This does not appease his enemies; he is more suspected than ever and not less hated. . . .' Barillon thought that Charles was not keen on 'the design of changing the government' but was 'drawn along by the Duke of York and the High Treasurer'.

This is so exactly the opposition's idea of what the Duke of York was up to, in collusion with Lord Danby, that its provenance is obvious; yet Barillon's despatches have been taken, by Dalrymple and by later historians, as evidence for James's absolutist intentions. He himself called these allegations 'stories' – inventions – and certainly neither his letters nor his actions suggest anything of the sort. All through April he was writing to William concerning his anxieties about the English troops already in Bruges and how to get reinforcements to them, and about a rumour that a Dutch squadron at Cadiz was to be withdrawn, which 'would be very prejudicial to us all, for then the French would be absolute masters in the Mediterranean, and not only destroy both your trade and ours but also very much trouble the Spaniard in all their coasts' (the English squadron there was not strong enough to deal with the French by itself).

It was in April too that James was approached by Lord Russell to let him know that if he would join with them 'for the good of the Nation' in prosecuting the Lord Treasurer 'they would remove his incapacity for being High Admiral.' James refused, saying that 'to fall upon the King's minister without the King's consent, unless he were visibly guilty of some great misdemeanour', would be 'very contrary to the good both of the King and of the Nation'. And he commented on the 'unsettled temper of the Factious Party, which one while was for attacking the Duke and at other times calling for his assistance to attack others.' It also shows that the opposition's policy was really aimed against government by the King; his Tory minister Danby and his military brother the Duke were equally targets, and if one could be used against the other, so much the better. But James would not play the power game.

In May the situation changed again. Continually baulked in Parliament, Charles started negotiating again with Louis and concluded another secret treaty, so secret that the King wrote it out himself, Danby not daring to be a party to it. In it he promised neutrality (instead of war) if the peace negotiations then in progress between the Dutch and the French failed, and accepted the usual cash bribe if he prorogued Parliament and disbanded his army. Dalrymple assumes that James was privy to these secret negotiations but he seems only to have learned of it when the treaty was completed, when he wrote an unusually long letter to William on 21 May, to warn him that reinforcements were now unlikely to be sent and to urge him to return to the Hague before the Deputies came back with the French answers, so as to be on the spot if peace were made – 'which will be whether you will or no; for as to Spain, you know as well as I the miserable condition they are in; and as to us here . . .' well, he had only to look at what went on in Parliament.

[83]

For now the ill men in the house strike directly at the King's authority: and should we have been engaged in a war now, they would have so imposed upon the King, as to leave him nothing but the empty name of a King, and no more power than a Duke of Venice; and how long they would have let him have that name, the Lord knows: I am sure it would not have been long. I say this to you, to let you see how necessary peace is, and how impossible it is for you to carry on the war . . . Pray let nobody see this letter, it is wrote only for you, and not fit for anybody else to read or to know.

In June came another reversal: Louis refused to hand back his Flanders conquests until his allies the Swedes received satisfactory terms from the German confederates. This caused uproar in the Netherlands and Charles, who had not yet received any money from Louis (because he had neither prorogued Parliament nor disbanded the army) changed his mind again and sent Sir William Temple to make a treaty with the Dutch, promising to assist them in war with France if King Louis did not within two months return the towns, regardless of what was happening to the Swedes.

On 26 July James was writing to William that the Duke of Monmouth was going on Sunday to Bruges 'and I shall take care for the embarking of those that are yet here as soon as possible, and be ready to go with them myself if occasion be.'

At this point the Dutch statesmen signed a separate peace with France, without waiting for the Spaniards, an event which so enraged William that he put the official letter announcing it in his pocket and attacked the French near Mons. It was a most bloody battle and like all too many of William's battles indecisive. James later condemned this action but at the time, unaware of the pocketed letter, he wrote that he was 'very much pleased with what you have done, for by what I hear on all sides, it was a very bold and vigorous action, and as bravely carried on.' The news of the separate peace, coming later, had 'stunned' him and 'so turns my head as I do hardly know what to say' – a phrase which reminds one how busy Pepys must have been at this time.

The Dutch peace did not necessarily mean the end of the war and James wrote from Windsor in August about sending over more troops, still hoping to go himself. But that was not to be; peace was made all round, the Emperor being last out as he was last in, the Flanders towns returned to Spanish hands, the Swedes contented and the Dutch able once more to trade with France. Charles, King of England, considered himself the chief mediator of the Peace of Nijmegen and he had got through another difficult year with his Parliament without dissolving it. Although much changed over the seventeen years it had been sitting, it was still the same Parliament he had called at the Restoration. Anything new might be worse.

James did not spend all the summer of 1678 organizing the embarkations for Flanders; some of it was spent in a new love affair – the child of it was born in March 1679. The girl was another Maid of Honour to the Duchess of York, Catherine Sedley, the only child of the poet and rake Sir Charles Sedley. As her mother was confined as mad at a convent in Ghent, Catherine grew up in her father's rackety household 'none of the most virtuous, but a witt etc,' as Evelyn commented in 1673, when she was only sixteen. Catherine was no beauty; she was brown of skin with bright eyes and dark curly hair, but she was lively and quick-witted, very much James's type, like a coarser Anne Hyde – and she was a friend of Anne's brothers, a Protestant Tory like them.

In spite of her reputation Catherine would have a dowry of £4000 and this was enough for Sir Winston Churchill to try to secure her as a wife for his son John, now a colonel in the Duke of York's (or Lord Admiral's) regiment. But John was madly in love with Sarah Jennings, who at seventeen had grown a tall girl with flaxen hair, blue eyes, a tip-tilted nose and a sharp tongue. Because she had virtually no money of her own (and nor had he) she was determined not to give in to his pleading for love till they were married. But his letters (which she kept, while insisting that hers were burned), though dementedly loving, contained no offer of marriage. Men writing of his courtship seem not to have noticed this, putting down Sarah's behaviour to coquetry.

But the prospect of the Sedley marriage forced Sarah to confide in the young Duchess and it was Maria who made it possible for Sarah to marry Churchill secretly, drawing her salary as a Maid till the marriage had to be made known, which it was by the spring of 1678, to the annoyance of Sir Winston. However, once married, Sarah proved a faithful though domineering wife and John continued to adore her to the end of his days.

[85]

Catherine Sedley, whose views on Churchill do not seem to be recorded, was having an affair with Colonel James Graham, an equerry and friend to the Duke of York. When the Duke made a bid for Catherine's favours, Graham retired, and the love affair begun that summer lasted on and off for some years. Catherine teased James; her witticism that she could not think what made him love her – 'It cannot be for my beauty, since I have none, nor for my wit, since he has not enough to know it' – has often been quoted to suggest that she despised him. But in fact she flaunted the relationship, got her babies acknowledged under the name of Darnley, and reacted strongly against William's usurpation in 1688, still corresponding with her royal lover when he was in Ireland. She was about twenty-one when she became James's mistress, a year older than his wife, who was to be made desperately unhappy by the liaison when she eventually discovered it.

She did not know of it that autumn. She and Anne planned to go over to Holland to visit Mary, 'very incognito' as James wrote to William. He was going to Newmarket with Charles, himself. Maria and Anne could not really remain incognito; they were received with lavish entertainment and much enjoyed themselves. On 18 October James wrote from London, 'We came hither on Wednesday from Newmarket, and the same night, presently after eleven, the Dutchess arrived here, so satisfied with her journey and with you, as I never saw anybody; and I must give you a thousand thanks from her and from myself, for her kind usage by you: I should say more on this subject, but I am very ill at compliments and you care not for them.'

He went on, 'As for news, this pretended plot is still under examination . . . and I do verily believe that when this affair is thoroughly examined, it will be found nothing but malice against the poor Catholics in general, and myself in particular.'

This letter shows that James's view of the Popish Plot was the same at the beginning as when he wrote of it in the memoirs: Oates's revelations were spurious inventions taken up by Shaftesbury and his party to rouse anti-Catholic feeling in the country which could be used to exclude the Duke of York from the succession – not because he was a future threat to the country, as they pretended, but because he was a present obstacle to their gaining political ascendancy, and a formidable one.

[86]

11 Hellish Conspiracy

Whole books have been written about the Popish Plot and I do not propose to do more than trace James's path through its complications and consequences. The first he heard of it was at the end of August 1678 when his confessor, the Jesuit Father Bedingfeld, brought him a sheaf of ill-written letters signed with the names of his priest colleagues but quite evidently not theirs, and containing dangerous rigmarole about murdering the King.

James immediately took these forgeries to his brother, who then told him that before he left Whitehall two mad clergymen had warned him of an assassination plot, which he had dismissed as nonsense. In the memoirs James said that 'a bundle of papers was left with his Majesty, but they being long, he gave them to the Lord Treasurer to peruse.' James pressed for them to be examined by the Committee for Foreign Affairs (which could meet in the holidays) but the King said they could wait till the Council due to be held in September, at which the informer, Titus Oates, was to appear. This was the first time James saw him.

Oates was an unappealing figure, fat and with a moon face in which his mouth seemed almost half-way up, so huge was his chin. He spoke with an affected nasal drawl, said to have been copied from courtiers. He was twenty-nine and had led a chequered career, thrown out of several educational institutes for homosexual practices, though he had succeeded in taking orders in the Church of England and had served briefly as a naval chaplain. In 1676 he had met the fanatical Israel Tonge and went abroad, pretending to be a Catholic, to gather information against the Jesuits. He made a brief stay at the English College in Valladolid (expelled) and another at St Omers in Flanders (expelled again); his short residence in Spain inspired him to call himself a Doctor (of Divinity) at Salamanca. He then came home and concocted the supposed plot of the papists to murder the King.

'As soon as Oates was brought in,' James wrote in the memoirs, 'he tould the King, He had ventured his life for his Majesty at Sea and his soul for him at land.' This dotty pomposity amused the royal brothers and James often afterwards used the phrase. Oates then 'began his Narration with so much assurance' as would almost have convinced the listeners, 'till by cross examination the vilainy of it began to appear'.

It was soon plain that the Bedingfeld letters were forgeries and in fact they were never used as evidence. In his narrative Oates referred to Don John, of whom Charles and James had vivid memories. 'The King asking him, what sort of man Don John was? he sayd he was leane, tall and black, whereas the King and the Duke knew him to be a litle, fat, and well-complexioned man, though he had brown hair.'

Charles was impatient of the whole affair. 'It would alarme all the Kingdom and put the thought of killing him into men's heads who had no such thoughts before.' But it was time to go to the races, so he left the business to Lord Danby.

James was convinced that Danby delayed dealing with the plot till the opening of Parliament because he saw in it a chance to divert the House's attention from himself; he was well aware of Shaftesbury's intention to bring him down. This delay moved Oates to deposit his narration with a magistrate, Sir Edmond Bury Godfrey, and the affair really blew up when Godfrey was discovered dead on Primrose Hill in mysterious circumstances. The murder remains a mystery to this day, though the latest investigator, Stephen Knight, has uncovered underground connexions which suggest that it was carried out on behalf of Shaftesbury's party. No real evidence ever turned up to fix it on the papists, which did not stop the populace from believing it a popish crime, master-minded by the Jesuits.

Shaftesbury is said to have remarked that he did not know who started the plot but that he was very sure he had the full hunting of it. He exploited the latent fear and hatred of popery which was soon aroused to frenzy, to try to exclude the Duke of York from the succession by Act of Parliament, so that Parliament could wrest supremacy from the King; henceforth kings would reign by licence of Parliament. It was the second act of the political drama which had begun in 1641 (date of dread to all who feared another civil war). The third act was to come in 1688 when Shaftesbury was no longer there to direct operations.

In the eighteenth century Dalrymple discovered some manuscript memoranda by Lord Keeper North, which showed that this old Tory lawyer had guessed that 'there must have been an invisible hand which directed the movements of the house of commons at this time.' He thought it strange that the Commons 'should be so earnest to persuade the King to enter into an actual war with France, and when he had made preparations in order for it, that the factious party should represent them as intended to enslave the nation, and that good men should be able to believe it. . . .' To get rid of the army it was called popish and 'the plot must be magnified.'

The invisible hand was Shaftesbury's, who had his Green Ribbon Club and his Brisk Boys to manipulate the London mob, spread rumours and organize demonstrations, like the huge funeral procession for Sir Edmond Bury Godfrey or the customary pope-burnings (with live cats sewn into the effigies for realistic screams) on 17 November, Queen Elizabeth's accession day. In Parliament the plot roused a passionate Protestant patriotism which could easily be turned against the King's heir, who was not only a Catholic but in command of the new raised army, which he had praised to William as better than he had expected: 'I never saw so many good looked men in my life.'

After James's letter of 18 October, mentioning Godfrey's murder, Dalrymple prints no more till December, but James was writing every few days to William and the letters survive in the Foljambe MSS, published by the Historical Manuscripts Commission in 1897, which keep his own spelling – Dalrymple 'modernized' it. Oates was now making accusations at the bar of the House of Commons 'and when he will make an end of accusing people the Lord knows,' James wrote on 29 October, 'but their chief malice is against me, for they think they have no sure way of ruining the King, as beginning with me. This day Lord Shaftesbury and his gange shewd their malice to me and would have got a thing done that might have proved very prejudicial to me, but they could not carry it in our House.' James attended the House of Lords every day during this frenzied session, when panic about the supposed papist plot reached lunatic proportions and all Catholics were ordered to leave London.

James told William he thought all the accused innocent, 'for I looke upon none but Colman to be faulty.' Colman, or Coleman, was an over-enthusiastic convert who had been the Duke's secretary till the King ordered his dismissal for his meddling in politics. He had been encouraged (and paid) by Barillon to work against the war with France and in 1675–6 had corresponded with the Jesuit Père La Chaise in Paris, full of plans to use French money to re-establish Catholicism in England, praising the Duke and running down the King. When he was dismissed the Duchess, sorry for Mrs Coleman, asked if she could employ him as her secretary. As he would only be writing formal letters to the Pope, Cardinals etc; this was allowed.

At the beginning of the plot scare Coleman was warned by Sir Edmond Bury Godfrey (no less) that his name appeared in the Oates depositions, and he went to the Duke for advice. James said that if he had any papers that might be misconstrued he had better destroy them. If Coleman destroyed any, he certainly did not destroy all. Knowing .himself guiltless of any murder plot, he actually gave himself up when a warrant was issued. His papers were seized and were afterwards passed round at the House of Commons, where members thought his three-years-past letters excellent evidence for implication in the recent conspiracy. Ever afterwards, when any member dared to suggest that the plot was a fabrication, the opposition would chant 'Coleman's Letters! Coleman's Letters!'

As Coleman had been the Duke's secretary his indiscretions inevitably seemed to implicate James. On 5 November, after commiserating with William on his troubles in Holland, he wrote:

> I am sure we have our belly full of them here, and I do not see how soon we are like to have an end of them, there being so many malitious persons in the world. I have been fallen upon in both houses . . . Tomorrow I expect to be fallen upon again in the Lords House, where I will defend myself as well as I can.

On 12 November, writing that he was very glad to hear his daughter Mary was better, for he had been 'in pain' for her illness, he went on:

> As for affairs here they do not mend, but every day grow worse and worse, so that I am to prepare for a very great storm to come upon me, and I do not see it is likely to stop at me and that their chief aime

in removing of me, is to come easier at the King . . . If I should write you all the newse and the malitious storys (that) are told, instead of a letter you would have a volume from me, but realy I am so tired with having been almost all day at the House, that I can say no more, but am yours, James.

Two more letters followed before he wrote on 22 November:

I have gott a proviso added to the bill for putting the Catholike lords out of the house and banishing all those of that perswasion from the Court, that nothing in that act shall extend to me; so that in this way my enemys have mist of their aime, for their cheif designe by the bill, was to drive me from his Majesty's presence.

On 26 November he said, 'But now there is another thing happened which I am sure will surprise you, which is that their great villain Oates did on Sunday last accuse the Queene of her having designed to poison his Majesty. . . .' Charles's reaction was to take more notice of Catherine than he had since Louise had gained ascendancy at court; he took her from Somerset House back to Whitehall and appeared often in public with her.

The anti-papist frenzy continued unabated. On 3 December James wrote to William complaining that the Commons were determined to disband the troops that were in Flanders; something they were both at one in deploring. He added, 'Mr Coleman was executed this morning, and declared, as he was ready to be turned off, that he had been falsely accused . . . that he knew nothing of a plot . . . and had never gone about to endeavour the alteration of religion by force.'

If James sounds uncaring about Coleman's fate, the secretary was partly responsible for his own plight, but the Jesuits were not guilty of anything; six were arrested in November and all their papers seized. Nothing remotely incriminating was found, which did not prevent proceedings against them on Oates's perjured evidence. James certainly cared about them; he admired the English Fathers of the Society and had let them hold their triennial conference in St James's Palace in the spring. Luckily this fact was never discovered. The crucial 'April meeting' was supposed to have taken place at the White Horse

Tavern, when Oates was in fact still at St Omer, though he flatly denied in court the witness of the young scholars of the College, brought over to testify against him.

In the memoirs it is briefly related that the King was persuaded to issue a proclamation banishing all priests from the country. When James asked that 'the Duchess's Jesuits might be excepted, as well as the Queen's and the Foreign Ministers' [ambassadors], it was absolutely refused as a privilege too great for a Subject.' It was then proposed that they should be included in the Queen's list, 'but her Majesty (tho the Duke and the King himself desired it) would never consent, which was a great tryal of their Royal Highnesses patience, to find themselves so soon abandon'd by one from whom they expected the greatest favours and support.' Catherine could not get over her jealousy of the Yorks, though they still had no living son to succeed Charles.

One of the Duchess's Jesuits was a Frenchman, Fr Claude de la Colombière, who had come over in the winter of 1676, one of the most severe for years. He had been chaplain at the Visitation Convent of Paray le Monial and was convinced of the authenticity of Sister Marguerite Marie's visions of Christ showing his heart as the sign of his love for men. Fr Claude introduced the devotion of the Sacred Heart in the Duchess's little chapel in her Bedchamber suite – she had never been allowed the use of the Queen's Chapel at St James's. Fr Claude's sermons touched many who came to hear them and brought into James's life the spirituality of the French Catholic revival in that century of great saints (the best known today are St François de Sales and St Vincent de Paul, founder of the Sisters of Charity).

Fr Claude was not strong and that summer he had been spitting blood; he was ordered back to France but forbidden by the doctor to travel in winter. In November he was arrested (at 2 a.m.) and thrown into the King's Bench prison. A few days later he was tried before a justice in the lower hall at Westminster, the witness against him (a renegade French servant) swearing he had said the King was a Catholic at heart. As he had had several private interviews with the King, this was dangerous. But Barillon was alerted (probably by the Duke) and Fr Claude was deported at the end of the year. He never recovered his health, dying in 1682. He had been deeply impressed with the

[92]

goodness, gentleness and kindness of the young Italian Duchess of York, in whose service he had lived in England – which he called 'the land of crosses'.

The English Jesuits, including Fr Bedingfeld (who died in prison) could not be saved; those who survived the rigours of imprisonment were executed in the June of the following year, but by that time James had been forced to leave the country.

An address from the Commons was made to the King in November 1678, demanding that the Duke of York should be removed from all the King's Councils. Charles refused but James recorded that next day he took his brother aside and asked him not to come any more to the Committee for Foreign Affairs. James replied that he would obey a command but could never do it of his own accord: 'first, he sayd, Because instead of stopping their mouths, it would on the contrary encourage his Enemys to press on farther if they saw his Majesty once give ground.' Secondly, if Charles were now resolved 'to content the people in reference to religion' it would seem to confirm the opinion that 'so soon as the Duke was out of the Council all things were done to the satisfaction of the Kingdom,' and people would infer 'what a mighty influence he formerly had in the direction of affaires,' and if he remained at court they would imagine that 'as soon as Parliament was up, he would infallibly reassume the same again,' and then they would demand his banishment from court too.

James was not mistaken; five days later the House voted an address for him to withdraw from the King's person as well as from his councils. The King withstanding this, the proviso which exempted the Duke was passed, the Duke of Monmouth going out before the debate ended, to avoid voting. James comments,

It is not to be wonder'd that the Duke of Monmouth, who had more ambition than judgment and more address to court an interest than prudence to manage it, should fancy himself within reach of a Scepter when he saw the Duke (whom he thought the only obstacle) soe furiously batter'd on all hands.

Baulked for the moment in the attack on the Duke, Shaftesbury's party turned their full attention to the Treasurer, and Ralph Montagu launched his attack in December. Montagu had been the King's ambassador in France; a furious letter from Barbara (now living in Paris) told Charles that Montagu had not only debauched their daughter the Countess of Sussex but called the King 'a dull governable fool' and his brother 'a wilful fool' adding that because of this it was better to have the King than the Duke, except that King always chose 'a greater beast than himself to govern him'.

Charles's retort was to dismiss Montagu, who immediately started negotiating with Barillon for full monetary support if he brought down the King's minister, Danby; he also managed to get himself a seat in Parliament, where he would be protected by Parliamentary privilege when he brought out his accusations against the Treasurer.

Montagu made known in the House the secret letters Danby had written to him at the King's command; uproar ensued and an impeachment was ordered to be drawn up forthwith. James wrote indignantly to William on 20 December, 'I am confident there never was so abominable an action as this of Mr Montagu's, and so offensive to the King, in revealing what he had trusted him with when he was employed by his Majesty: all honest men abhor him for it.' He added that he was sure the Lord Treasurer would defend himself very well – 'I am sure his Majesty is bound to stand by him.'

His Majesty did stand by Danby to the extent of proroguing Parliament and then spent the Christmas holidays wondering whether to dissolve it. James took time off to go hunting.

Barillon was kept busy with suggestions from different quarters which are summarized by Dalrymple. In November the Duke of York proposed that the army be kept on foot, Parliament dissolved and the union between Charles and Louis be renewed; he wanted his intervention kept secret from the King and Danby.

Montagu, in January, was urging Barillon to advise Charles to dismiss the army and give up Danby; assistance from France to be promised if he consented.

Finally, Charles himself was pressing for more aid from King Louis, saying that 'the attack upon the Catholicks was only an attack upon the common cause of royalty.' Barillon had answered that Charles ought to disband his army first – 'car c'est le point essentiel.' The French were not really interested in the cause of royalty, of Catholics, or the fate of

Charles and James Stuart; what was essential was to keep England from being an active member of the anti-French alliance.

But Charles could not disband his army without money to pay the troops and as Louis refused to provide the wherewithal he decided to dissolve Parliament, call a new one and disband the army if it provided the means and – send his brother abroad; in effect banish him, not only from the court and the Council as the Commons had desired, but from the country.

He first broached it to James in the middle of February 1679. Although James said he was ready to sacrifice everything if necessary, he did not believe banishment was the right policy; it seemed to be admitting the case against him and would prevent him from defending himself. Charles, under the impression that if James publicly returned to the Church of England it would remove the pretext for the current attacks, sent the new Archbishop of Canterbury to him. This was William Sancroft, appointed in 1678 on James's advice, in preference to Henry Compton.

So the Archbishop and the old Bishop of Winchester, who was now eighty but a loyal royalist, called at St James's on the morning of 21 February and were admitted to the Duke's closet. Of this meeting we have not only James's account in the memoirs but Sancroft's notes, published in 1765 with the Clarendon Correspondence.

James says that the Archbishop began with a well-ordered discourse, wondering that the Duke should leave the Church of England for the Church of Rome, which held many doctrines contrary to the Word of God; its priests hindered people from reading the Scriptures and required blind obedience from all lay people. The lecture lasted nearly half an hour but James heard it 'without interrupting him in the least'. Restraint must have been difficult if the Archbishop expressed himself according to his own notes on Roman Catholics 'who absolutely give themselves to serve the secular interests and designs of the proudest, the cruelest, and the most uncharitable church in the world'.

'But we hope better things of you, great sir,' he proceeded, promising not to lead him into 'hard and thorny questions' but adjuring him to leave the stepdame Rome and return to his 'true dear and holy mother the Church of England'.

James says he replied that he did not doubt they meant well, and that it would be 'a presumption in him, who was an illitterate man, to enter into controversial disputes with persons so learned as they' but that he would have given the reasons for his conversion if he had had time, assuring them that he had not done it without careful study, 'nor without a previous foresight of the inconveniences which have already happen'd', and he ended by apologizing for having to dismiss them now 'by reason of the greater hurry of business'.

Two days later the King asked his brother what had happened and found 'that project was ineffectual'. He then asked James's own opinion on what was to be done. James pointed out how hard it was for him to decide his own case; 'that if he gave moderate counsells it would be looked on as an argument of fear; if vigorous ones the world would say, he cared not how he embroiled the King now his own condition was so desperate.' So he would submit his will entirely to the King. 'So the King told him he was convinced it was absolutely necessary to yeeld to this torrent, accompanying his discourse upon it, with great expressions of kindness for his Person and sorrow for the occasion, and in conclusion desired that he would withdraw for some time out of England.'

James then asked for 'something to show the world, what was the motive of his complyance', knowing that otherwise it would be put down to fear or guilt or both.

So, on 28 February 1679 Charles wrote:

I have already given you my reasons at large why I think it fitt that you should absent yourself from me for some time beyond the seas; as I am truly sorry for the occasion, so you may be sure I shall never desire it longer than will be absolutely necessary both for your good and my service: in the mean time I think it proper to give it you under my hand, that I expect this complyance from you and desire it may be assoon as conveniently you can. You may easily believe with what trouble I writ this to you, there being nothing I am more sencible of than the constant kindness you have ever had for me. And I hope you are so just to me as to be assured that no absence nor any thing els, can ever change me from being truly and kindly your C. R.

This kind tone softened the blow of banishment though it did not ease the Duke's apprehension that it was a mistaken policy. He was to be gone before the new Parliament opened, which gave him only a few days to collect himself and his belongings; he and the Duchess took ship on 4 March. The King, who came to see them off, at the last minute said they could not go on board, the wind was contrary. Seeing tears in his eyes, Maria broke out, 'What, sir, are you grieved? – you, who send us into exile! Of course we must go, since you have ordained it.'

When telling the nuns of Chaillot in later life of this youthful outburst, she blamed herself, saying that she now realized it was not Charles's fault. 'He was placed in a cruel strait, and was compelled to yield to the clamours of our enemies.' But at twenty she passionately identified with James's cause.

So the Duke of York left England, a banished man.

12 Frustrations of Exile

James had written to William that he was coming on another private incognito visit but when he arrived at Rotterdam the Prince of Orange met him in state and conducted him to the Hague, where the guards were drawn up to give him a salute of honour. Nevertheless, William was quite relieved when James soon decided to move to Brussels, taking up residence in the Prince de Horne's house where he had stayed with Charles just before the Restoration, nearly twenty years ago.

In April he hurried back to the Hague, on hearing that Mary was ill again; her recurrent fits of ague continued for some time after this crisis was past. Maria was writing to Modena, 'no further hope of a child, since she has passed the nine months since her pregnancy in great loneliness, which strongly displeases us.'

The marriage was not going well. William, when not at war, went off hunting for weeks on end, staying in one of his other castles; even when he was at home he dined with his male friends, leaving Mary to dine alone. She had nothing to do but play cards, do embroidery and write weepy letters to Frances Apsley. Ill and miserable, she clung to her father, so ready always to dash off at a moment's notice to visit her.

He was back in Brussels by the first week in May, writing to William with startling news from England. When abroad James switched to the new style of dating. England, still refusing to accept the Gregorian calendar, corrected by the papal astronomers almost a hundred years earlier, was now ten days behind the rest of Europe and was to lag still further till the middle of the eighteenth century, when the adjustment was at last made. The news which so surprised James was that the King had remodelled his Council and made none other than Lord Shaftesbury its President. James could not see the sense of that and dreaded the consequences. His final (and typical) comment was: 'A little tyme will lett us see much.'

In Brussels James suffered the usual frustration of political exiles, watching events from a distance, impotently. When the first Exclusion Bill was brought in, he wrote to William that if the King and the House of Lords

> stick to me, then one may expect great disorders, nay a rebellion: if his Majesty and they shall consent to what the commons may do against me, I shall then look on his Majesty as less than a Duke of Venice, and the Monarchy and our Family absolutely ruined and given up; but what to do or what to advise as things now stand, is very hard to say.

It might be a good idea for William to go to England, but he dared not propose it, not knowing whether it would suit his present affairs in Holland.

Writers of later centuries have made merry over James's fears lest the King of England should become a mere Duke of Venice – a state figurehead. Perhaps this is because that is just what he did become in the century after the Revolution, when the real power was held by Parliament. Only, as the King or Queen was not elected (like the Doge) but inherited the Crown, the fiction of Monarchy could be maintained, and a very useful fiction it has proved, providing a stabilizing and unifying influence without which the conflicting parties in Parliament would have torn the nation apart long ago.

In judging James's reactions to the Exclusion issue these writers seem to forget that he could not look forward to the constitutional monarchy of modern times; he could only look back, and what he saw in the immediate past was the rebellion of Parliament, the disastrous Civil War, the judicial murders of the King his father and the subsequent republican experiments under the Commonwealth which were so generally disliked by the people that they welcomed the Restoration of the Monarchy with rejoicing. It was natural that James should expect that the victory of the Parliamentary faction would lead to a republic; many others thought so too, especially those who called themselves 'all honest men' but whom their opponents were soon to call Tories.

Before the first vote on Exclusion the Tories had lost their leader, Lord Danby. Danby's fall was not as complete as Clarendon's chiefly because he was a far more wily politician than the old Chancellor. When Charles dissolved his old Parliament, he tried to persuade Danby to follow Clarendon's example and flee abroad; he gave him a royal pardon to protect him against impeachment. But Danby, convinced that given the chance he could prove the charges unfounded, surrendered on 15 April (old style) and was imprisoned (fairly comfortably) in the Tower. And there he stayed (impatiently) for five years.

In taking Shaftesbury, the Earl of Essex (Capel) and other Whigs on to his Council Charles, who had a low opinion of men's motives, hoped to satisfy their desire for power while keeping ultimate control in his own hands. By allowing the fantastic Popish Plot trials to go on (and soon the executions) he hoped to persuade people that he would not abandon the Church of England, while maintaining his secret friendship with the French King.

Because Charles, after three years of political touch and go, emerged more or less the victor, whereas James, when it came to his turn, was defeated, James has been denied any political sense at all. However, he was right about one thing: that giving in to the opposition only made them grasp at more. Now that they had succeeded in banishing the Duke, they pressed on with blackguarding his name to facilitate the passing of Exclusion. As he sarcastically put it in the memoirs, the Committee of Secrecy (for examining the plot) was 'informed by my Lady Shaftesbury's buttler, that the French King was to be on the Sea coast by the middle of June with an army of 60,000 men, who were to be transported to England to assist the Catholicks and that the Duke, who was run away, they sayd, to save his head, was to return along with them.' And he recorded their vote on 27 April, 'That the Duke of York being a Papist had been the principal encouragement to the papists in their designes against the King.' He also made a dry comment on the new House of Commons: 'whatever any old manager moved, the new factious Members still cryd up and applauded, like so many young spaniels that run and bark at every lark that springs.'

James also details the arguments used in Parliament by his Tory friends against any tampering with the succession. Attempts to alter it, even by Henry VIII, always failed. And Scotland 'would catch at such an occasion to separate again from England and have not only their lawful King but a King that would live among them.' Moreover, to bar a lawful claimant would only cause bloody conflict, because there would always be some who would follow him. (A preview of Scottish Jacobitism?)

It is ironic that James was suggesting William should go to England as representing the legitimate succession, just when William was beginning to see the way opening to the throne of England for himself, as husband of the Protestant heir. In June Henry Sidney was sent by the King as a special envoy to the Dutch government, but undercover he came to sound out the Prince of Orange from a cabal of the King's new ministers who did not like the way faction supporters were turning to the Duke of Monmouth. The two managers of this new enterprise were George Savile, now Viscount Halifax, and his brother-in-law (Sidney's young uncle) Robert Spencer, second Earl of Sunderland.

George Savile was an exact contemporary of James, born on 11 November 1633, and had been favoured by him in the sixties. He rose to prominence in the seventies, gaining a reputation for political ability and a philosophic mind. He had a close relationship with his mother-in-law the Dowager Countess of Sunderland (Sidney's much older sister Dorothy). Her letters to Halifax, printed in the Sidney Correspondence, are enlightening on the intrigues in court circles at this time.

Her son, Robert Spencer, Earl of Sunderland from his infancy, was a strange creature. A portrait of him as a faunlike youth in classical robes, leaning elegantly on a monument, was painted in Rome, whither he had escaped with uncle Henry Sidney from the marriage arranged for him with Anne Digby, a daughter of that Earl of Bristol with whom James had clashed in exile. But in 1664, at twenty-three, he came back and married her after all. They had several children and because one of their sons married the Churchills' daughter, the family became Spencer-Churchill and the Sunderland title subsidiary to that of Marlborough.

Gossip said that Anne Sunderland was Henry Sidney's mistress. Sidney was possibly bi-sexual, since he never married but was credited with affairs with both sexes. Sunderland, who never appeared to have extra-marital affairs, may have had similar leanings in youth and perhaps accepted marriage as a safe solution. He, his wife and Henry Sidney remained a close trio all their lives and worked together in the political scene.

Sidney saw the Prince of Orange in July (1679) and William took an immediate liking to him; people later said that Sidney was the only Englishman William ever did like. Sidney's proposition was that William should come to England and take his place in the House of Lords as Duke of Gloucester. The Prince favoured the idea, except that as a Dutchman he could not take any oath of allegiance to the King of England. In September they discussed Exclusion and Sidney said the Prince now favoured it; he did not think the Duke of Monmouth would ever have the crown but 'he would be very willing to be put into the way of having it himself.'

Meanwhile in England, after two readings of the Exclusion Bill in Parliament, the King suddenly prorogued it till August and left Whitehall for his usual summer holiday at Windsor. Sir William Temple recorded that Shaftesbury was so angry that he declared 'whoever had advised the King to that measure should pay for their presumption with their heads.' This threat shows the height of Shaftesbury's power that summer, but it was a power without means of expression when Parliament was not sitting.

James, delighted at the King's move, at once urged him to stop disbanding the army and to recall him home.

He knew very well that when Parliament was up, these factious men had no other way to compass their ends but by open force; which considering the flame they had blowne themselves in too, was no ways improbable; wherefore he ceased not conjuring the King, to pursue the method he was now in, and not to immagin those men's good nature would be wrought upon by complyance, which was the fatal rock on which his Father miserably split. . . .

James had already written a long letter to the King which he began: 'I do assure you I can bear any misfortune with patience so long as you are so kind; I have but one life to loos, and I shall always be ready to lay it downe in your service, and at the rate things now go there is too great a probability an occasion may not long be wanting: They will never be satisfy'd unless your Majesty unking yourself. . . .' He went on, very cautiously, to warn his brother against the Duke of Monmouth ('pardon me for naming him') and the friends who were driving him on, especially Sir Thomas Armstrong and 'young Gerrard (Lord Brandon), who were such earnest agitators against me in the House'.

Urging Charles to make sure of the garrisons in his forts, in case of rebellion, he ended,

> and certainly the speedyest way of breaking their measures is to break the Parliament itself, and proportion your way of liveing to your revenue, rather than to ly any longer at the mercy of these men, who by that vilainous vote to revenge your death upon the Papists, can have no other meaning than to expose your life to the bloody hand of any desperate fanatick.

The sudden prorogation seemed like an answer to this plea (made in May) but though he wrote again, James received no answer. Charles's silence worried him. 'It is strange his Majesty has not written to me,' he wrote to his naval friend George Legge (afterwards Earl of Dartmouth). '. . . I am not used like a brother nor a friend.' When Charles did at last answer he disarmed James as usual by his kind and affectionate tone but he would not recall him. One letter from the King is quoted in the memoirs: 'If you should come over at this time, it would be of the last ill consequence both to you and to me. I am sure there is nothing troubles me more than to be deprived of your company, nor can I write any thing more against my heart than this, but when I consider it is the last stake . . .' it could not be allowed. In another letter he wrote that James's return would give the Popish Plot new life, 'neither durst he answer that his person would be in safety, such was the hatred the people were in against Popery and him, as its cheife support.'

James did not feel like a chief support to the unfortunate Catholics in England; he could do nothing to help them. The execution of the Jesuits in June 'went to his heart' and various names are given in the memoirs of those known to him who suffered imprisonment, fines or worse. The King had delayed signing the warrant for the innocent priests but had given in at last; he was to feel deep remorse and is said to have kissed their picture in Queen Catherine's Bedchamber, begging their pardon.

James continued to write but knew he was making no headway. 'The Duke knew very well from what fountain these arguments sprung, and that so long as Little Sincerity (a cant word betwixt the King and him for my lord Shaftesbury) sat at the head of the Council, the King would be eternally byased against him.' Shaftesbury was a small slight man, who suffered from an unhealed wound sustained in a carriage accident, which had to be drained through a silver pipe; Tories thought it might account for his political bile. He frequently used the phrase 'in all sincerity' – hence the nickname the royal brothers used.

James, realizing that he was in for a longer exile, sent for his own hounds and hunting equipment and asked permission for his daughters to visit him, which (Parliament not being there to object) the King was able to grant. They came over with Lady Bellasys and the Earl of Peterborough and his wife, still faithful friends of the Duke.

Anne was now fourteen and growing tall; she had developed a slightly sulky prettiness and was already under the spell of Sarah Churchill – married but still in the court circle. Her letters home, however, were to Frances Apsley whom (copying Mary) she calls Semandra and signs herself Ziphares. But they were not romantic outpourings but prosaically described her room – with a chimney 'made a-purpose for me'. Shocked at the calvaries and statues at street corners in Brussels she had to admit that her father made no attempt to take her into Roman Catholic churches.

In July Maria's mother, the Duchess of Modena, arrived on a visit. It was five years since she had seen her daughter and Maria had grown so tall she hardly recognized her. Duchess Laura wrote back to Prince

Rinaldo, 'my lord duke adores her and has thanked me again for having given her to him. Certainly he is a most excellent and aimiable gentleman.'

A few weeks later the Duke received alarming news from England: the King had been taken ill, so seriously that his ministers, Halifax, Sunderland and Laurence Hyde, were so afraid he might die that they decided to send for the Duke, not out of loyalty to him but for fear Shaftesbury would make Monmouth King, as a puppet for his party.

Monmouth was now at the height of his popularity. In May the fanatical remnants of the Covenanters had murdered the Archbishop of St Andrews while he was out driving with his daughter, and then they had broken out in rebellion. Monmouth was commissioned General to go north and crush the rising, which he easily did at Bothwell Bridge, and then increased his popularity by his leniency to the leading rebels – though 200 men were transported to the American colonies. If the Duke of York had been in the country this command would not have gone to Monmouth. When he came back to London he was received with wild rejoicing by the anti-Catholic populace, who lit bonfires for 'the Protestant Duke' and toasted him as Prince of Wales.

James, on his unexpected summons, acted with his usual promptitude. He had been told to come secretly, pretending to do it of his own accord, so he travelled in disguise – a plain black stuff suit, without his Garter star, and a black wig. He took only Churchill, who acted as the chief gentleman of the party, Lord Peterborough, a barber and a groom. They spent one night on the road to the coast but then had to wait another at Calais till the contrary wind changed; they landed at Dover on 11 September, or as it was in England, the first, old style. The Postmaster recognized the Duke but had the wit not to show it, telling Churchill he was glad to see him but would be even more glad to see a better man than he – with a glance at James. It was a good omen; the Duke was evidently not so unpopular as he had been led to believe.

Leaving the elderly Peterborough to follow by coach, James and Churchill rode post to London, where they stayed the night with Sir Allen Apsley. Laurence Hyde and Sidney Godolphin were sent for 'and tould him his comeing was still a secret, that neither the Duke of Monmouth nor any of his gang knew or suspected it.' So he made an early start next day and reached Windsor 'by seaven a'clock, just as his

Majesty was shaveing'. Acting according to instructions James knelt and asked pardon for returning without leave. Charles, already much better, received him 'very kindly'. Charles's illness was a severe fever, cured (according to Dorothy, Lady Sunderland) by the new medicine known as Jesuits' bark – quinine.

'This scene being over, all the Courtiers flock'd about him to make their compliments, his Enemys as well as his friends, for his presence always forced an awe and respect even from those who were the worst affected to him.' All the same, his situation at court was precarious. 'The Ministers that had agreed to his return he knew were not his friends in the bottom.' He also discovered that Monmouth had tried to get Sunderland 'to have the Duke writ to not to stir' and so was the more surprised to see him there, but even he had to pay his respects, because the King ordered it.

Not knowing that Sidney was treating with William, James wrote to his son-in-law,

I found his Majesty upon the mending hand, who received me very kindly; and now, God be thanked, he has got so much strength that he walks into the park ... I am very glad to find I have so many friends here, and that his Majesty has been undeceived in one thing that had been told him, which was, that there would be a rebellion, and that the city would rise in case I came back; but neither of these have happened, and the city is very quiet, and most of the rich men there are pleased with it.

The merchants, unlike the mob, were loyal to the Duke who had always promoted commerce and overseas trade.

James was not so pleased to be approached by some of the ministers to join in persuading the King to 'lay aside' the Duke of Lauderdale; he refused, just as he had refused over Danby, but felt that this refusal probably 'gave a helping hand' to the decision to send him back into exile; they 'found his spirit was not yet so broke with his adversities' as to 'enter blindfould into all their measures' just because they had recalled him in a moment of crisis. He added, shrewdly, 'they had reason to suspect that his credit with the King would always be too hard for theirs.'

The King showed his trust in his brother by involving him in the new secret treaty he was negotiating with King Louis; in fact Louis, suspicious of James ever since his conversion to William's policy of the Flanders barrier, insisted on his cooperation. As the first article of the new treaty promised that Louis would not invade Flanders or Holland, James was able to approve it. Charles in return was not to ally with France's enemies and would receive a pension again, paid quarterly. Louis stipulated that he was not to call a Parliament and Charles naturally hedged on this; he might have to call one.

Considering that Barillon, who was doing the negotiating, was also heavily involved with his ring of opposition members of Parliament – with Montagu, dunning for his payment for ruining Danby, and with Buckingham, who was always coming in with fantastic schemes and boasts of his power in the city, his Plantagenet blood, etc – one sometimes wonders why Louis bothered with Charles at all. Evidently it suited him to keep both sides going but it would not suit him to have either on top.

This treaty eventually fell through, but not till James had left London. While there he wrote to King Louis to show goodwill and sent Churchill to Paris to expedite the treaty, thereby annoying Henry Savile (Halifax's brother) who was ambassador there and suspected Churchill was out for his job. Henry, fat and amusing, was enjoying life in Paris.

In spite of consulting James on the treaty Charles was persuaded to send him away again, which James meekly accepted, thinking 'complyance' would do him more good with the King than argument. However 'many of his antient friends were hugely troubled at it' and persuaded the King how ill-advised it was to put the heir to the crown into the power of a foreign prince: surely better to send him to Scotland? Charles agreed, and told James he would not leave him there long, just while Parliament was sitting. And he made the order more acceptable by deciding to send Monmouth too out of the country, for his misbehaviour in the city.

Monmouth (furious, but unable to prevent this) was to leave first, then James. Monmouth went over to Holland, where William received him in a friendly manner, telling Sidney that now there was no need for him to go to England.

James got back to Brussels early in October and immediately swept up his family, princesses, Duchess of Modena and all, and carried them off by water to the Hague for a brief farewell visit to Mary. They stayed only a couple of days but William and Mary accompanied them to the coast, where loving farewells were said. Although none of them knew it, this was to be the last time James saw his daughter Mary. The last time too that he and William met face to face.

13 A Sort of Vagabond

Two frigates had been sent to the Downs so that the Duke could tranship and sail direct for Scotland, but as the weather was so dreadfully rough that the seasick Duchess was vomiting blood, James sent Churchill ashore to ride post haste for Whitehall and get permission to land. Of course Charles gave it; he tried to persuade Maria to stay in London, promising that as he was going to prorogue Parliament again the spell in Scotland would be short.

James was mollified by the prospect of prorogation and positively gleeful when Charles dismissed Lord Shaftesbury from the Council. He wrote to William: 'I hope the little man's being out of employment here may help to break those measures' – for Shaftesbury was corresponding with the republican Loevestein peace party in Holland, William's enemies.

The Duke had to leave at the end of October. It had been raining for weeks and the roads were in a terrible state, but nothing would persuade Maria to stay in London; she was determined to share all her husband's trials. In the memoirs James wrote 'but it was a sencible trouble to his RH to see the Dutchess thus obliged to undergo a sort of martirdom for her affection to him, and he to humour the peevish and timorous disposition of some Councillors be then sent a sort of vagabond about the world, not only to his own, but to the King his Brother's visible disadvantage.'

So, reluctantly leaving Anne and Isabella in approved Protestant hands, the Duke and Duchess left London on 27 October 1679, on what proved a very tiresome journey, sometimes doing only ten miles a day along the muddy roads. The first night was to be spent at Hatfield House, the palatial residence of the Earl of Salisbury, descendant of Queen Elizabeth's minister William Cecil, but when they reached it they found the great house deserted. The anti-papist Earl had removed himself, most of his household effects and his staff to another house, leaving it empty and unlighted.

Refusing to be downed by this insult, James sent his servants into Hatfield to buy what was needed and find accommodation there for some of his gentlemen, while the house was made habitable for the night. In the morning he directed his Comptroller Sir John Worden (still with him from his days as a volunteer in Turenne's army) to leave money for what they had used, since he was 'unwilling to be burdensome to so poor a lord'.

Proceeding on their slow and soggy way they reached York on 6 November where another cold welcome awaited them, the Mayor merely calling privately on the Duke when he was installed in the Treasurer's House. This medieval house, improved in the seventeenth century, now belongs to the National Trust; in the hall stands an upright chair traditionally said to have been James II's. The guidebook seems dismissive but the chair has the same two cherubs' heads carved on it as appear on the stools (now at Knole) which were part of the Bedchamber furnishings for James's marriage to Maria in 1673. As one can hardly imagine James bringing the chair with him and leaving it at the Treasurer's House, it must have been collected later, just as the stools at Knole were taken as 'perks', after the death of Queen Mary II, by Lord Sackville, who had been her Chamberlain. He took the bed too and there it is at Knole, with James's ducal coronet carved on the bedhead.

The Duke's reception in Scotland was, in contrast, magnificent. He was met at the border at Berwick by the Scots Guards, commanded by the Marquis of Montrose, by the Lord Chancellor of Scotland and thirty-eight Lords of the Council, accompanied by sixty noblemen and many of the principal gentry, making up a splendid cavalcade of about two thousand horse. In spite of the rain the Duke got out of his coach and walked to meet them, taking off his hat (royal courtesy in the etiquette of the day) while the principal persons kissed his hand. The

Duchess's hand was kissed too, as she sat in the coach. Maria's youth (she was just twenty-one) her beauty and graciousness were always a great asset to James on ceremonial occasions.

They stayed at Lethington, the Duke of Lauderdale's house, till 4 December, when they made their public entry into Edinburgh and took up residence in Holyrood Palace, where the Duke and Duchess were soon holding splendid receptions in royal style.

James took his seat on the King's Council, after out-manoeuvring Montrose, who wanted him to take the (new) oath first, by saying he had taken the oath long ago when he first took his place on the Privy Council at Whitehall. Although on this first visit he had no official commission from the King, he was able to exercise a pacifying influence after the recent rebellion, which was much appreciated. He kept up a 'newtrality' between parties, taking care not to offend any. His industry, application to business and his kind reception of the gentry gained him general credit. It is recorded in the memoirs that Shaftesbury 'some time after, bewailing as it were the impotency of his malice, complain'd that the persecuting of the Duke in England served only to make him reign as it were in Scotland.'

The King meanwhile prorogued Parliament again and kept his promise to recall his brother in February 1680. James decided to go home by sea. He wrote to Laurence Hyde, 'If you were a seaman, I could make you understand that it is better going from Scotland to London by sea in winter, than back thither at this time of year. There will be a light moon at the time I name, and both the Duchess and I have a great mind to go back by sea, having been extremely tired by our land journey to Edinburgh.'

This time the voyage was without incident and they reached Deptford by 24 February, where they transferred from the royal yacht to a barge, going up the river to salutes of guns from the Tower, to be received by the King in person as they landed at the privy stairs in Whitehall. Courtiers crowded round to kiss their hands and the City lit bonfires. The Lord Mayor gave a banquet for the King and the Duke which ended with their being escorted home at two in the morning with drunken loyalty.

The previous year the King had been inundated with Petitions, organized by Shaftesbury 'and his gang', to call Parliament, but now the

Tories had got going and 'Abhorrences' were coming in – expressions of abhorrence for the proceedings of the faction and of support for the King's government. James was pleased to note that an address from Norfolk thanked the King for recalling the Duke of York.

Convinced that the tide had turned, James went with the King to Newmarket for the spring races. Maria stayed at St James's, feeling unwell. Possibly she had a miscarriage, for James made her a flying visit, coming one day and returning the next, satisfied that she was recovering.

At the end of May Charles had another attack of fever, serious enough to revive the alarms of last year but as soon thrown off. However, this second illness lent urgency to Shaftesbury's determination to get rid of the Duke of York. Without Parliament, nothing could be done about Exclusion and meanwhile it was getting difficult to keep the Popish Plot frenzy going; the last victim, the Irish Archbishop Oliver Plunket, convicted on the evidence of some Irish renegades, was so saintly that his execution in July was counter-productive to the Protestant cause.

Monmouth's supposed legitimacy was being widely trumpeted abroad, on the strength of a Black Box containing his mother's marriage lines, a box which nobody ever saw but many believed in. On 3 June Charles issued a solemn denial on oath that he had ever been married to anyone but his Queen, Catherine, but this made no impression on Monmouth's popular following, who continued to cheer him as Prince of Wales. He had come back to London without permission the day after the Duke left for Scotland, but he was not allowed at court.

Shaftesbury now arranged for James to be indicted as a recusant before a Grand Jury by Lord Russell and Lord Cavendish (heir to the Earl of Devonshire); proof of his having heard mass was provided by a renegade. Under the penal laws two-thirds of his estate could then be seized and he would probably be driven out of the country. 'And then', continues James dryly, in the memoirs, '(to put him in good company) he desired at the same time, the Duchess of Portsmouth might be presented too as a common nuisance.'

Charles was so annoyed at this piece of impudence that he drove from Windsor to London to see Lord Justice Scroggs (the terror of the

Popish Plot trials) who promptly discharged the jury as unfit. So for the time being the case was dropped.

James comments that Shaftesbury gained something from it all the same, for 'this frighted her (Louise) into an Allyance with him against the Duke, and she having a great influence over the King was the enemy of all others that brought his RH the greatest mischief.' In the days of final exile in France Louise herself told James that she had gone down on her knees to Charles to beg him to pass the Exclusion Bill. She was also soon scheming with Lord Sunderland, who had now decided to go along with Exclusion, though in favour of William of Orange rather than Monmouth. Louise's own idea was to get her son, the infant Duke of Richmond, adopted as heir. Why not? She was told that Henry VIII had done just that (though the youth died before he did) and Monmouth was not the only illegitimate son of Charles.

James did not know at the time of this new gang against him, or a certain meeting at Althorp, Sunderland's country house, which took place in the middle of June when Henry Sidney was over from Holland and Halifax was staying there. Halifax was not in favour of an Exclusion engineered by Shaftesbury but he wanted to keep the Duke away from the King, whose Catholic sympathies he suspected. Sunderland's wife (Anne Digby), who corresponded with Sidney, had written triumphantly, 'That you may guess how well it is, I shall only tell you that I take the Duke to be undone.'

Sunderland's mother (Dorothy Sidney) writing to her son-in-law Halifax when he was at his own country house, Rufford Hall, in July, reported, 'His Highness smiles, dances, makes love and hunts.' Evidently he was unaware of the gossip and the plotting. 'The Duchess of York is not with child. She prays all day almost. She is very melancholy, the women will have it for Mrs Sedley. She looks further than that, if she has so much wit as she is thought by some.' (*Mrs* was then applied to unmarried women.)

On 19 July the Dowager was writing again, about riots at the choosing of the sheriffs for London. There was 'a loud outcry, No Yorkist! No Papist!' and when one was proposed they set on him and beat him, 'still crying, A Yorkist, none of him!' Instead, one of the faction was chosen but Lord Russell had said he was sorry, 'for he was as great a Commonwealth's man as Algernon Sidney. I wonder what his lordship is, if he is not so too, and goes so far towards it.' Algernon Sidney was her brother; much older than Henry, he had escaped abroad at the Restoration, but Charles had recently allowed him to return, when he immediately took up with the faction, though as a determined republican he did not always hit it off with the other leaders.

Lady Sunderland continued, 'My Lord Shaftesbury says, if the Duke should go away, that is nothing! If he should take the oaths, go to church, receive the sacrament, abjure transubstantiation, that is nothing!' So determined was he to get rid of the Duke altogether that he brushed aside as unimportant the religious issue which was supposed to be the ground of objection to James's succession. She added a piece of gossip about Buckingham, who had talked of his troubled conscience to 'some fanatics' who fixed a time to come and complete his conversion. But when they did 'he could not be found and afterwards they heard he had been with a wench all that day.'

The campaign against the Duke of York had now reached outrageous proportions in pamphlets and cartoons directed at the populace. The licensing law had lapsed in 1679 and could only be renewed in Parliament, which the King was trying not to call. A representative cartoon is reproduced in the book on James II by Peter Earle in the *Kings and Queens of England* series. In the centre is a huge horrific figure, half man, half devil. The man-half is blowing flames up to a burning London while hooking up the crown with his foot. The devil-half's hoof is poised among skulls (labelled 'Ruins and Murders without Mercy') while he sets a torch to the faggots burning martyrs tied to stakes; a balloon from his mouth declares 'Thus Ile Govern Hereticks or Godfrey um' and to make sure the point is taken, under the torch is written: 'This A hopefull Successor, is it not.'

Such an identification of the Duke with all the imagined horrors of Popery was the strongest weapon in Shaftesbury's hands and the one that most alarmed the royalists. As James put it in the memoirs, 'The Duke was blamed for giving the first handle to the party. This was perpetually buss'd also in his Majesty's ear by those who had the greatest credit with him.' New efforts were therefore made to get James to renounce the Catholic faith, which he found trying not only because it was against his conscience but because he was convinced that the

faction was really aiming at monarchy rather than popery. Shaftesbury's remarks as reported by Lady Sunderland confirm this view.

The Whig tradition after 1688 so sweepingly dismissed James as
stupid, bigoted and unpopular, that he appears a negligible figure and
the concerted attack on him organized by so clever a politician as
Shaftesbury, inexplicable. But it should be looked at the other way
round: Shaftesbury would not have concentrated all his energies on
getting James excluded and banished during his brother's lifetime if he
had not presented a formidable obstacle to the success of the party's
political aims then as well as in the hypothetical future.

James's attempts to convince the King and his ministers that it was
not for his papist but his monarchist principles that he was being
attacked, failed. 'Still the cry went against him, as the Jonas for whose
sake these stormes were rais'd.' And when the King announced in
August that he was calling a Parliament to meet on 21 October, 'all the
world cast about to save themselves and the Duke like that Prophet
must be sacrificed for the public quiet.'

Some of his friends informed him that an impeachment would be
brought against him for high treason, others told of a bill of limitations
on a Catholic King of England 'which once passed, they would look
upon a commonwealth as in a manner settled.' (Because Parliament
would show that it controlled the monarchy.) Others were for sending
the Duke away again. There were suggestions of a bill to have *all* Catholics banished; James knew 'my lord Halifax had long meditated this
project.' James comments that 'he was astonished that men of sence
did not see that Religion was only the pretence and that the real contest
was about Power and Dominion, that it was the Monarchie they designed to banish, without which other banishments would give them little
satisfaction.' Yet his personal fate naturally dominated public debate.

Lady (Dorothy) Sunderland wrote to Halifax on 20 August:

You will wonder perhaps that no discourse is so common in
everybody's chamber, and every coffee house, as of the Duke's going
away before the Parliament, some saying he will and others that he
will not. Upon this, his servants and friends, and they say himself too,
take all occasions to declare that he will not stir, and this is so much
done that I do a little wonder at it.

[113]

Halifax was back in town for the meeting of the Council after the King (and the Duke) got back from Newmarket in October. Of course James was not allowed to sit on the Council now, so his fate was decided in his absence. He suspected that the King was being influenced against him. When he next saw Charles he found him 'so changed that it gave him great reason now at last to aprehend what he had been oft tould but never believed, That his Majesty would abandon him in the end.'

This was unnerving, but James was not going to give in without a fight. He put his case strongly to the King who promised he would take the advice of the Privy Council which was called for 13 October, the day before James's forty-seventh birthday.

Henry Sidney had been in England since September, not only meeting Halifax and Sunderland but dining with other key figures and relaying the news to William, who was then making a tour of German states, persuading their leaders into a league against France. 'There was a great debate in Council what should be done with the Duke,' wrote Sidney, no doubt informed by Sunderland. 'Some were for his going away, others for his staying till 'twas seen what Parliament would do, and others were for the King's sticking to him. It was carried that he should not go. We were mightily out of humour, and thought our matters would go ill.' This shows that James was right in seeing his banishments as an advantage to the opposition.

Steps were taken by them, however, to get the King to call another Council on 15 October. We know more of this meeting since notes were taken by Lord Anglesey (then Lord Privy Seal) which survived among the Clarendon papers and were printed by Dalrymple. 'At the Council October 15, 1680, till late at night: Never any yet condemned for reconciling to the church of Rome; shall your brother be the first?' It was the threat of impeachment, more than the Exclusion Bill, which preoccupied them. The sole charge of treason which could be made against James was his reconciliation to Rome. And as this had been known when he had been exempted from the measures taken against the other Catholic peers, 'will your Majesty now revive it alone?'

What would the King do if an impeachment was brought? Would he dissolve Parliament? If so, it would be better to do it after granting the Duke a pardon, 'for this is in maintenance of the prerogative; the other is in maintenance of popery' – if a pardon had not been granted beforehand, dissolution would be simply to save his brother from the anti-Catholic laws.

Somebody must have raised the consequence of attainder – execution as a traitor – for the next note reads: 'If there is not one lord that would advise execution, which is the end of the law, how can anyone advise what leads thereunto?'

After more discussion the notes end: 'If not execute, but dissolve, rather why not pardon. I saw the K (King) was turned against his B (Brother) but I and most of the council did our dutys.' Eleven voted for the pardon, seven against it; yet the King chose to follow the minority and decided not to grant it.

This decision came as a shock to James, but though he argued vigorously with the King for a pardon, he failed to move him, and began to fear for his life if he refused another banishment. Barillon had a long conversation with the Duke while he was in this desperate state, and says he 'showed great marks of misery; he thinks himself entirely abandoned, and does not reckon upon being long in Scotland.' He thought he would either be arrested and sent to the Tower or be banished 500 miles from England for the King's lifetime, if the Exclusion Bill was passed. He told Barillon that he had a considerable party in Scotland – and more in England than he had realized till this summer – who would rally round him if the worst came to the worst. Barillon interpreted this as a threat to rebel against Charles and wrote off to King Louis who, delighted to cause even more divisions in England, responded at once with promises of help for the beleaguered Duke of York.

Of course, James did not mean he would start a rebellion against Charles but that if the faction started one he could, from a base in Scotland, make things pretty hot for them. It was not to be long before the opposition recognized this possibility too; but at present everybody thought his papistry would make him powerless as well as unpopular anywhere in Britain.

Why Charles refused the pardon (which he had given to Clarendon and to Danby) is not apparent but to soften the blow of banishment he named James his High Commissioner in Scotland, replacing Lauderdale, who was now old and ill, and charging him with full powers to settle Scottish affairs, which were still in a disturbed state.

The Duke and Duchess of York left London on 20 October 1680 and the King accompanied them to Leigh to demonstrate, as far as he could, that his brother was not in disgrace.

14 Reigning in Scotland

The Duke and Duchess of York had their usual bad weather at sea; storms prevented their coming into harbour at Kirkcaldy till 25 October and Maria had been so sick that they did not land till eleven the next morning. But then they were greeted by the Duke of Rothes (Lord Chancellor of Scotland) and a crowd of local gentry. Rothes entertained them at Leslie House till Friday the twenty-ninth when they left, after presenting their hosts with Lely's latest portrait of Maria with an Italian greyhound; it was also his last, for he died that year.

At Burntisland they went on board the *Charlotte* yacht (called after Charles's illegitimate daughter the Countess of Lichfield) to ringing of bells and salutes of guns. They arrived at Leith to more salutes from Edinburgh Castle and men-of-war at anchor, and were received on shore, amid cheering crowds, by the Earl of Linlithgow, Colonel of the King's regiment of Guards, at the head of several companies. A huge cavalcade formed up and they drove to the watergate at the Abbey of Holyrood, where they were met by the Lord Provost, magistrates and town council of Edinburgh and escorted to the Palace, received in the hall by the Archbishops of St Andrews and Glasgow and the Lieutenant Governor of the Castle, who presented the Duke with its keys.

Bells rang half the night, bonfires blazed in the streets, healths were drunk to the descendant of so many Scottish kings and nobody seemed to be worrying about popery at all. Only one discordant note sounded; the great gun Mons Meg cracked when it was fired in salute – by an English gunner, needless to say. (But it is still there to this day, a showpiece.)

Since their visit last year the new wing of Holyrood had been completed, its splendid rooms decorated in the then modern style, with ornamental plasterwork on the ceilings. The Duke's court at Holyrood was the first royal court held in Scotland for a long time and it became a great centre of interest for the nobility and gentry. Maria held Drawing Rooms and introduced the ladies of Edinburgh to tea, a new drink in England which had not till then penetrated to Scotland. She charmed everyone, as she always did.

James was soon in a fair way to charming everyone too. As the King's Commissioner he was Viceroy for Scotland, presided at the Council and soon got to know all the great lords and notables of the country, gaining understanding of the family feuds which complicated the politics of the nation. Apart from business he took up golf, which endeared him to all Scots, especially as he made a point of choosing as his partner one of the ordinary citizens. Once on the links at Leith they beat the Duke of Lauderdale and when he handed over the prize money, James presented it to John Paterson, saying it was his skill which had won them the match.

However, at first James was naturally preoccupied with what was happening in Parliament in England; the Exclusion Bill was first brought up in the House of Commons just two days after he arrived at Holyrood and all through November and into December he was hearing from Hyde and others of the impassioned debates which ensued, and recording it all in his memoirs. The bill, brought in on 2 November, had its third reading by the eleventh. James noted that among its provisions was one declaring that if he tried to return from banishment he 'should be deemed a Traitor and suffer as such' – in fact, exile on pain of death, simply for becoming a Catholic. There was also a proviso that nothing should affect the next heir if the Duke was dead (safeguard for Mary and William) and the act was to be read in the churches every year and at every Assize during the lifetime of the Duke of York.

The bill was introduced by Lord Russell and seconded by Sir Henry Capel, brother of the Earl of Essex. The burden of the speeches was that all the ills England had suffered since the Restoration were the fault of the papists and that, as the Whig Colonel Titus said, the expectation of the Duke's succession gave life to the Popish Plot. Mr

Harbord (Pepys's enemy) was strong on the nefarious influence of the Duke; he was on Barillon's payroll but hardly needed to be paid for his heartfelt oratory.

James recorded the defence his friends put up, Laurence Hyde, Sir Leoline Jenkins the present Secretary of State, Mr Seymour and others, but they made little headway. The bill was rushed through in ten days and Lord Russell then presented it in the House of Lords, a crowd of MPs accompanying him who 'as soon as it was deliver'd, gave a mighty shout, which tumultuous and barbarous way of proceeding had too great a resemblance to forty one, not to convince all judicious persons, that this would.prove a prelude of the same tragedie if not timely prevented.'

James comments that now the King himself realized that firmness was necessary, 'because he saw the more aversion they shew'd to the Duke, the less reason they had to attempt any thing against his own person, so long as the Duke was to succeed him.' Charles's *bon mot* is often quoted: 'Nobody would kill me, James, to make you King.' It is usually told as a quip *against* his brother, but as James was aware of the reason behind it, this is more like a shared joke, like those in happier times when Pepys caught the royal brothers winking at each other at the Council table.

The Exclusion Bill came before the Lords on 15 November. The King, who had put his guards on alert in the city, spent the whole day, in his robes, at the Upper Chamber, and his presence no doubt encouraged the lords who spoke against the bill. Among these the star turn was Halifax, to the bewildered fury of the Sunderlands and other Orange supporters. Evidently he feared a victory for Shaftesbury's faction more than a Catholic heir, at this juncture, and his eloquent speech did much to sway the house. When it divided, at nine at night, there was a majority of thirty-three against the bill. It fell, and great was the fall of it.

The enraged Exclusionists tried to impeach Halifax, but really had no grounds for it. He became the King's favourite adviser and was made a Marquess. Sunderland, who had voted for Exclusion, was dismissed in disgrace.

A new proposal was next introduced for stringent limitations on a popish king: a council of forty-one was to hold the power of government; foreign treaties to be transacted by commissioners; Ireland to be governed by it too and Parliament to exercise the final authority. James wrote at once to the King that this was 'wors than Exclusion and would give a greater shock to the Monarchy by vesting the power in the Parliament and to drop the Government more gently into a Commonwealth, that Algernoon Sidney and his partie had express'd as much. . . .'

Someone else was exceedingly agitated by the proposed limitations and that was William of Orange. He was corresponding with Sir Leoline Jenkins and his letters (written in French) are translated and printed by Dalrymple. 'You know how I have always willed a good intelligence between the King and his Parliament,' he wrote on 10 December (new style) from the Hague, and lamented that this did not seem to be happening. He was 'much surprized to learn of the mitigations of the royal authority being spoken of in case the crown should fall to a papist king' and feared that 'if they had once taken away from the crown such considerable prerogatives as are talked of, they would ever return again.'

So alarmed was William at the idea of future kings of England being reduced to mere dukes of Venice that he got his friends in the Dutch government to write a memorial to King Charles, urging him for the sake of Christendom to agree with his Parliament and pass Exclusion if that was necessary. Charles was extremely angry at this interference from abroad and though William disclaimed participation neither of his English uncles ever quite believed in his innocence.

Meanwhile, letters had been coming to Henry Sidney from Sunderland's wife Anne, frantically urging that William should come over to England at once. While Exclusion seemed sure to pass she wrote on 7 November (old style) 'If not, tis the Duke of Monmouth must be the King, and if the Prince thinks it not worth going over a threshold for a kingdom, I know not why he should expect anybody should for him. The case is much changed since you were here . . . if you could see all that is to be seen, the Prince would not be such an ass, and so farewell.' But William still could not make up his mind whether it would serve his interest to go over at this critical moment. After the Exclusion Bill fell she wrote 'All things are coming to the last confusion . . . At present Lord Halifax is the King's favourite and hated more than ever the Lord

Treasurer (Danby) was, and has really deserved it; for he has undone all.'

James's view was naturally different. The bill's rejection in the Lords, he says, 'struck the Commons like thunder'. A proposal to adjourn was really only to give an opportunity for 'private caballs to get to work' so that Parliament would be recalled only to pass their plans – 'by which means this devolved the government not only from the King to the Parliament, but from Parliament itself to the Sunn Taverne and King's Head Clubbs.' These were coffee house clubs like the Green Ribbon, used by Shaftesbury for disseminating propaganda. The King's Head (appropriately) was in Fleet Street.

No adjournment was made but instead of turning to business 'the house could think and talk of nothing but Popery, which they pretended hung so dreadfully over their heads; it obsessed them like a Specter, and wherever they turned their eyes they fancy'd it stared them in the face.' For instance, Colonel Titus sought to prove from history that 'country went with King in Religion' so that a popish king was bound to bring in popery, instancing Queen Mary.

James's comment deserves quotation for it gives his decided opinion.

People considered not the different circomstances of those times, and the temper and power of Princes in those days; the Protestant Religion was then new, and tho' the liberty it encouraged made many embrace it, yet in Queen Mary's time the memory of what they had been was not so entirely forgot, but that by example and authority of the Prince they were easily brought back again; whereas now, after a long settlement of a Religion which had layd aside all those hard points of Doctrine either as to faith or practice, which the Church of Rome obliges too, it was not reasonable to presume the people would be so susceptible of a change and return to a Religion which besides its opposition to liberty they were so prejudiced against by Education, as to look upon it with detestation and horrour.

James never entertained any idea of a forcible conversion of England.

On 29 November was published that popular work of fiction, Oates's *Narrative of the Plot*. James exclaims that 'in future times it will not be credited that so numerous an assembly of persons chozen for their wisdom and abilitys to compose the representative of the People of England, could . . . have believed such folly' as that a handful of oppressed Catholics could have carried out such a plot, even if they had wished it.

Yet members of Parliament showed their belief at the solemn trial for treason of William Howard, Viscount Stafford, which opened in Westminster Hall on 30 November 1680. John Evelyn, just elected President of the Royal Society, who had admired Stafford's father, the collector Earl of Arundel, was present at the trial, held before the King, Lords and Commons – 'all the sides on both hands Scaffolded up to the very roof, for Members of the H: of Commons.' He did not think much of the evidence against Stafford, produced by Oates and two other informers. Stafford, one of five Catholic peers thrown into the Tower on suspicion, was a mild, cultivated, rather hypochondriac character, completely unsuited to political plotting or to defending himself against false charges of treason. But the scare of popery was still strong enough to secure his condemnation by his fellow peers, who voted 'guilty' by fifty-five to thirty-three. All his own family voted against him except the young Earl of Arundel, his great-nephew. Halifax, to his credit, voted 'not guilty'.

Charles, who did not believe in the plot at all, let alone Stafford's implication in it, yet felt obliged to sign the warrant for execution; but he exercised his royal prerogative of mercy to commute the hideous penalty to beheading. In the Commons Lord Russell passionately protested that the King did not have the right even to do this; something that Charles did not forget.

Stafford was executed on 29 December 1680. In Scotland James was deeply shocked, both at the farce of the trial and at Charles's consenting to his death. Like Evelyn he noticed the similarity of the victim's name to Strafford's, for whose execution Charles I had felt guilt and remorse to the end of his own life. Stafford was not of comparable importance but he was innocent of treason; his only crime was to be a Catholic. James also noted that Oates had now begun accusing the Duke of York of complicity in the plot and of compassing Godfrey's murder.

Perhaps Oates was jealous of Dangerfield, a new informer who had told the Lords, just before the Exclusion Bill was brought up, that the

Duke had proposed to him to kill the King, Lord Peterborough being present and Lord Anglesey acquainted with the design. This so frightened Anglesey that he voted for Exclusion, but Peterborough 'sayd so much in his vindication, that the Lords thought it not proper so much as to commit him.'

In another place in the memoirs James records what Oates was saying of him: 'he calls the Duke a Rascal, a Papist and a Traitor, he shall be hang'd, says he, and I hope I live to see it, we will have no more regard for him than if he were a Scavenger of Kent Street; he hoped, he sayd, to see him at the barr of the house of commons, where there were many better men than he; if the devil has a hotter place in Hell than an other, he hop'd he would bestow it upon him. These were the flowers of his eloquence.'

After Stafford's death the King prorogued Parliament for a fortnight but on 18 January 1681 he dissolved it and summoned a new one to sit in March at Oxford, away from the excited atmosphere of London. He left the old cavalier Earl of Craven in command of the guards in the capital while he took the best part of a regiment with him to Oxford. But these precautions did not stop him from calling at Burford races on the way there, with the Queen, the Duchess of Portsmouth and Nell Gwyn all in tow.

At the opening of the Oxford Parliament new limitations were suggested (probably devised by Halifax) including the possibility that the Prince and Princess of Orange should be regents, if James should outlive Charles. (James was disgusted at the idea of being put in the charge of his own children 'like a lunatick or an idiot'.) But Shaftesbury spurned all compromise; it must be Exclusion. Why, since such a regency would safeguard the country from popery if James ever did become king? Obviously because he wanted to get James out of the way at once and for good, not from fear of popery but as an obstacle to the supremacy of Parliament.

Charles outwitted him. He smuggled crown and robes into Christ Church Hall where the Lords were sitting, summoned the Commons and formally ordered the Chancellor to dissolve the Parliament forthwith. He then went straight out and took coach for Windsor, having arranged relays of horses on the way. There was uproar in Oxford but nothing worse, owing to the presence of the guards; the members

[122]

dispersed, the Exclusionists in indignant frustration, and Shaftesbury found himself without his base of operations.

Soon afterwards the King issued a Declaration, giving his reasons for the dissolution and calling for national unity and loyalty. It was to be read in all the churches so that everybody in the kingdom would be aware of what had happened and why. Members of Parliament were after all a tiny proportion of the people: Charles was addressing the whole nation. He was to get a positive response that was almost overwhelming, showing that the faction was in no sense representative of public opinion.

James, rejoicing at the dissolution which he had so long advised, naturally expected to be recalled at once. But the King put him off till things were more settled. James recorded sadly that his friends 'would not let him injoy this little glimps of sunshine, but by renewing their old sollicitations assure him it would be impossible to keep his head above water, or for any of his friends to abide by him, unless he did the only thing which would extricate himself, the King, and all his friends from inevitable ruin . . .' give up the Catholic faith. But that he could not in conscience do.

So he settled down to the task of reigning in Scotland.

After the 1688 Revolution the victors tried to make out that James had persecuted the Covenanters in Scotland and even indulged in watching their torture – still legal in that country, though no longer in England. But the Convenanters by then were the fanatical remnant of the movement, who believed in murdering kings and had actually murdered the (Anglican) Archbishop of St Andrews. When some of these Cameronians (nicknamed after their leader) were brought before the Council the Duke offered pardon to all who would say 'God save the King.' But most of them regarded this as bowing the knee to Baal and refused. Six young men whom James had offered to take into his own regiment in Flanders began cursing the Council instead, and so he had them removed forthwith lest they should convict themselves out of their own mouths.

It was not contemporaries who accused James of persecution but eighteenth-century writers who were building up an heroic (and legendary) history of the sect. One of these, Wodrow, said that the Duke had been present at the torture of Spreul, a fanatic who had

[123]

threatened to blow up Holyrood with their Highnesses inside it. It seems unlikely, since he makes an inquiry as to the result, in a letter, but he did not intervene to prevent it. There is no other evidence remotely relevant.

Agnes Strickland (a high Anglican of Victorian vintage) appends a footnote in which she castigates Macaulay for 'endeavouring to deprive James of the convincing evidence of his innocence afforded by the privy council records, by stating that "all those relating to the period of his residence in Scotland had been carefully destroyed."' She then triumphantly states that she herself gained access to the royal record office of Scotland and there studied the 'Decreets of the privy council of Scotland for 1679, 80, 81 and 82.' There were notes of business at about ninety sessions when James presided; she says most of them refer to maritime and trade affairs 'and the rectifying of previous abuses, especially in the way of monopolies'. She adds that 'the romance of the torture matinées rests solely on the unsupported assertion of Burnet, in the History of his Own Time, which is contradicted by another passage in the same work.'

Malcolm Hay, pursuing the same question in *The Enigma of James II* (1938) details the growth of the torture fantasy (which grew to horrendous proportions in the nineteneth century) before citing some contemporary witnesses of James's rule in Scotland who uniformly praise his justice, moderation, and refusal to take sides in the ferocious internal conflicts of the day. Cameron himself, in a sermon in May 1680 (between James's visits) said, 'Yea, many in Scotland cried there was no trouble while the Duke of York was in the country; and though he be a papist, he will persecute none on account of his religion.'

Hay also quotes a letter of Sunderland's to Henry Sidney:

I will venture to say the King's affairs (in Scotland) are in a better condition than they have been these seven years. We apprehended he (the Duke) would have disordered them, but we find quite the contrary. Take this on my word, for I do positively affirm it to you.

In June 1681 James was writing to his niece Charlotte, Countess of Lichfield, that all things were 'very quiat and like to continue so, for here fals witnesses dare not come, perjury being death, if it had been so in England so many innocent people had not suffred, and things would have been much quiater than they are.' He signed this letter, 'Your most humble servant, James.' In a later letter he said, 'Pray do not write to me with ceremony' and all the letters to Charlotte, though brief, are cheerful in tone. She was seventeen and had been married at thirteen to George Lee, made Earl of Lichfield for the occasion. They were to live happily together for forty-two years and she had eighteen children.

About this time James got permission for his daughter Anne to join them; sadly, little Isabella had died in March, just before the Oxford Parliament. Her death, James said in the memoirs, was 'the more afflicting because they had not the satisfaction of seeing and assisting her in her sickness.' She was not quite five years old and the last of Maria's three children to die. Since the baby Charles's birth and death in 1677 no other child had been born.

Anne, now growing tall and blooming, sixteen years old, arrived at Leith on 17 July 1681 after what Maria called, enviously, 'a very fine passage, being but four days upon the sea'. She added, 'I thank God I am in perfect health and much pleased to have the Lady Anne with me. . . .'

James, encouraged by his success in calming the disorderly state of Scotland, and reorganizing its finances, petitioned Charles for permission to call a Parliament there, knowing that it was conducted on different principles from the English Parliament. Permission granted he opened the Scottish Parliament on 28 July 1681, riding in procession from Holyrood up the Canongate to the Parliament House, which had been rebuilt by his father in late medieval style, like a college hall, and survives now as a ceremonial part of the law courts. James's Duchess and his daughter, going by coach, were present in the hall, in splendid robes, to the astonishment of the Scots, who did not expect ladies to be admitted to these solemn proceedings.

From James's point of view the session was a great success. Having allowed them to impose a Test of their own, slanted more against 'fanaticks' than against papists, he was pleased when they went on to uphold the rightful succession and pledge their loyalty anew to the King and his lawful heirs. Then several 'grievances' were brought up to be redressed and celebratory banquets were held, with lords at one table and commons at another, the Duke of Albany and York presiding in the place of honour.

Now began a season of entertainment, indoors and out. James made progresses to other towns, seeing and being seen, knighting deserving royalists, receiving loyal addresses and settling local disputes; it was now that he gained the nickname James the Just.

It is typical of James's story that virtually the only thing remembered of his time in Scotland is the condemnation of the Earl of Argyll for treason, because he would only take the new Test with private reservations. James's own account is that it was 'neither the King's nor the Duke's intention to take away the Earl of Argyle's life, but to make use of this occasion to get him more in their power and forfeit certain jurisdictions and superiorities which he and his predecessors had surreptitiously acquired and most tyranicaly exercised.' The King's orders were that the sentence should be passed 'but stopp'd'.

However, Argyll did not wait to test the King's clemency but escaped, dressed as his daughter's footman and, 'carrying up her train as she went out, passed undiscerned by all the guards.' The memoirs add: 'Some of the Council were for having his daughter whipped through the streets of Edinburg, but the Duke prevented it, by saying, they were not used to deal so cruelly with Ladys in his country.' Typical of James to think of himself as an Englishman, even in his ancestral Scotland.

He comments, somewhat bitterly, that in London he was blamed for pressing things too far and 'prosecuting Argyle out of pique'. The Lauderdales had a great share in these reports; they were annoyed with James for his criticisms of the misconduct of people they had appointed. Lauderdale's wife, Countess of Dysart in her own right, was a formidable lady who had been involved in secret cavalier plots before the Restoration. James had often visited them at Ham House near Richmond, where much of her furniture and Lely portraits survive, now in the care of the National Trust.

Meanwhile, James's activities in the Scottish Parliament 'wonderfully ashtonished the Duke's enemies in England' and cheered his friends, who began to agitate again for his recall. Unfortunately this was made conditional on his return to the Church of England, to which most of his Tory friends belonged. James wondered whether his being present at prayers in Parliament, or his concurrence in the Scottish Test Act, had made people 'fancy a further step'. His reason for this policy was 'to convince the world that the Duke was not so blindly zealous in his Religion, as that if it were ever in his power he would force those who would not go to mass to go to Smithfield (as his enemies industriously gave it out.)' But perhaps it had appeared not as a sign of tolerance but only of wavering.

At any rate, when Laurence Hyde came north on a mission of reconversion, 'the Duke was amazed to find himself (he knew not how) blown farther back than ever, just when he thought he had wethered the storme and was entring into a secure harbour.' Laurence, now Baron Hyde, had once been a sharer in theatre parties with Nell Gwyn (who called him Lory) and could never quite believe in James's Catholicism; he had deplored his going to Brussels in 1679 for fear of its Catholic influence. 'I cannot be more Catholike than I am,' James had written irritably to George Legge, his Protestant naval friend.

After two or three days of argument, 'then my lord Hide pulled a paper out of his poket writ by the King himself, profering That in case he would promise to go to church without doeing more, he should have libertie to come to court. . . .' James had long since made up his mind that such deceit would do no good to the monarchy and destroy his own credibility. So, 'the Duke persisting in constant denyal' Lord Hyde 'left him with the comfortless view of being abandoned by all the world, charged with the ruin of the King's affairs which went nearer his heart than that of his own, and of ending his days in the most uneasy banishment and afflicting circomstances that fortune could possibly reduce him too.'

However, the King was mollified by Hyde's report of the Duke's great success in Scotland and asked him to make his own report on Scottish affairs. This was just what James could do well and he set to and made a very full report, which is summarized in the memoirs. James held that the mismanagement of Scotland came chiefly from 'private animosities' and remarked that many whom the King had trusted had 'governed more by their own than the King's interest – such men must be layd aside.' But he thought that anyone put in Lauderdale's place would soon be as unpopular as he had become and suggested that in future there should be two Secretaries of State for Scotland, one there and one in England, changing places every year or half-year, and that five or six of the Scotch Privy Council should attend the King's court and be changed too at regular intervals.

Then the standing forces needed experienced officers; most knew nothing and owed their posts to friends in power. Moreover, they neglected their men and 'put most of the mony in their own pockets'. James's advice on the Highlands was that the four great lords should be paid what was now given to the companies to keep order (about £700 apiece) and be responsible for making good whatever their dependents plundered from the Lowlands. Nor was there any need of seven Lords of the Treasury to manage the small revenue of £60,000 a year. When the farms of customs and excise expired it would be better to collect the duties as in England, for the 'farmers' had grown rich at the expense of the government.

The King approved everything James had suggested and thereafter always took his advice on Scottish affairs. After his return James acted as liaison with Scotland and, as his correspondence with Lord Queensberry shows, his knowledge of the conditions and the persons concerned was invaluable. After his accession, he continued to write in person, in his usual plain, blunt style.

Charles's latest reason to keep James away was that the trials of Shaftesbury and Lord Howard of Escrick were due in the autumn; in the event the Grand Jury was still sufficiently under Shaftesbury's influence to bring in an *Ignoramus*, and the trial fell. He and Howard were bailed, bells were rung and bonfires blazed in the city. Moreover, it looked as if the King would be forced to call a Parliament, because King Louis was trying to get round his promise not to invade Flanders by laying claim to Luxembourg, the fortified capital of the Duchy, then under Spanish rule. As Charles had a treaty with Spain it looked as if England would be forced into action against France – just what William of Orange was trying to effect, and why he was using the Spanish and Dutch Ambassadors to press Charles to call a Parliament.

At one point Charles was persuaded to recall his brother but the order was countermanded a few days later. 'This quick relaps was oweing to my Lord Halifax's arguing, who was always for cleaving a hair in his advice,' James commented sarcastically. Halifax thought the

Duke ought to return if there was a Parliament but not before. He wrote to tell the Duke it was all for his best interests and he hoped he would not think otherwise. James rather did think otherwise. So did Hyde, who 'was not satisfied with his Trimming'. (Trimmer was Halifax's nickname, which he interpreted as trimming the ship of state, though other people were less complimentary.) Charles was considering where to hold this unwanted Parliament, perhaps at Cambridge – nice and near to Newmarket! But in the end he managed to wriggle out of the situation, at the cost of ditching Luxembourg, and no Parliament was called. According to Barillon Charles told him the factious Parliament men were devils who were out for his blood.

Throughout this autumn, so fraught in London, James was writing cheerful little notes to his niece Charlotte, Countess of Litchfield, as he always spelt it. On 18 October he told her, 'Some tyme we go to the plays, these players come out of Ireland and are pretty tolerable. . . .' On 26 November he wrote, 'I assure you that we here do not passe our tyme so ill as you in England thinke we do, for we have plays, ride abroad when tis good weather, play at Bassett (cards) and have a greate deale of good company, but for all that one wishes oneself with ons friends at London. . . .' He went on to tell of Anne's acting in a play (as Semandra in Lee's tragedy of *Mithridates*) 'there were five of them that did their parts very well and they were very well drest, so that they made a very fine show, and such a one as had not been seen in this country before.'

There were also balls at Holyrood Palace and Anne danced with her father in the country dances. Maria could not dance because she had suffered a bad riding accident, being dragged along the ground by her horse, her habit catching in the saddle as she fell. In December James wrote to Charlotte,

You will by the last post have heard what a terrible fall, especially to look to, the Dutchess had and realy t'was a miracle she was not spoyled, and tis a great mercy she had no more harme, she is now God be thanked as well as can be expected after such an accident, and her legs mend apace but yett she is tyde to ly on hir bed or sitt in a chaire and it must be yett some days before she must walk.

[129]

James did not approve of young married women riding but was too soft-hearted to forbid Maria's enjoyment of the exercise. He even had a portrait done of her in her riding habit, a coat of mannish cut with a lace cravat, which always hung in his Bedchamber.

In January 1682 he was writing to his niece, 'We have now doone right winter weather . . . so that there is no sturring abroad, which is a great mortification to me, that love best the divertions outdoors than those within.'

Charlotte evidently told him of the visit of some outlandish ambassadors (Evelyn describes them) for James replied that he had little news to give from Edinburgh, 'where we have no Morocco nor Russian Embassados to divert us, nor God be thanked such disorderly yonge men as Mr Harry Wharton, to disturb the playhouse or kill horses. . . .' The weather had cleared and James was now 'abroad every day and playing at Goffe'. One of the ways he took out from Holyrood is called to this day 'Duke's Walk'.

The end of his exile in Scotland was approaching, though he could see no sign of it then.

15 Old Jemmy's Come Again

It was the Duchess of Portsmouth's greed which eventually got James back to England. She was going to Bourbon to take the waters and to show off her splendour at the French court and she wanted to make a large investment in France for the future; Charles, hard up as usual, could not find £100,000 and someone suggested it should be granted out of the Duke of York's revenue from the Post Office, he being given an equivalent from the excise. James, always sharp on finance, knew his revenue could not be alienated except by act of Parliament, but he kept quiet about this and humbly agreed, only stipulating that he must come himself to manage the business. The King agreed, inviting him to Newmarket, on condition he left his Duchess in Scotland to show it was not an official recall. Privately, however, he sent George Legge to tell James he meant him to return for good.

So on 4 March 1682 James embarked on the *Henrietta* yacht and after a rough passage landed at Yarmouth, going straight on to spend the night at Norwich. He says he was well received in both places; this is an understatement, for there was popular rejoicing and seamen could be heard singing: 'The glory of our British line/Old Jemmy's come again.' In spite of the propaganda of the faction the Duke's reputation was still high on the east coast.

At Newmarket the King met him 'with all immaginable demonstrations of kindness' and James pleased him by declaring that he would not 'meddle in publick business'. Charles took him back to London and there the Attorney General discovered that an act of Parliament was necessary to alienate the Duke's revenue – surprise, surprise. It was the King who eventually paid up for his Fubbs's investment, quarterly out of his French allowance.

Meanwhile the Duchess of York was languishing in Edinburgh, 'in an advanced state of pregnancy' as she told the nuns of Chaillot in her widowhood. 'I felt myself so greatly depressed in his absence that, unable to struggle against the melancholy that oppressed me, I wrote at last to tell him so; on which he determined to come by sea to fetch me.'

Charles now really wanted his brother at his side; James's energy and ability in the practical side of government were badly needed after the confusion and intrigue of the Shaftesbury era. Pepys was among those delighted to see the Duke back and commented to his old friend James Houblon that he was 'plumper, fatter and all over in better liking than ever I knew him'. And he thought that 'his political state of body seems to be much mended too, since his nearer partaking of his brother's sunshine.' He added that the King 'seems in no point less fortified against mortality than the Duke, but in one particular more, namely . . . he hath the prayers of the very Whigs for his health, while we Tories are fain to pray by ourselves for his brother's.'

When James set out for Scotland on 4 May, it was aboard the flagship *Gloucester*, accompanied by several smaller vessels, including the *Catherine* yacht, in which Pepys got a passage, and lucky for him he did, for at half past five in the morning of 6 May the *Gloucester* struck the Lemon and Oare shoals.

James, with his dog Mumper, was asleep below. He was roused by Churchill, who urged him to leave the sinking ship at once. At first he refused, thinking she could be saved, but then a great wave lifted her and smashed her down on the shoals so that her back was broken and water began coming in fast. The longboat was lowered and James was persuaded to get into it, annoying Churchill by insisting that he must have the box containing his papers – the basis of the memoirs – something he obstinately stuck to through all the vicissitudes of his life.

Burnet (who was not there) later asserted that James's only care was to save his priests and his dogs, a slander which annoyed the second Lord Dartmouth whose father (George Legge) had been in the *Gloucester* and knew what really happened. The longboat could only hold six besides the rowers and Churchill with drawn sword prevented its being swamped with frantic passengers; Legge himself had to swim for it. All the same James insisted on picking up Montrose and later one of his musicians who could not swim.

As the boat drew out from the stricken ship the seamen raised a cheer when they saw the Duke was saved. A few minutes later the ship went down and most of them were left struggling in the water. Luckily it was fairly calm and daylight was strengthening, so that many castaways were picked up by other ships. George Legge was taken up by the *Catherine* yacht and so was Sir Charles Scarborough, the famous physician, who had been struggling for possession of a floating plank with the Duke's dog Mumper. (Presumably poor old Mumper was saved too.) Maria's Italian priest-secretary saved himself by swimming.

Nevertheless, many were lost; Maria says that the Duke was 'almost beside himself with grief at the calamity which had been attended with the loss of so many lives'. He saw that compensation was awarded to the widows of the seamen drowned. But that was for the future; his immediate care was to reach Edinburgh before the news of the wreck, which he succeeded in doing. Maria often said that if she had heard of it before she knew he was safe, the shock would have killed her. She certainly might have lost the longed-for baby she was carrying.

Edinburgh's reaction was to celebrate the Duke's escape with bonfires; the Scots did not at all want to lose 'great Albany' as the balladmakers called him, renowned for his fairness to all people and parties.

Pepys, who arrived soon after in the *Catherine*, saw the Duke in action when James invited him to two sessions of the Council, which impressed him as being much superior to the English Privy Council 'in order, gravity and unanimity of their debates'. As to the Duke himself, Pepys said his authority was 'being maintained with so much absoluteness and yet gentleness, to the rendering it morally impossible for any disquiet to arise in his Majesty's affairs.'

This letter is quoted from Sir Arthur Bryant's three-volume *Life of Pepys*, a mine of information about the times. Pepys had dared to stick up for the Duke of York in 1679, maintaining that whatever his religion he had been the best Lord High Admiral the country had ever had. And when Pepys was struggling to clear himself from charges of treason he wrote to the Duke, then in Brussels, and James wrote to the King, 'Give me leave to say, your Majesty is bound to do something for him that has spent so many years in your service to your satisfaction.' Pepys, largely through his own efforts, got free at last and was now back at the Admiralty and hoping that somehow the Duke might be reinstated.

In spite of the wreck of the *Gloucester* the Duke intended to go home by sea and the Duchess was determined to go with him. When they embarked at Leith on the *The Happy Return* James had devised a chair and pulley for hauling his pregnant wife on board. Maria was to describe it to the nuns at Chaillot, saying that she feared nothing so long as she was with her husband. Just looking at him encouraged her: 'I seemed to have power to confront every peril.'

This time the voyage was uneventful, they arrived on 26 May and were met on the river by the King, who had come specially from Windsor, bringing the Queen with him. There was a tremendous welcome from the Lord Mayor and citizens of London as well as from the court; instead of toasts to the Duke of Monmouth people were singing glory to *old* Jemmy. It was indeed a Happy Return.

Maria was expecting her baby at the end of August and the Scots and the Yorkists confidently hoped it would be a boy. The Exclusionist Whigs began spreading reports that if it was a girl, a boy would be secretly substituted – the Duchess of Modena, who was coming over from the Low Countries for her daughter's confinement, was supposed to be bringing over a Dutch boy for the purpose.

In fact Maria went into labour a fortnight sooner than expected and the child was born on 15 August 1682, only three days after the Duchess of Modena arrived. It was a girl and was christened Charlotte

Maria by Dr Compton, the belligerently Protestant cleric who had charge of the religious education of the princesses Mary and Anne. No more was heard of the Dutch boy.

Sadly, Charlotte Maria lived only eight weeks and died of 'convulsions'. The appearance of a comet about that time had caused some enthusiasts to predict a great future for the royal child. Edmond Halley, observing this comet, came to the conclusion that it was the same that had appeared in 1607 and on earlier occasions at intervals of seventy-five or -six years, and predicted it would return in 1758. Sure enough it was sighted on Christmas day that year, though Halley was not alive to see it. Called after him, it has recently (1985/6) made another return, though barely visible from England. The point about Halley's discovery was that till then nobody imagined comets could orbit the sun; all were believed to be one-off heavenly visitors.

James, like Charles, was interested in the sciences and a patron of the Royal Society. In the new Greenwich Observatory there were hung two huge portraits of the King and the Duke in court dress and robes. When James was King, in 1687, Halley, who had persuaded Isaac Newton to publish his *Principia Mathematica* (and paid the cost) presented it to his Majesty, with a treatise on the tides which he knew would be of special interest to him. Foreign scholars were also patronized by James, including several Huguenots of distinction.

Scientific curiosities formed part of the Ashmole collection which Oxford University first housed in the Old Clarendon building; James was invited to open it in May 1683, when he and the Duchess of York, with the Princess Anne, visited Oxford. (In 1983 the Ashmolean Museum celebrated this as the tercentenary of its Foundation.)

The Duke and Duchess of York came over from Windsor and were met in state at the Eastgate (and presented with gloves) by the Mayor, and greeted with poems at Christ Church. They spent several days in Oxford, visiting the colleges, the Bodleian Library and the Sheldonian Theatre, then a new building designed by Christopher Wren, and from there walked across to inspect the 'rareties' collected by the Tradescants, which Elias Ashmole had given to the university – still to be seen today in a special room at the Museum. They were also shown some scientific experiments and then entertained to a banquet. At Convocation next day several courtiers were made Doctors of Civil

Law, including, rather incongruously, John Churchill. When they left, the Vice Chancellor presented the Duke with *The History and Antiquities of the University of Oxford*, bound with its plates; the Duchess received the plates bound separately and Plot's *Natural History of Oxfordshire* while the Lady Anne was given 'a fair English Bible'.

This royal visit took place after the King's spring expedition to Newmarket, which had ended earlier than usual because of a fire in his house there; but before the revelation in June that by this unexpectedly early return the King and the Duke had escaped a murderous attack by an armed gang planned to take place at the Rye House, near Ware in Hertfordshire.

A man called Keeling betrayed a group of ex-republicans and Cromwellians who had plotted this assassination, which was linked with the activities of some great men who were scheming for an insurrection; Russell was named, and Lord Howard of Escrick, the Earl of Essex and Algernon Sidney – and Monmouth.

Lord Howard was caught hiding up a chimney and he turned King's Evidence, confessing that there had indeed been conferences with a view to an insurrection. Russell, Algernon Sidney and Lord Essex were arrested and sent to the Tower. Monmouth disappeared.

Reports went about that the King was looking sad and grim; no wonder, for it looked as if his beloved bastard had been plotting the murder of the father to whom he owed everything. A warrant went out for him, but Charles did not try very hard to find him.

Meanwhile, Russell was put on trial and on the very first day, when the King and the Duke were visiting the Tower, a message was brought to the Governor that the Earl of Essex had cut his own throat. This shocking news seemed to confirm the guilt of Russell and the others. Because of this the Whigs, then and later, tried to make out that Essex had been murdered – at the instigation of the Duke of York, of course.

During Russell's trial it became plain that though he could only be proved to have met the Rumbold gang once and had then declared against 'lopping' (as the desperadoes called the assassination) yet he had been involved in conspiratorial meetings with Shaftesbury and others. Lord Howard's evidence was crucial but other things supported it and Russell was condemned. His family begged for his life, even offering the King money, but Charles remained unmoved. 'If I do not

[135]

have his life, he will have mine,' he is said to have averred. However, he did commute the sentence to beheading. 'Lord Russell shall find that I am possessed of that prerogative which he denied in the case of Lord Stafford,' he said grimly.

Dr Gilbert Burnet was one of the clergymen who attended Russell in the Tower; he was writing memoranda, some of which he later used in compiling his famous *History of his Own Time*, others he omitted but they survived and were printed in 1902 by H. C. Foxcroft as *A Supplement to Burnet's History*. These often give a rather different picture from his later accounts. For instance, he was to omit the fact that he had failed to get Russell to admit that it was unlawful to take arms against the King, and that he found him 'cold' in religious matters. Nevertheless, he undertook to edit and publish Russell's 'dying words' which soon became part of the Whig martyrology.

Russell had told Burnet there were 'never anything but embryos of things' which, given the ill-assorted conspirators, one can well believe. Still, there is a good deal of evidence that the conspiracy had been going on for some time, and had been started by Shaftesbury, timed for November 1682; it was when this had failed to come off that Shaftesbury fled to Holland, where he died early in 1683. Lord Grey of Warke (Ford Grey, who was made Earl of Tankerville under William) asserted as much in the confession he made after Monmouth's rebellion, which was countersigned by Sunderland, then James's Secretary of State. Grey was an unashamed Whig and Exclusionist and Monmouth's chief friend and abettor. Younger than Monmouth, he was as dissolute but a good deal more shrewd, at any rate in pursuit of his own ends. In 1685 he exonerated Russell as well as Monmouth from implication in the murder plot, but not from the conspiracy.

Of course, in the Rye House affair, the King cared most about the conduct of his son and after some time Halifax succeeded in bringing about a reconciliation. He advised Monmouth to write a letter to the King, in which he swore that he knew nothing of the murder plot and that his own intention had simply been to get the King away from his ill-advisers and effect a reconciliation between him and Parliament.

This worked and a meeting was arranged between the King, the Duke of Monmouth and the Duke of York, at which James took notes.

He said Monmouth freely owned the knowledge of the whole conspiracy except the assassination; he named persons and did not contradict anything Lord Howard had said 'except one particular which was not material'. Monmouth had 'very well remembered what Rumney had sayd of my lord Russell, who, when Trenchard had failed him, sayd he would put on his boots and go down to Taunton himself and make the people rise.' Monmouth spoke of Wildman, the republican agitator, and wondered no more witnesses had come in against him, 'since no man, he sayd, had been more active in the conspiracy than he.' (Wildman had got away and was to come over with William.) He also gave information about the Scottish connexion with Argyll and named Booth (afterwards Lord Delamere and an Orange supporter) as 'the man they depended on in Cheshire'. Monmouth further 'owned his having visited the Guards in order to a surprise'.

All this agrees with what Lord Grey wrote in 1685 and shows that the 'embryos' Russell spoke of to Burnet were fairly near to parturition. The King required Monmouth to put all this in writing 'not only as a ty upon him but for publick satisfaction, it being so hard to stifle the groundless suggestions of those false and factious men against the plainest matters of fact in the world.' This was the Whig contention that the whole business was a put-up job by the government to get rid of the leaders of the opposition. William of Orange also took this view, calling the Rye House Plot 'a contrivance'. No doubt he was arguing from his own experience, for he was fond of contrivances which exposed assassination plots against himself at critical moments.

James records that 'Assoon as the Duke of Monmouth got his pardon, he began to herd as formerly with his factious Counsellors . . . the truth of it was, they had got such a dominion over his unstable mind that they soon overthrew all his new made vows of Loyaltie.' Although he had been exempt from witnessing against his friends he could not rest till he had got his written confession back, which Charles weakly handed over, 'whereupon he flew back immediately and deny'd every word he had sayd.' James wrote to William on 7 December 1683, about Monmouth's denial, which was actually published in the *Gazette*, 'and now tis visible to all the world, that he only designed by his coming in, to get his pardon, and to keep his credit with his party still, both which he has now done.'

[137]

He ended this letter, 'Algernon Sidney was beheaded this day, died very resolutely, like a true rebel and republican.' On 4 January 1684 he was writing that it was thought fit to have Sidney's paper printed 'that the world might see what his principles were, and what both he and the rest of the conspirators drove at, and its being published has really done good.' James also sent Mary a printed copy of the state trial. Sidney had got his deserts but could be respected for his resolution and openness.

Banished again for this new flouting of the King, Monmouth went to Holland, where he was welcomed by William with lavish entertainment, in which Mary was allowed for once to take part, dancing with her cousin and even skating with him, with her skirts tucked up. Monmouth was treated more like a visiting prince than a disgraced exile. In June 1684 this was still going on, regardless of protests from Charles's ambassadors, and James wrote to his daughter Mary to complain how it scandalized 'all loyal and monarchical people here', and to suggest that she might speak to William about it. 'And let the Prince flatter himself as he pleases, the Duke of Monmouth will do his part, to have a push with him for the crown, if he, the Duke of Monmouth, outlive the King and me.' William, however, continued on his subtle way.

With the failure of the Whig conspiracy James was soon restored to all his old positions, first on the Foreign Affairs Committee in May 1683, then taking his place on the Privy Council, and finally made High Admiral again, in May 1684, though officially everything had to go through the King's hands, so that James would not have to take the Test oath. His return to the Admiralty pleased not only Pepys, who had helped to bring it about, but Evelyn too. He said, 'everybody was glad of this Change: those in the late Commission being utterly ignorant of their duty, to the greate damage of the Navy Royal.'

It had been a very cold winter. In December 1683 James wrote to William, 'last night it froze so very hard that this morning the boys began to slide upon the Canal in the park, though last night at sun-set, there was not one bit of ice on it; 'tis like to continue, the wind being north-east.' It did continue; the Thames froze so hard that a kind of fair was held on the ice, with booths selling meat and drink. Everybody went out on the frozen river, including the entire royal family, whose names were printed on cards by an enterprising huckster: *Charles, King . . . Catherine, Queen . . . James, Duke . . .* etc.

In that party Anne appeared, with her husband the Prince of Denmark and 'Jack in the Cellar' – she was already pregnant. Anne's marriage was important, as Mary remained childless and Maria's children had all died. The final choice was George, brother to the King of Denmark; he was a Protestant, but as Denmark was an ally of France King Louis was favourable, so the match should suit everyone. As it turned out George, fair, stout and stolid, suited Anne too; with him she enjoyed the novel sensation of being the dominant partner, so different from her subordinate rôle to her adored Sarah Churchill, now her Mistress of the Robes. The Prince and Princess of Denmark were set up with their own household in the fine Cockpit lodgings, now vacated by Monmouth, and Anne retained her important place in the royal succession.

But with the dissolution of Parliament and the scotching of the insurrection plot and Monmouth's disgrace, the question of the succession dropped into the background. James's application to business was appreciated by all the ministers, even those like Halifax who did not want to see him succeed his brother. But that contingency did not seem imminent. The King was in good health; he went to Newmarket as usual that spring, though he was much taken up with his plan to build a new palace at Winchester. The land was bought, Sir Christopher Wren designed a great building in the classical style, with a view towards the sea, and the work was put in hand at once.

Charles was now on excellent terms with his brother. James says that the Duchess of Portsmouth became suspicious of their tête-à-tête conferences in the King's closet; she thought they were talking politics but in fact they were discussing religion. James was the only person Charles could talk to on that subject now.

The icy winter was followed by a very hot summer and prolonged drought – 'never so dry a season in my remembrance,' noted Evelyn (now overy sixty), 'the leaves dropping from the Trees as in Autumn' – just as they did in our recent very dry summer.

In September there was what now would be called a Cabinet reshuffle. Laurence Hyde, made Earl of Rochester recently, was removed from the Treasury to be Lord President of the Council, when

Halifax coined the phrase 'being kicked upstairs'. Sidney Godolphin was made a Baron and first Lord of the Treasury (which was put into commission); it was the right place for him which he kept for several reigns to come. And Lord Middleton, a contemporary and friend of James (he was a Scot) was made a Secretary of State. Sunderland, through Louise's wiles, was back in office again. Hyde was suspected of mismanagement in the Treasury; he was certainly rather grasping, having risen to an Earldom without much in the way of estates.

Probably in August of this hot dry summer Catherine Sedley bore James a son, christened James Darnley. It was Rochester who had brought Catherine back into James's life, in an attempt to draw him into Protestant circles again. It caused great misery to Maria; she had lost all her children and not only had she not conceived for some time but she was in poor health; coming back to England had not been such a triumph for her as it had been for James.

A portrait was begun this year of James, by Godfrey Kneller, which was finished after he became King. In armour and holding again his baton as Admiral, he looks sturdy and hearty, almost smiling. He was back at his brother's side, Whig conspiracies were foiled and England was at peace with itself again.

The celebrations for Queen Catherine's birthday on 15 November were lavish: 'there was such fire works upon the Thames before White-hall,' writes Evelyn,

> with pageants of Castles, Forts and other devices of Gyrandolas, Serpents, the King and Queenes Armes and mottoes, all represented in fire, as had not been seene in any age remembered here . . . It is said this sole Triumph cost 1500 pounds: which was concluded with a Ball, where all the young Ladys and Gallants daunced in the great Hall: the Court had not ben seene so brave and rich in apparell since his Majestie's restauration.

It was nearly twenty-five years since that glorious and ever memorable event.

II KING

February 1685

King Charles II, taken ill on 2 February, died on Friday 6 February 1685, between eleven and twelve in the morning, having his senses till within an hour of his peaceful death.

The account from the memoirs proceeds:

Assoon as the breath was out of the King's body, the Duke (whom henceforth we must call by the name of King James II) to avoid the importunity of compliments which were then crowding in upon him, retired immediately to his closet, haveing more inclination to satisfy his grief and anguish at the late sorrowfull object than to please himself with thoughts of a Crown so unexpectedly fallen upon his head, which with all its glettering charms was not able to asswage that sencible affliction he suffer'd, in parteing with a Brother he loved and honour'd so much; haveing therefore for some time given full scope to his tears, necessity and order (tho much against his inclination) obliged him to appear and receive at last the compliments and congratulations of those who waited with impatience to make them.

Evelyn, who wrote up his accounts on Sunday evening (8 February) says,

His Majestie dead, the Duke (now K. James the 2d) went immediately to Council, and before entering into any businesse, passionately declared his sorrow, Told their Lordships, That since the succession had fallen to him, he would endeavour to follow the example of his predecessor in his Clemency and tendernesse to his people: that however he had ben misrepresented as affecting arbitrary power, they should find the contrary, for that the Laws of England had made the King as greate a Monarch as he could desire; that he would endeavour to maintaine the Government both in Church and State as by Law establish'd, its Principles being so firme for Monarchy and the members of it shewing themselves so good and loyal subjects.

James's version, essentially the same, goes on, 'therefore as I will never depart from the just rights and prerogatives of the Crown, so I never will invade any man's property. I have often ventured my life in defence of the Nation and will go as far as any man in preserving it in its just rights and privileges.'

Impressed, the lords asked if this speech might be published. James, who had spoken impromptu, had nothing in writing, but Mr Finch had taken notes and presented a version which the new King approved. The Councillors then swore allegiance, the ministers were to keep their offices for the time being, and the proclamation of accession was sent out. Evelyn accompanied the heralds to Whitehall Gate and into the City, where James was proclaimed at Temple Bar and the Exchange, with trumpets and kettledrums, ending with the people's acclamations. No trouble at all.

Coming back to Whitehall, Evelyn went with the rest to kiss the hands of the King and Queen. 'He had ben on the bed, but was now risen, and in his Undresse' – informal day clothes. 'The Queene was in bed in her apartment, but put forth her hand; seeming to be much afflicted, as I believe she was, having deported herself so decently upon all occasions since she first came into England, which made her universally beloved.'

On Sunday, though the services were as usual in the Chapel Royal, the new King went openly to mass with the Queen 'in the little Chappel of St James's', and had the doors left open because, as he said himself, 'as he was resolved not to invade other men's Religion, so neither would he conceal his own.'

The funeral of King Charles presented some problems, because of his having died a Catholic. Not wanting to disturb people by publishing this abroad, James decided it should be held at night, then a common practice. (King William was also to be buried at night.) All the Privy Council, the household, and the lords in town attended, and the lying in state beforehand was, according to James, 'very solemn'.

Evelyn on the other hand wrote on 14 February, 'the King was (this night) very obscurely buried in a Vault under Hen. 7th Chapell in Westminster, without any manner of pompe, and soone forgotten after all this vainity.' However, there was considerable popular mourning and the funeral statue was displayed at Westminster Abbey; it is still there.

After the funeral, Evelyn notes, 'the face of the whole Court exceedingly changed into a more solemn and moral behaviour: the new King affecting neither Prophanenesse, nor boufonry.' Lent, which began soon after, gave James the occasion for this reform.

The ministry was now reorganized: James appointed his brothers-in-law to high posts, Laurence Hyde, Earl of Rochester, to be the Lord Treasurer and Henry, second Earl of Clarendon, Lord Privy Seal. Halifax became President of the Council (kicked upstairs in his turn); Lord Godolphin was made Chamberlain to the Queen and the Earls of Sunderland and Middleton were continued as Secretaries of State. James made a point of continuing Charles's appointments, even though he was aware that Sunderland and Godolphin had ratted on him over Exclusion.

James also announced that he would call a Parliament, to sit after the coronation, which was fixed for St George's day, 23 April. He told Barillon, 'Many people will say that I determine too hastily in calling a parliament; but if I waited longer I should lose the merit of it. I know the English; you must not show them any fear in the beginning; the malcontents would have formed cabals to demand a parliament, and thereby gained the favour of the nation, which they would afterwards have abused.'

Barillon, incidentally, paid up the allowance due to Charles and recorded James's gratitude to King Louis. All the same, when James had secured the revenue for life which he was asking from the new Parliament, he made no further financial deals with France. He did not want to be dependent in any way on foreign aid. And such was his financial ability that he did not need to be. But he told Barillon that he was grateful because 'the King your Master helped me at a time when it could not be known if there might not be a sedition in London, and whether I should not be driven out of it.'

If Shaftesbury had been alive or Monmouth still in London, there might well have been trouble, but Monmouth was in Holland at the time of King Charles's death. He had been over in England secretly in December; Halifax had once more arranged a meeting for him with his father and he thought he was soon to be recalled. James was to be sent to Scotland again, to hold another Scottish Parliament.

At Charles's sudden death, Monmouth had written in his pocket book, 'O cruel fate'.

1 Coronation and Rebellion

St George's day fell on Thursday in Easter week in 1685. Exactly a week before on Maundy Thursday, James revived the medieval practice of the King's washing the feet of poor men, in imitation of Christ. There were fifty-two of them because he would be fifty-two in October next. He also touched for the Evil persons suffering from scrofula (a form of tuberculosis) as Charles had done all through his reign. The King laid his hands on their heads and faces, while prayers were read. Then each was given a gold piece (the origin of the royal Maundy money) which was usually bound on the arm. (William discontinued what he regarded as a superstitious rite; Anne revived it but she was the last to practise it and Samuel Johnson, as an infant, one of the last to receive the royal touch.)

James prepared carefully for his coronation, which was to be carried out in full by the Archbishop of Canterbury, except for receiving the Sacrament. Sancroft was supported by the Bishop of Durham (Crewe, James's old friend) and the Bishop of Bath and Wells – Ken, who had been chaplain to James's daughter Mary in Holland.

The Queen was to be crowned too and new regalia had to be made for her, since no Queen Consort had been crowned for a long time. In her coronation portrait she looks beautiful, still young – she was in her twenty-seventh year – and with her dark hair in long loose locks over her shoulders in the fashion that was soon to give way to a stiffer style. As a royal gesture, she paid the fines of small debtors, so that they could be released from prison.

James, in the interests of economy, had cancelled the night spent at the Tower and the state procession from there to Westminster. Maria slept at St James's, the King at Whitehall, and they met at Westminster Hall for the procession to the Abbey. Carrying the left-hand front pole of the canopy over the King's head was Samuel Pepys, Baron of the Cinque Ports and Secretary to the Admiralty.

Evelyn did not attend, because he had just lost his beloved daughter Mary, who had died of the small pox. So it was left to Gilbert Burnet to write up the coronation of King James (which he did not attend) detailing ludicrous incidents, such as the crown's hanging down over James's face. The crown certainly did not fit well for Maria mentions that there was difficulty in keeping it in place. Probably, as it was made for Charles before wigs came in, it sat too high rather than too low on the King's head. In his earlier (unpublished) memoirs Burnet says the King was 'more intent on the ceremony of the splendour of that day than became a man of his age'. Did he leave this out later because it suggested that James was entering into the spirit of something very like a sacrament of ordination to the office of king? Whatever Burnet thought, this was in James's mind, for he had taken care to be anointed beforehand by a Catholic priest, to make sure that the grace of kingship was validly conferred.

The coronation of James II was very fully attended by the lords spiritual and temporal and everything was set down in writing, engravings of the scene were made and the whole bound up in folio, and copies can still be seen and studied today. Music was specially composed for this great occasion, including several anthems by Purcell. 'My heart is inditing' is the one now most frequently performed.

James received the coronation ring, which he managed to keep through all the vicissitudes to come. He made the traditional oath to rule according to the laws and customs of England; it did not then contain any specifically Protestant wording. And the Archbishops, Bishops and peers all in turn did homage and swore loyalty to him and to his heirs.

After the ceremonies were concluded, the company went to banquet in Westminster Hall, where everything was done in traditional style, with the King's Champion riding in to defend his right. Nobody challenged it *then*. Later in the evening there was a great display of fireworks over the river which the King and Queen, Princess Anne and Prince George, the courtiers and ministers watched from Whitehall. Pepys kept a print of the coronation fireworks. To a Tory royalist it was all very satisfactory.

Not so to Burnet, who left England in May. After the Rye House Plot he had been dismissed by King Charles from his place at the Rolls Chapel for seditious sermonizing – perhaps one reason why he says that at the end of his reign Charles became 'cruel', though he blames the ruthless pursuit of the plotters mostly on the Duke of York. Now that the Duke had become King, Burnet began to feel nervous. His unpublished memoir relates that when he got Halifax to ask if he might kiss the King's hand 'the King not only refused it but spoke sharply of me. Upon which I desired Halifax to ask the King's leave for me to go beyond the sea, which the King said he agreed to with all his heart.' James's ironic humour shows here, as it so often does in the memoirs.

King James opened his Parliament on 22 May 1685. Thanks to Charles's policy of calling in charters and re-ordering corporations (continued by Sunderland) there was a comfortable Tory majority. Evelyn, who had got a good place in the House of Lords through his friend Lord Clarendon, was amused that the Catholic Queen, who came in with the Princess Anne, had to hear the lords taking the Test oaths and 'the Pope, and worship of the Virg:Mary etc renounc'd very decently'.

'Then came in the King, the Crowne on his head etc and being sate, the Commons were let in, and so the house being fill'd, he drew forth a paper, containing his speech, which he (read) distinctly enough. . . .' The speech repeated his promises to the accession council and asked the members in return to settle the revenue for life. In his usual blunt style James said 'that some might possibly suggest that it were better to feede and supply him from time to time onely, out of their inclination to frequent Parliaments; but that that would be but a very improper Method to take with him; since the best way to engage him to meet oftener, would be allways to use him well.' Evelyn further reports that 'at every period of this, the house gave loud shouts etc.'

At the end of his speech James announced that he had just had news that Argyll had landed in Scotland and published two treasonous declarations. 'It is sufficient to tell you that I am charged with usurpation and tyranny,' he said, according to the memoirs. He did not doubt their giving him zealous support against this threat. 'At which there followed another *Vive le roy* etc,' reports Evelyn.

The new Commons unanimously voted the revenue for life. James's Parliament backed him up against Argyll and equally so when the news broke soon afterwards of Monmouth's landing near Lyme in Dorset, 'which wonderfully alarm'd the whole kingdome, fearing the joyning of disafected people,' as Evelyn put it.

In the memoirs James gives his second speech to Parliament on 18 June, thanking them 'heartely' for settling the revenue for life and promising he would only use it for necessities. Among these the navy held pride of place. 'I cannot express my concern on this occasion more sutable to my own thoughts of it, than by assuring you I have a true English heart, as jealous of the honour of the Nation as you can be.' He noted with satisfaction that

they seemed so sencibly touch'd at some expressions, particularly that of his haveing an English heart, that they waited not for the usual formes of thanking him for it, but by their very jestures and countenance while he was actualy speaking, gave him so much the more unfain'd testimony of their satisfaction, as that manner of showing it was less capable of being counterfeet or unsincere.

James made the typical comment on Argyll's furious declaration that 'it was no small advantage to the King that he had to doe with such fiery patriots and plain spoken enemys.' He always preferred a straight fight and could count on the support of those who disagreed with the rebels' views; Monmouth's declaration (actually written by Ferguson the plotter) made equally wild accusations: James was planning to subvert the government by turning the limited monarchy into an absolute tyranny; he was behind the fire of London in 1666, the murder of Godfrey, the cutting of Lord Essex's throat, suborning witnesses and the 'horrid parricide upon the late King his Brother'. Parliament was disgusted with these charges and immediately put through an Act of Attainder, which meant that if Monmouth were captured his life would be forfeit without further trial. It also meant that anyone who joined him now was assisting a proclaimed traitor.

Argyll and Monmouth had both set out from Holland, 'a country which was ever liberal to the King in presents of that nature,' James remarked, with irony. This shows that this account was written after 1688; but his comments, though written with hindsight, bluntly express what he came to think later. Fagel, the Dutch Pensioner (head of government) had told the Prince of Orange to play off the King and Monmouth against each other. 'If the Duke of Monmouth succeeded, he saw it would be easy for him, that was a Protestant as well as he, and in right of his wife the next heire, to shove him out of the saddle, if on the contrary the Duke of Monmouth was worsted, he got rid of a dangerous rival, and was sure all his partie would then have recourse to him, which proved accordingly, and was his main support when his turn came to try for it.' In 1685, of course, James had no idea William might make a grab for the Crown while he himself was still alive. He recognized Mary and William as his present heirs and had commissioned portraits of them by Wissing, which were hung in places of honour at Whitehall, and very handsome they look too, if somewhat larger than life.

With Parliament behind him James organized the military response to the rebellion. He put Louis Duras, Lord Feversham, in charge of the small but trained force at his disposal: 2000 Foot and 500 Horse, he says, adding that Monmouth (who had landed with only some 200 men) now had 'near 6000 men but more than he could arm or feed'. Churchill went ahead with such speed that he was operating in the west within a few days. Monmouth wrote hopefully to his one-time comrade in arms but Churchill sent his letter straight to the King. He was annoyed at having Feversham put over him but had no wish for Monmouth to be King.

The campaign was over in a few weeks. Monmouth and Grey fled the field of Sedgemoor and were taken by Lord Lumley, the son of an old Catholic family who had become a Protestant during the Popish Plot terror and was to be one of William's collaborators in 1688.

Charles, James and Mary,
children of Charles I and
Henrietta Maria: By Sir Anthony
Van Dyck

James, Duke of York, as a boy at
Oxford in the Civil War: By
William Dobson

James, with his father Charles I at Hampton Court in 1647: *After* Sir Peter Lely

Left: James as a General in his first exile: By Charles Wautier. *Above:* James as Duke of York: miniature by Samuel Cooper 1661

Charles II at the Restoration:
miniature by Samuel Cooper

James, Duke of York: miniature by
Samuel Cooper

Anne (Hyde) Duchess of York: By Sir Peter Lely

James, Duke of York: By Sir Peter Lely

Mary, eldest daughter of James and
Anne, as Diana: By Sir Peter Lely

Anne, second daughter of James and
Anne, as a child: By Sir Peter Lely

Maria Beatrice d'Este, second wife of James: By William Wissing

James, Duke of York, presented by Elias Ashmole at the opening
of his Collection at Oxford in 1683: By John Riley, in a frame
by Grinling Gibbons

Princess Anne, at her marriage to Prince George of Denmark: By William Wissing and Van der Vaart

St James's Palace c.1690

Princess Mary of Orange, 1685:
By William Wissing

William, Prince of Orange
(1677): *After* Peter Lely

Royal Portraits: Charles II:
c.1680: By Edward Hawker

Royal Portraits: James II, 1685:
By Godfrey Kneller

James as King, 1685: By Nicolas de Largillière

James in ordinary dress: By Anne Killigrew, Maid of Honour and gifted amateur, who died in June 1685

Catherine Sedley, Countess of Dorchester: James's mistress, from whose daughter were descended Marquesses of Normanby, and later Barrett-Lennards, also descended from Henrietta, daughter of James and Arabella Churchill, who married the first Baron Waldegrave: *Studio* of Peter Lely

James FitzJames, Duke of Berwick, son of James and Arabella Churchill, as a young man: By Sir Godfrey Kneller

Prince James Francis Edward
and Princess Louise Marie,
children of James II and Maria of
Modena, *c*.1695: By Nicolas de
Largillière

The Château of St
Germain-en-Laye

James II and VII in his last exile at St Germains: By François de Troy

James Francis Edward in 1701 at
the death of his father: By
François de Troy

Maria of Modena in widowhood:
Artist Unknown

Monmouth wrote a long moaning letter to James, which is printed in the *Life*. He swore he had never intended to take up arms against James: 'but my misfortune was such as to meet with some horrid people, that made me believe things of your Majesty, and gave me so many false arguments, that I was fully led away to believe that it was a shame and a sin before God not to doe it.' He went on to beg that he might speak to the King, 'for I have that to say to you, Sir, that I hope may give you a long and happy reign.' He went on for half a page more of anxious remorse, 'and could I say but *one word* in this letter, you would be convinced of it, but it is of that consequence that I dare not doe it. . . .'

James was uncertain what to do about this request. He sent his equerry and friend Ralph Sheldon to meet Monmouth, and when Sheldon came back to report, it happened that Sunderland 'came into the closet on pretext of business'. The King pressed Sheldon, and after an awkward silence he blurted out that Monmouth had told him Sunderland was 'of intelligence with him'.

'At which my Lord Sunderland seemed extreamly struck, so that the King could not but observe it; but soon recovering himself, said with a fain'd laughter, If that be all he can discover to save his life, it will do him little good.' He 'succeeded in wiping off the suspicion' is the comment, and another is added that Sunderland had probably been promised a place in the new government. Ferguson, it seemed, 'when at sea with Monmouth, advised him to keep imployments for baits, at which Monmouth said he had promised none but Sunderland.' This must have come from Ferguson himself who, strange as it may seem, later changed over from the Williamite to the Jacobite side.

Knowing, as we do now, that it was William with whom Sunderland was in touch, through Henry Sidney, it seems unlikely he was backing Monmouth, though of course he may have let him think so. There is yet another slant on this business. Argyll was extremely indignant when Monmouth proclaimed himself King (as James II – his uncle was merely Duke of York) because this had not been in their agreement; a commonwealth had been proposed, which many of those who followed Monmouth would have preferred. Yet a third suggestion was that the Crown had been promised to the Prince of Orange; if so, Sunderland may have planned to be in a position to manage the transfer. What is certain is that Monmouth was in a thorough muddle about the whole business; he astonished James by saying he had not even read his own declaration.

James decided that he ought to grant the interview. It proved exceedingly embarrassing and useless. Monmouth simply fell on his knees to beg for his life; he was 'crawling on his knees to embrace those of his Majesty'. No 'one word' was spoken, no warning about anyone or anything, only a pathetic begging for mercy as if this man of thirty-six were still the pretty boy who had so captivated his father and been so spoiled in his youth.

> The King inclined of his own nature to spare him, [runs the account in the *Life*] but he was soon made sencible, how cruel a compassion it would be, to expose the publick peace to so great a hazard, and the lives of thousands for that of one man's, who had deserved so little to live; that considering how great numbers had joind him, even after he was attainted by Parliament, and how the people were intoxicated with an Idea of his personal merit, and pretended zeal for the Protestant Religion, no one could answer for the consequences if he were at libertie again; the fabulous inventions of the late King's being married to his Mother, tho' ridiculous in themselves and disowned by the King, however had imposed upon many . . . ;

all this convinced James that he could not pardon him.

Monmouth was sent back to the Tower; he hinted at becoming a Catholic and James sent some priests to him but when he realized that conversion was not going to save his life he reverted to his Protestant faith. Then James sent clergymen to him but he shocked them by refusing to confess that his connexion with Lady Henrietta Wentworth was sinful. He maintained that he had been so young when the King married him to Anna Scott that it could not have been a true marriage of consent, and we may feel he had a point there. Henrietta was his wife 'in the eyes of God'. The clergymen could not agree and refused him the sacrament.

Monmouth, when all was lost, recovered his courage and died bravely, horribly butchered by an inexpert executioner. 'Poor unfortunate man,' James calls him, 'born to cross and contradict himself.' He maintains that he had long been a friend to Monmouth in his youth, till

Shaftesbury had set him against his uncle. Monmouth's character was ruined by his spoilt youth and his weakness for flattery; he seems to have remained a permanent adolescent, unable to think of anything but himself.

James breakfasted with Monmouth's deserted wife the day after the execution and promised that her children would not be under the ban of attainder and would be allowed to inherit all the estates, which were really hers. That is why Monmouth's descendants are Dukes of Buccleugh. It was only the title of Monmouth that was lost.

As for the rebellion, John Evelyn commented: 'For my owne part, I looked upon this deliverance as absolutely most signal; such an inundation of Phanatics and men of impious principles, must needs have caused universal disorder, cruelty, injustice, rapine, sacrilege and confusion, an unavoydable Civil-War, and misery without end: but blessed be God, the knot was happily broken, and a faire prospect of Tranquilitie for the future likely to succeede if we reforme, be thankfull, and make a right use of this Mercy.'

Undoubtedly this view was widely shared in the country. It was not the defeat of the Rebellion that was later used to blacken James's reputation but the measures taken against the defeated rebels afterwards. But it should be remembered that the story of savage retribution was first put out in 1689 and the authors of the pamphlets *The Bloody Assizes* and *The Protestant Martyrs* (and of later re-hashes) were Titus Oates and other writers of Popish Plot fame. It was they who painted the horrific picture of Judge Jeffreys which has survived to this day, in spite of a careful examination of the evidence by G. W. Keeton, a legal expert who had made a special study of historical treason trials. In *Lord Chancellor Jeffreys and the Stuart Cause* (1965) he points out that Jeffreys was the chief of four judges who went on that circuit and that the official prosecutor was Henry Pollexfen, a Whig lawyer who was to defend the Bishops against the King in 1688 and prospered exceedingly under William III. Ordinary Assize business was done as well as the trials of the rebels; when he reached Bristol Jeffreys came down hard on the kidnapping merchants who had been selling off poor boys to settlers in Jamaica. Bristol was always a great slaving centre; white as well as black were among its victims.

Transportation was the fate of most of the rebels found guilty but this was not a new invention. Cromwell had used it in Scotland and Ireland. Monmouth had sent off about 200 after Bothwell Brig, who had been drowned at sea. Some of the rebels of 1685 died before they reached the West Indies but those who did get there were not put into sugar plantations like black slaves – they usually held craftsmen's jobs. They were 'sold' for a specified term, ten years in the case of the Monmouth rebels. It was the equivalent of 'ten years' hard labour' – a form of punishment not then invented. Incidentally, after the Revolution it was several years before orders came through to release them and quite a number stayed on to work or trade for themselves.

Bryan Little, in his meticulously researched book *The Monmouth Episode* (1955) reckons that about 800 to 850 were condemned to transportation and about 750 actually arrived. The number of executions is harder to assess but not all those condemned were actually executed; in Bath, for instance, six were to be executed, the warrant was made out for four and in the end the tythingmen were paid for being present at two. Little reckons that there must have been about 150 in Somerset, perhaps 230 in all four counties together. Out of the thousands who joined Monmouth, this is not a high proportion but Little emphasizes that it was enough to create fear among the people of the west, few of whom made any move to join William when he landed three years later.

It was only in Dorchester that executions took place while the judges were still in the town; most of the sentences were carried out after Jeffreys had returned to London. His record seems to be no more 'bloody' than that of other judges of the period, possibly less so than Scroggs, the bullying judge of the Popish Plot trials.

As far as James was concerned, he was anxious that people should have a fair trial – and some did get off for lack of evidence. There was also a careful follow-up the next year, reimbursing local people for expenses feeding the prisoners and for making good the damage to bridges and so on. Property confiscation went on, with petitioning and counter-petitioning. The biggest confiscations were exacted from the richest rebels and were granted to the chief officers of the royal army. Churchill laid the foundation of his later fortunes with the estates and business interests of John Hucker, the Taunton serge-maker who was Monmouth's host there. Jeffreys struck up a bargain with Prideaux of

Ford Abbey, realizing £14,000 with which he bought an estate in Leicestershire. And Laurence Hyde, Lord Rochester, did very well out of Lord Grey. In fact, this may have been one reason why Grey was given his life, because if he were dead Rochester would lose the income he was already drawing from Grey's estate since the Rye House Plot.

If all this sounds like corruption on a grand scale, it was not, in the context of the time. Just the same went on under William (his Dutch generals being the main beneficiaries) and had gone on for generations before. The loyal had to be rewarded and the disloyal punished and this seemed the obvious way of doing it.

James was evidently surprised to be accused in 1689 of exacting savage penalties after the suppression of the rebellion. In the memoirs he points out that in the cases of the 'great men' which came on in London, and for which he was responsible in so far as he had the power of pardon (*pace* Lord Russell) very few were executed. He divides the ex-Rye House plotters from the others as being already attainted and outlawed; two were executed at once. Sir Thomas Armstrong (whom James thought the worst influence on Monmouth) already outlawed, was captured abroad and brought back to execution.

James deferred the trials of those who had rebelled against himself till after the next session of Parliament. Lord Brandon ('young Gerrard', son of Charles Gerrard, first Earl of Macclesfield) who had been with Monmouth abroad, was tried and found guilty, but James pardoned him. After the 1688 Revolution Brandon wrote to William to explain why he had not joined him; he could not in honour turn against the King to whom he owed his life.

James writes in the memoirs, 'Mr Hampden pleaded guilty and though sentence of death was passed, he was also pardon'd.'

Lord Delamere (Henry Booth son of George) was tried in the House of Lords, and though everybody (even Burnet) knew he had been in communication with Monmouth, no evidence implicated him and he was found 'not guilty' by his peers. Afterwards, when a crucial witness, Saxton, was accused of perjury, he was tried, found guilty and punished. James had a horror of the perjured witnesses in the Popish Plot trials and was determined his enemies should not be condemned in like manner.

When he went down to the west next year, in August 1686, James was distressed to see rebel quarters still hanging on the gibbets and ordered them to be taken down and buried. On this visit he was well received everywhere, visited the site of Sedgemoor and stayed in Bridgwater, and at Bristol with the 'kidnapping' Mayor, still in office, in spite of Jeffreys.

Already on 10 March 1686 James had issued a general pardon and though quite a number were excepted, most of them were either already abroad (like Ferguson) or paid fines; others were pardoned later.

It had been James's opinion, ever since the Restoration, that oppressing the dissenters for nonconformity in religion drove them into rebellion – and many rebels in the west were dissenters. In 1686 the King was already taking steps to set them free from the religious penal laws. In his view rebellion must be sternly put down for the sake of the whole country, but if wrongs were righted in time there would be no rebellions.

2 The King in Action

At the beginning of September 1685 James appointed Henry Hyde, Earl of Clarendon, as Lord Lieutenant of Ireland. He did not deprive him of his office of Lord Privy Seal but put it temporarily into commission and Clarendon nominated Evelyn to be one of the commissioners. They went to Windsor to kiss hands and the King received Evelyn with 'extraordinary kindnesse'. On Sunday, when their Majesties went to mass he withdrew to admire Verrio's 'stupendious painting in the Hall' and thought these new decorations surpassed anything he had seen abroad.

On 16 September Evelyn went with Pepys in his coach to attend the King on his first visit to Portsmouth since his accession. They arrived at Winchester to find the King at the Dean's house, discussing miracles with Thomas Ken, Bishop of Bath and Wells. Some dubious marvels ascribed to the Spanish Saludadores were mentioned which Pepys afterwards told Evelyn were frauds but that he had not liked to interrupt the King, who was telling of them 'so solemnly'. However, Evelyn also recorded that James had said 'that he was so extreamly difficult of Miracles, for feare of being impos'd on, that if he should chance to see one himselfe, without some other witnesse, he should apprehend it some delusion of his senses.'

Bishop Ken told of cures caused by the blood of King Charles the Martyr and presently James was reminded that as his brother was dying he had called to him to take out what he had in his pocket, which James thought must be keys, but turned out to be a gold cross with a relic of the true cross inside it, found by a workman in St Edward's tomb. James took this relic from his own pocket and showed it, putting it in Evelyn's hands so that he could see the 'inscription in Latin and Gotic'.

Evelyn recorded with approbation that the King had said he was going to insist that 'the Negroes in the Plantations should all be Baptized, exceedingly declaiming against that impiety of their Masters prohibiting it, out of a mistaken opinion that they were then *ipso facto* free.' Even if they were, they still ought to be baptized, and Ken blessed him for this Christian piety.

While he was in Winchester Evelyn went to look at King Charles's palace, which had nearly reached roof-level; he heard that it had already cost £20,000 but that the present King did not intend to continue it. Nor did he; James wanted all the money he could get for his navy and for the regiments raised against the rebellion, which he intended to keep as a small regular army. These five regiments celebrated their tercentenary in 1985 but virtually nothing was said in honour of the founder of the British regular army.

Evelyn went on to visit the Cathedral, 'a reverend pile and in good repair', and finally back to his lodging 'very wett, it having rained the whole day.' Next morning it seems to have cleared up. Pepys and Evelyn got to Portsmouth first, driving through the crowds who had come out in their best clothes to see the King. He came riding on horseback and was met with speeches from the Mayor and salutes of guns from the Port and the Garrison, with soldiers lining the streets. After viewing the new fortifications and shipyard (which he had commissioned) the King was entertained to a magnificent dinner at which all the gentlemen were invited to sit down with him.

Evelyn had a prior engagement to dine with Sir Robert Holmes, now

[155]

Governor of the Isle of Wight, but afterwards he 'went to waite on his Majestie againe, who was pulling on his boots in the Towne Hall . . . and then having saluted some Ladys etc: that came to kisse his hand; he took horse for Winchester, whither he returned that night.'

'By what I observed in this journey,' Evelyn wrote with unwonted enthusiasm,

> I find that infinite industry, sedulity, gravity, and greate understanding and experience of affaires in his Majestie, that I cannot but predict much happinesse to the Nation, as to its political Government, and if he so persist (as I am confident he will) there could nothing be more desired, to accomplish our prosperity, but that he were of the national Religion: for certainely such a Prince never had this Nation since it was one.

Soon after this a matter of religion came up, when Pepys asked Evelyn to come and see something he might not have another time. This turned out to be copies of two papers written by King Charles II on the arguments in favour of Roman claims. Pepys now had free access to the King and they had been talking alone in his closet when Pepys took courage to ask if it was true that King Charles had died a Catholic. James told him he had and took the papers out of a cabinet to show him, lending him the copies.

Evelyn, though he thought all the arguments easily answered and digressed at length on the menace of Rome, concluded,

> As I do exceedingly preferr his Majesties free and ingenuous profession, of what his owne Religion is, beyond all concealments upon any politique accounts what so ever; so I thinke him of a most sincere and honest nature, one upon whose word one may relie, and that he makes a Conscience of what he promises, to performe it: In this confidence, I hope, the Church of England may yet subsist; and when it shall please God to open his Eyes, and turne his heart . . . to flourish also.

Soon after, Evelyn was present at 'a solemn Ball at Court' for the King's birthday, 14 October – not too solemn, one hopes! 'And

Musique of Instruments and Voices before the Ball. At the Musique I happened by accident to stand the very next to the Queene, and the King, who talked with me about the Musick.' He does not say what it was, but Purcell (twenty-six this year) wrote a birthday ode 'Why are all the Muses mute?' which was sung at one of these birthday celebrations in James's reign. The musicians had cause to rejoice for they were now at last regularly paid, after petitioning often vainly in Charles's reign. James kept on all the Chapel Royal staff – Princess Anne attended the services sitting next to the empty chair of state and received the three genuflexions from the preachers customarily made to the sovereign. James formed another choir to sing in the new Catholic royal chapel he was building at Whitehall.

It was part of a new range of lodgings for the Queen designed by Sir Christopher Wren (also kept on as Surveyor) which included a new Council Chamber and offices next to the south end of the Banqueting House, as well as the chapel itself, which must have been beautiful, with carvings by Grinling Gibbons. It was all burnt down in the great Whitehall fires of William's reign, though some of the carved angels from the altar reredos, taken away earlier, are thought to have survived in a church at Burnham-on-Sea in Somerset. A bathroom of Italian marble was built for the Queen in her new apartments, but she really preferred her old ones at St James's, disliking the bustle and crowds at Whitehall. The removal was not made till the end of the next year, 1686.

In spite of the new building, James soon effected notable economies at court; the Venetian and Florentine Ambassadors were astonished at what he had already achieved. To do this he did not cut salaries but paid them on time, thus removing the excuse for the black market in 'perks' which had flourished in Charles's day – so that he once complained he had no cravats to wear, the valets had flogged them all.

The same black market went on over supplies to the navy during the years of the Commissioners; now that James was King he and Mr Secretary Pepys set about cleaning things up. James also reorganized the garrisons in the chief ports, the Office of Ordnance and other institutions involved in the defence of the realm. Many of his reforms and ordinances were later revived by Churchill, when Duke of Marlborough, and yet again a century later by the Duke of Wellington. Both great generals recognized James's organizing ability in military affairs.

Yet it was on a matter connected with the army that James first fell out with his Parliament, in November 1685; significantly the issue was also religious. All Parliaments, especially since the rule of Cromwell, were suspicious of a standing army, and some members now wanted the new regiments disbanded as soon as the rebellion was crushed. James pointed out that the Militia was worse than useless; some had actually joined Monmouth in the west. It was necessary for security to have a regular force at the government's command for deployment in emergency. While most members were able to accept this, they found the admission of Catholic officers quite unacceptable. James had decided to keep on those who had volunterred in the recent emergency. To do this he had to dispense them from the Test oath. He got advice from all the judges as to whether the King had this right under the royal prerogative; they decided he had. A test case was set up: Sir Edward Hales (son of a loyal cavalier family and a convert) was reported as a recusant and therefore ineligible to hold his commission. But the court upheld the King's right of dispensation. In the House of Commons, however, objections were raised so loudly that James lost his temper and prorogued the Parliament; later, following Charles's tactics, he prorogued it again and again, though he did not actually dissolve it till 1687.

Dispensing a few Catholic officers from the Test oath was only the beginning of James's efforts to secure religious toleration, the chief aim of his reign. It was unfortunate that just at this juncture Louis XIV revoked the Edict of Nantes which their common ancestor Henri IV had passed a century earlier, granting a limited toleration to the French Protestants, Calvinist in theology, known as Huguenots. For some years before the Revocation of the Edict of Nantes there had been a campaign of conversion, when Protestants had been compelled to attend sermons and various incentives and disincentives had been introduced to facilitate a change of allegiance. Quite a number had conformed and were known as New Catholics. In 1685 Louis announced (and possibly believed) that the majority were converted and the Revocation was presented as the regularizing of a *fait accompli*. It even contained a clause that no one who refused to change should be molested.

[158]

This accounts for the congratulations Louis received from the Pope, who afterwards criticized the methods employed, when he heard about them. It also explains why Barillon was able to report to his master that the King of England was delighted to hear of the numerous conversions from heresy; James imagined it was a change of heart brought about by preaching. But soon rumours spread of 'dragonades', some of lurid atrocity. The dragoons were legally quartered in private houses in France so that it was possible for the authorities to declare that no intimidation had been authorized. Thus Barillon and other French ambassadors at Protestant courts were denying reports of atrocities and denouncing a book by a minister named Claude as lies and defamation of King Louis, which is why James ordered it to be burnt by the hangman in London.

But soon the refugees, at first fleeing to Holland, were also arriving in England, and it was clear that their flight was from compulsion, intimidation, harassment and restrictions on their trades – they were mostly craftsmen and men of business. James's attitude immediately changed. He sponsored a national collection in aid of the refugees and contributed £500 from the privy purse; he eased the process of naturalization and pacified complaining English tradesmen by ordering that for every Frenchman the new entrepreneurs employed, they must employ two Englishmen. They were also allotted a church for their own form of worship.

In January 1686 James was writing to William about the rumour he had heard that members of religious orders were to be banished from Holland and hoping William would not allow it. When William replied that they were not after all to be banished James said he was glad to hear it, 'and do easily believe you are not for prosecuting any merely for their religion: I always was and will be of that mind; and am of your opinion, that it was the very hard usage the Huguenots had, and have still in France, which made that affair of the regulars be talked of where you are.'

The persecution of the Huguenots in France revived all the old hatred and fear of popery in England, even in cultivated minds like Evelyn's, rousing his suspicions against the King he had been praising only a few months before. It never seems to have occurred to Evelyn that in England Catholics had been treated very much as the

Protestants were now being treated in France. The mass was proscribed, priests liable to the death penalty, men of property to heavy and recurring fines for not going to the established church; no Catholics could hold any official position, civil or military; they had no votes, could not be Members of Parliament, could not have Catholic schools and were prohibited from publishing any books of doctrine or devotion. All this had been going on for a hundred years or more. It would seem that in the matter of persecution the English Protestants were hardly in a position to cast the first stone. Of course they did not think of it as persecution; popery was evil and therefore it seemed quite in order to enforce church attendance on all and (since the Test Act) make receiving the sacrament in the Church of England a condition of holding any office in the state. But was this very different from Louis XIV's decree that everybody in France ought to be Catholic, with certificates of Easter communion for the New (and reluctant) Catholics?

James, at any rate, disapproved all such state coercion of conscience. He wanted freedom for all, not just for Catholics, as Protestants imagined. When he spoke to Barillon of his desire to establish Catholicism in his kingdoms he did not mean to make it the state church but to establish its legal right to exist. That this was his intention is proved not only by the preamble to the Declaration on Liberty of Conscience but by what he actually did for the Catholic Church in England – largely ignored by Protestant historians. Even Catholic ones, like Dom Basil Hemphill, in his book *The Early Vicars Apostolic of England* (1954) prefaces his account by repeating the old story that James was trying to transform the Church of England into a Roman Catholic establishment, even though the facts he then relates simply contradict this.

James was determined that the Catholics of England should once more be organized according to the rules of the Church, but that organization was to be entirely separate from the Church of England. The first need was a bishop; there had been no Catholic bishop in England for fifty years. After consulting the senior secular clergy, known as the Old Chapter, he petitioned Rome for a bishop in ordinary, who would have the normal episcopal jurisdiction. But Rome considered the proscribed remnant of Catholics in England to be under the jurisdiction of the Roman Congregation for the Propagation of the Faith (*Propaganda Fide*) which controlled missions in non-Catholic countries and would only allow a Vicar Apostolic, that is, a bishop whose title was not territorial but taken from some defunct see *in partibus infidelium* (usually Middle Eastern places overrun by Arabs and Turks) and whose power derived directly from the Pope or rather from the Congregation. The blow was softened by the appointment of Dr John Leyburn, the man James had requested as bishop, who had been head of the college at Douay (in Flanders) where English secular priests were trained, and himself held a doctorate of the Sorbonne in Paris.

Leyburn was consecrated in Rome and arrived in London in October 1685, where he first had to pacify the suspicious members of the Old Chapter; luckily most of them were well-known to him. He divided England into four districts and put a Vicar General at the head of each, he himself being based in the London District, which included the home counties and part of East Anglia. Two years later the three Vicars General were consecrated bishops and became Vicars Apostolic. Although at the 1688 Revolution these four Catholic bishops either had to flee abroad or endure imprisonment, the organization survived and functioned until the restoration of the hierarchy in 1850. James paid his bishops out of the privy purse. They were forbidden to lay claim to any Anglican property but must buy land for any chapels or schools they were to build. The King could hardly have made it plainer that he considered the two churches quite separate institutions.

But the awkward fact remained that in virtue of Henry VIII's unilateral decision that he and not the Pope was the supreme head on earth of the Church of England, James, simply by being the King, found himself automatically in that invidious position, which meant that he was responsible for Crown appointments and judgements in that Church. He solved this problem by appointing an Ecclesiastical Commission to act for the Crown, inviting the Archbishop of Canterbury to preside. Sancroft, while approving the institution, declined, on the score of age and infirmity, to lead it. James then called on his old friend Dr Crewe, Bishop of Durham; Bishop Sprat of Rochester also sat on it. Lay members (all Anglicans) were Laurence Hyde, Earl of Rochester and Lord Treasurer; Robert Spencer, Earl of Sunderland, President of the Council; Lord Chancellor Jeffreys and the Lord Chief Justice, Edward Herbert.

The Ecclesiastical Commission first sat at Whitehall in August 1686 and its first business, unfortunately, was the case of Dr Compton, Bishop of London, who had refused to suspend Dr Sharp, Dean of Norwich, for preaching violently anti-Catholic sermons in London, where he also held a living. Polemical preaching had been prohibited in a decree at the Restoration (more honoured in the breach than the observance) which James had reissued at the beginning of his reign.

As Compton refused to suspend Sharp, the Ecclesiastical Commission suspended him, but did not cut off his temporal emoluments. The Bishops of Durham, Rochester and Peterborough were to exercise jurisdiction in London for the time being and when preferments in Compton's gift fell vacant they allowed him to nominate for them. Thus he could not really be said to be persecuted by a popish King for defending Protestantism but that is exactly what he did say, complaining of his fate to the Princess Mary of Orange whom he had confirmed and married. Thereafter he worked for the Orange cause and was to manage the clergy and the Princess Anne during the 1688 Revolution.

It was unfortunate that the new Commission had to deal with such a belligerently Protestant bishop (and noble – he was the youngest son of the second Earl of Northampton) at its first session, especially as the King had already dismissed him from the Privy Council in December 1685 for a speech in the House of Lords when he had asserted that both the civil and ecclesiastical constitutions were in danger. Protestant-minded Anglicans became suspicious of the Commission as the tool of a papist king. But it is hard to see what alternative existed, since if James had personally exercised the royal office of Supreme Governor it would have been even more bitterly resented.

One of the things that annoyed the Protestant clerics most was the King's granting licences for Catholic books to be printed. James took care that these were not polemical but plain statements of the true doctrine of the Church, which he rightly thought would surprise those fed so long on fantasies about popish idolatry, superstition and priestcraft. Malcolm Hay (in *The Enigma of James II*) lists translations of the *Short Christian Doctrine* by Robert Bellarmine, the Jesuit theologian of the Council of Trent; an *Exposition of Catholic Doctrine* by Bossuet, the famous contemporary French Bishop of Meaux; and an *Abstract of the Douay Catechism*, based on the Tridentine Council.

Even when controversy (inevitably) entered in, the chief Catholic contribution was John Gother's *A Papist Misrepresented and Represented* which compared genuine Catholic teaching with the no-popery fantasies. Replies, vindications, attacks and counter-attacks followed each other in a long pamphlet war through the next year or two. Bossuet's *Exposition* (which had converted James's hero Turenne in 1668) was translated by Joseph Johnstone, an English Benedictine who was one of James's chaplains. When Anglicans accused Bossuet of insincerity – the real doctrine was not what he said it was – Johnstone replied: 'We declare this is our doctrine . . . We who refuse to take these oaths which thwart our consciences, though we lose all our temporal advantage by the refusal, are yet ready to take any oath that this is our doctrine: but yet we must not be believed.'

On the continent Bossuet's *Exposition* was widely read and discussed by Protestants; one was the philosopher and mathematician Leibnitz and he corresponded with James's cousin Sophia (daughter of Elizabeth of Bohemia) who had married the Elector of Hanover and was the mother of the future King George I. Leibnitz was a pioneer of Christian reunion but as Sophia remarked in the autumn of 1688, nobody wanted to hear about reconciliation in England.

James was concerned with the necessary preliminary for any possible reconciliation, liberty of conscience, and that he intended it for all is shown by his acts from the beginning of his reign. In 1685 he commanded that the Jews should be relieved of all restrictions and instructed the Attorney General to stop all proceedings against them, so that they should 'quietly enjoy the free exercise of their religion, whilst they behave themselves dutifully and obediently to his government.'

The Attorney General was again instructed in March 1686, 'Not to permit any process to issue in his Majesty's name against any Dissenter whatsoever.' (Quoted from the records of the Privy Council by Malcolm Hay.) In November that year the King remitted a sentence of imprisonment for seditious libel which had been inflicted on the nonconformist minister Richard Baxter who, incidentally, believed Oates's revelations about popish wickedness.

[163]

In March 1686 the amnesty was issued for the Monmouth rebels of the summer before, many of whom were dissenters, and so it no doubt seemed an appropriate time to make a start on religious freedom. It was at this date that James released from prison about fourteen hundred Quakers, taken up in the reign of Charles, whom they had petitioned, vainly, in 1684. The poor Friends had a miserable time of it, not only starving with cold in the prisons but losing most of their property, which could be seized by the informers. They probably owed their special treatment to James's long-standing friendship with William Penn (son of the Admiral) who now, like Pepys, had free access to the King. James, as Duke of York, had been instrumental in getting Penn himself released from prison in Charles's reign.

In this March James began sounding out the Scottish lords and bishops, who were soon to meet in their Parliament, on toleration. The Archbishops of Glasgow and St Andrews thought it seemed reasonable 'to take off the sanguinary laws touching religion' and did not see 'any danger or insecurity arising to our Protestant religion by so doing'. (Quoted by Malcolm Hay from a collection of letters to Archbishop Sancroft, published in Edinburgh in 1848.)

But the Scots temporal lords were concerned about toleration for the politically subversive Cameronians and even proposed to limit it to Catholics, who were not numerous outside the Highlands. This led to Barillon's telling King Louis that James wanted liberty only for Catholics, which Dalrymple (in the eighteenth century) thought proved James's real intentions. In fact, toleration in Scotland was eventually extended to all, with the proviso that the minority sects should only meet privately in their own houses.

In Ireland, where of course Catholics far outnumbered Protestants, James had instructed Clarendon to forbid anti-papist sermons and ease the restrictions on Catholics, without undermining the Settlement imposed after the Restoration. The Irish question was deeply involved with property, which both sides claimed as theirs by right and each side had, on different occasions, seized by force. Clarendon, as English, Tory and Protestant, could be relied on to uphold the Settlement but James suspected that he was lukewarm on Catholic rights and eventually decided to recall him and transfer his powers to Dick Talbot, now made Earl of Tyrconnel, a Catholic, if hardly a pious one, whose career had been military rather than political. But this exchange, which was to alienate Clarendon from his royal brother-in-law, did not take place till the winter of 1686-7, when several other personal crises came to a head for James.

3 Domestic Politics

Once the rebellions were crushed and Argyll and Monmouth executed, James seemed settled on the throne and his reign began to take shape. Just as he had kept on most of Charles's ministers, so he continued his policies in foreign affairs, though he conducted them in his own very different style. His principal aim was to keep Britain neutral and out of continental conflicts, but possessed of a trained army and professional navy sufficient to command respect and discourage attack. He intended to keep on good terms with the Dutch and the French, while not being dependent on secret subsidies and treaties, as Charles had been.

Because Mary was still his heir, it was essential to maintain close relations with William, and James continued to write to him personally and regularly as he had always done. William had used Monmouth's rebellion to demonstrate his family loyalty by sending over the Scotch regiments in Dutch employment. They did not arrive in time to do any fighting but the King was very pleased with them. 'They do truely look like old regiments' he told William in July 1685, thanking him again for sending them. A few weeks later, recording Monmouth's execution – 'He died resolutely and a downright enthusiast' – he added that 'Mr Bentick' would inform William of everything. James was always rather hit or miss with foreign names. George Legge, now Earl of Dartmouth, noticed that Mr Bentinck was on tenterhooks till Monmouth was dead; he warned the King that the Prince of Orange was probably a greater danger than Monmouth, but James did not take this seriously. Disagreements with William were fairly frequent but never broke the correspondence.

In the autumn of 1685 there was serious domestic trouble at the Hague. The King's ambassador, Sir Bevil Skelton, was informed by

Mary's chaplain, Dr Covell, that the Princess was very unhappy because of the Prince's coldness to her and his relations with Elizabeth Villiers, one of her Maids of Honour and generally believed to be William's mistress. Skelton passed on this information to Mary's uncle, Lord Rochester.

Mary eventually decided to face William with his unfaithfulness. Unusually for a royal couple they slept in the same bed (but only slept, according to Mary's entourage) but William often came to it very late, delayed by business, according to him, but according to Mary's attendants by Elizabeth Villiers. So one night Mary lay in wait at the foot of the stairs leading to the Maids' apartments. When William appeared (at 2 a.m.) she boldly reproached him. He was furious and declared 'there was no crime'. Mary is said to have burst into tears and embraced him, forgiving all.

But it gave William the chance to get rid of Mary's English attendants and he hoped of Skelton too. He got his secretary to intercept one of Dr Covell's letters to Skelton and this gave him grounds for dismissing the chaplain and his wife, and several others. They were forbidden to speak to Mary again and were given two days to pack and leave Holland. Although Mary tried to get rid of Elizabeth Villiers too, she failed, and the woman remained part of her entourage, to her discomfort.

William's connexion with Elizabeth Villiers is undoubted but it may not have been physical. Married off to the Earl of Orkney at the age of thirty-eight (after Mary's death) Elizabeth bore three children. Neither she nor Mary ever produced children by William and there is some doubt that Mary was ever pregnant; her early miscarriage being discounted as such by her attendants. Some said William was impotent; whether or not this was true, he must certainly have been infertile. He was also believed to be homosexual and undoubtedly used much warmer language to his male friends than ever to his wife. Much later he told Bentinck that there had been 'no crime' between himself and young Keppel, when their familiarity shocked the old favourite into remonstration. It seems likely that what attracted him in Elizabeth Villiers (who was not handsome, and squinted) was her shrewd mind; she shared his political preoccupations and continued in his confidence when he was King of England.

Mary's unhappy relationship with William was radically changed in 1686, largely by the intervention of Dr Gilbert Burnet, who came to Holland that year at William's invitation and soon became deeply involved in the Orange cause, as his memoirs written before the 1688 Revolution (but only published by Foxcroft in 1902) show clearly enough.

Burnet, the son of a Scottish lawyer, born in 1643 (ten years younger than James) was a big burly man, boisterous and strong in his own conceit, but clever and with a journalistic gift for writing which he was now to put into service for the Prince of Orange. He had begun his career under the Duke of Lauderdale but later turned against him. It was James who got him a post at court as chaplain but in 1674 King Charles dismissed him for being too 'busy' in political affairs. He then secured a position at the Rolls Chapel in the City and associated with Whigs of Lord Russell's party; during the Popish Plot he received the thanks of both Houses of Parliament for his timely *History of the Reformation*. Although he disapproved of Monmouth's supporters he was in correspondence with Argyll and it was probably this that led him to leave England in May 1685. He went first to France and only a year later to Holland.

Burnet's treasonable correspondence had come to the notice of the English government, which requested his extradition from Holland; William showed Burnet a letter from King James. Burnet declared himself innocent of treason but took care to safeguard himself by taking out Dutch naturalization and marrying a rich Dutch woman of English descent, by whom he was to have a large family. He had none by his first wife, a rich and well-born Scottish lady many years his senior – a marriage which had to be kept secret to avoid the rage of her family. She was dying in the spring of 1685 but as she was then senile Burnet felt justified in leaving before she actually died.

Soon after Burnet's arrival in Holland William told him of the conversation he had had with the Quaker William Penn, who had come over to put forward King James's plans for religious toleration. Burnet noted, 'He is a man of good parts but extremely vain; he loves mightily to hear himself talk.' A case of the pot calling the kettle black?

William found Burnet's knowledge of the English political and religious scene useful; still more his influence on Mary, for it was

Burnet who persuaded Mary it was her religious duty to back her husband in rescuing England from popery. William's efforts had been ham-fisted to say the least. Mary had always kept 30 January, the day of Charles I's 'martyrdom' in fasting and prayer, as it had been kept in James's household. On that solemn day William had suddenly summoned her to dine with him in public, took no notice of her pleas or her refusal of the lavish dishes, and afterwards insisted that she should be present at a comedy. This treatment certainly broke Mary's will to resistance, but did not change her mind or her feelings.

But Burnet made Mary believe that wicked popish priests had got control of her father's mind and that he was intent on turning England into a Catholic tyranny on the model of Louis XIV's France. Mary, harrowed by the plight of the Huguenot refugees, shuddered. She had last seen her father in 1679 when she was only seventeen; it must have seemed long ago by 1686.

A story is told that Mary once asked Burnet how her father had been able to make her mother a papist (presumably his view of Duchess Anne's conversion) and he replied, 'When he found her in bed with Mr Sidney, he could make her do anything.' William, who was in the same room, observed dryly, 'Pray madam, ask the Doctor some more questions.' True or not, this neatly hits off Burnet's mixture of gossip and propaganda, which has fascinated many besides Mary. His racy anecdotes about Charles II, for instance, have appeared in all the biographies of that monarch, with no doubts expressed as to the veracity of the *raconteur*, to whom it is highly improbable that the King would confide comments on his brother James, or his son Monmouth.

It seems from his unpublished notes that Burnet was already apprehensive, before he left England, that Princess Anne might be converted to Catholicism and preferred before Mary in the succession. This bugbear was raised in the summer of 1686 by the Dutch Ambassador, Van Citters, who got hold of a document called 'A Remonstrance made to the King of England by his Council' which suggested this very possibility. James told Van Citters that this document was a forgery and on another occasion said that his affection for his eldest daughter would preclude any such plan. He was not believed and in November that year was imagined to be behind another suggestion, that his marriage to Anne Hyde had not been valid, and this in spite of the fact that the author of this forgery, Edward Getthing, was convicted and fined £500. (Henry and Barbara van der Zee, whose book *William and Mary* makes use of Dutch archives, plainly think James was behind all these schemes for ousting Mary from the succession; of course Burnet may have made Mary believe it.)

But all this explains the correspondence set up between Mary and Anne in the spring of 1686. (Some of Anne's answers, preserved by William, were printed by Dalrymple and a modern edition was made in 1968, using transcripts at Althorp, by Beatrice Curtis Brown.) Anne fervently proclaimed her attachment to the Church of England, thought the ceremonies of Rome were 'plain downright idolatry' and promised not to employ any popish servants. In August she was writing, 'But because you think in my last I seemed more at ease, I must justify myself and tell you I don't think that I am at all more secure for the kindness the K. has showed me lately. For I am of your opinion, that it is more likely he will use fair means rather than force; and I am in as great expectation of being tormented if he had not some hopes that in time he may gain either you or me.' And in November she was assuring Mary that she would rather beg her bread than ever change. There was not much prospect of Anne's having to beg her bread while her father allowed her £30,000 a year and the fine Cockpit lodgings which had been Monmouth's. Nor of her being persecuted to convert to Rome while she deputized for the King every Sunday in the Chapel Royal.

In December she had to admit that nothing had been said to her about religion except once, when the King had noticed her 'talking to somebody or looking another way' when a priest said grace before she dined with the King and Queen. James asked her whether she did it on purpose and she admitted that she did. 'Upon that, he said it was looking upon them as Turks, and looked disrespectfully to him; and he said he found by this that I had a very ill impression made on me about his religion.' Anne untruthfully assured him that 'nobody had ever opened their lips to me, which he said he believed, but saw very well what strange opinions I had of their religion. He said also he would not torment me about it but hoped one day that God would open my eyes. Just as he said this, the Prince (George) came into the room and he immediately fell upon another discourse. This is all.' And this continued to be all, in spite of her fears.

[169]

Most of her November letter had been taken up with explaining why she had not made a promised visit to Holland in October; Prince George had changed his mind about going to Denmark and did not want her to go away while he was at home. Since it was soon being said that James had prevented Anne from visiting her sister, it is interesting to have her own explanation. And most of the December letter is an ardent defence of Lady Churchill, to whom Mary had evidently taken exception, with an assurance from Churchill himself that rather than change his religion he would be willing to lose all his places and all that he had. This marked the beginning of the Churchills' involvement with the Orange cause, though Churchill never was asked to change his religion, or threatened with loss of place.

Anne's letters always ended with great expressions of love for her dear sister. Burnet wrote (in his unpublished memoirs) 'So now we are out of a danger which I confess I apprehended more than all other when I came out of England.' Now that he was in Holland he was able to throw himself into the cause of William and Mary and he soon achieved a major advance for it. William had thought much on what his own position would be if Mary succeeded but had never liked to broach the question with her.

Burnet had no such inhibitions. He recorded his conversation with Mary in the *History*. If she succeeded, what would be her husband's position? Mary said she assumed that as her husband he would share in everything that came to her. Not so, said Burnet. Philip of Spain had been called the King but he was only King-Consort to Mary I with no share in the government of England and no rights in it after the Queen's death. Burnet then hinted to Mary that if she assigned her right to William 'it would lay the greatest obligation on him possible, and lay the foundation of a perfect union between them, which had been of late a little embroiled.'

Mary saw her advantage and made up her mind instantly. Burnet related the interview at which she promised 'to give William the real authority as soon as it came into her hands'. She made a stilted little speech, wondering that the laws of England should differ from the law of God in Scripture, which pronounced the wife to be in subjection to the husband, but added that if she followed Scripture in obeying her husband, she hoped he would follow it in loving his wife. In fact relations did improve now that William had got what he wanted and grew closer as the design on the Crown of England developed. Mary was content with her bargain; William would rule by her consent and therefore would have to treat her well.

Meanwhile, James, unaware that schemes were being laid against him using religion as a pretext, made his biggest political mistake when he dismissed Mary's uncle Lord Rochester from office, alienating many Tory Anglicans who thought he had been dismissed for refusing to turn Catholic. But Rochester's fall was involved with James's own domestic affairs, which during the past year had been in some disarray. Catherine Sedley was the cause.

In January 1686 Evelyn recorded that he passed the Privy Seal on the creation of 'Mrs Sidly' to be Countess of Dorchester, 'which tis certaine the Queen took very grievously: so as for two dinners, standing neere her, she hardly eate one morsel, nor spake one word to the King, or to any about her, who at all other times was us'd to be extremely pleasant, full of discourse and good humour:' and he added, not without relish, 'The Roman Cath: were also very angrie because they had so long valu'd the Sanctite of their Religion and Proselytes etc.'

It seemed to Maria that Catherine Sedley was setting up to play the part of a Duchess of Portsmouth in the new reign. (Louise had been packed off to France, James insisting that she should pay her debts before she left.) Moreover, Catherine was backed by Lord Rochester, who encouraged the liaison as a means of keeping James in his old Tory Protestant circle. The boy Catherine had borne to James had died soon after he became King but the daughter, also called Catherine (Darnley), was about seven years old. James allowed his mistress £5000 a year and granted her an estate in Ireland, so that she had to go over there to take possession. But Catherine came bouncing back, as bold as brass, into the Queen's public Drawing Room.

Maria was Italian and passionate; she would not stand for it. She faced James, with several priests standing by her, and told him that if Catherine remained at court, she herself would leave and enter a convent.

James, shamed, promised to make the lady leave the court, but it was easier said than done. Catherine sat tight and jeered at him, saying that

[171]

if he wanted her to go he must come and turn her out of her house himself; she was a freeborn Englishwoman and would live where she pleased. James refused to see her and eventually got her to go by threatening to cut off her pension if she did not. So Catherine capitulated; she took a house in Weybridge and though she sometimes came to London she did not present herself at court. Of course, gossip said the King continued to visit her at Weybridge on his days out hunting. If he did, Maria took care not to notice. It was enough that there should be no rival queen at court, flaunting her power, as Portsmouth had done.

During this domestic drama, while Rochester had backed Catherine, Sunderland, whose chief ambition at present was to get rid of Rochester, had backed the Queen. He was also professing a serious interest in Catholicism, the better to secure his hold on the King. Since the King's conscience was already on the Queen's side, they were bound to win.

Sunderland had already been angling for the Lord Treasurer's post, hinting that Rochester was mismanaging the Treasury. It is possible he was; he was quick to make whatever profit he could, especially now that Lord Grey was pardoned and living quietly in the country. (Uppark was his favourite seat.) James, so careful of money himself, was thinking of putting the Treasury into Commission, as a measure of financial reform.

At this critical point Sunderland suggested to the King that Rochester himself was thinking of becoming a Catholic. It was James's weak point. Eagerly he arranged one of the debates he was fond of holding, in which Catholic priests at last had a chance to answer the attacks of Protestants and put forward the true and undistorted Catholic doctrine. Rochester attended, but almost before the debate got under way he jumped up and said he was more convinced than ever of the truth of the Church of England. James lost his temper and when, shortly afterwards, he dismissed him from his post, it appeared to be for not changing his religious allegiance. As James settled a large pension on him (£4000 a year) and continued to receive him at court, it did not appear to him in that light. But when he recalled Lord Clarendon from Ireland and gave his post to Lord Tyrconnel, it was no wonder people took it as demoting Protestants in favour of Catholics. (Clarendon got a pension too and stayed on the Privy Council, though the Privy Seal was not returned to him.)

However, James did not make Sunderland Treasurer. In the memoirs he says he would not 'trust his purs to one who could never keep any money in his own'. Sunderland was an inveterate gambler. The King put the Treasury into Commission with Godolphin at the head of it, a judicious choice and a Protestant one. Nevertheless, Sunderland consolidated his power as chief Secretary of State; Lord Middleton, the other Secretary of State, who had charge of Northern European affairs, was a secondary figure. He was a bit of a sceptic in religious questions, which did not prevent James from liking and trusting him, a trust not misplaced.

In spite of the suspicions of Protestants James trusted his old Anglican royalist friends to be loyal, though he was inclined to trust those who had become Catholics, like Jermyn (now Lord Dover) rather more than they perhaps deserved. Thomas Bruce, who had succeeded his father as Earl of Ailesbury, tells many anti-Dover stories in his memoirs (his taking bribes, etc) and shakes his head over the King's refusal to hear anything against him.

As to the King's putting Catholics into office (and dispensing them from the Test) there were actually only a few in government posts, all minor ones. James's chief ministers were all Protestants, for even Sunderland did not actually become a Catholic, only went to mass and pretended interest. Perhaps James's biggest mistake was to appoint the Jesuit Edward Petre to the Privy Council. Petre came of an old English noble family and seems to have given moderate and sensible advice, but just because he was a Jesuit he was totally unacceptable to English people and after the uproar of the Popish Plot James ought to have realized this. That he did not was probably because *he* knew that popular fantasies about Jesuits were nonsense and Petre trustworthy. In the same way *he* knew he had not demoted the Hyde brothers for refusing to become Catholics and so he did not realize that their demotion signalled the beginning of serious disaffection among the Anglican Tories who had backed him during the Exclusion crisis. And he was about to alienate them still further by suspending the religious penal laws which ensured the monopoly of the Church of England.

[173]

4 Consciences

1687 turned out a good year for James, the best of his reign. In March he prorogued Parliament till November and on 4 April he published his Declaration on Liberty of Conscience. In the preamble, after setting out his aim, he said: 'We cannot but heartily wish, as it will easily be believed, that all the people of our dominions were members of the Catholic Church. Yet we humbly thank God it is, and hath of long time been, our constant sense and opinion (which upon divers occasions we have declared) that conscience ought not to be constrained, nor people forced in matters of mere religion; it has ever been directly contrary to our inclination as we think it is to the interest of the government, which it destroys, by spoiling trade, depopulating countries and discouraging strangers; and finally that it never obtained the end for which it was employed.' The failure of the various acts of uniformity to unite the country in religion was set forth and the King then issued the Indulgence, 'making no doubt of the concurrence of our two houses of Parliament when we shall think it convenient for them to meet.'

In the first place we do declare that we will protect and maintain our archbishops, bishops and clergy and all other our subjects of the Church of England in the free exercise of their religion as by law established and in the quiet and full enjoyment of all their possessions, without any molestation or disturbance whatsoever.

We do likewise declare it is our royal will and pleasure that from henceforth the execution of all and all manner of penal laws in matters ecclesiastical, for not coming to Church, or not receiving the Sacrament, or for any other nonconformity to the religion established, or for by reason of the exercise of religion in any manner whatsoever, be immediately suspended; and further execution of the said penal laws . . . is hereby suspended.

This freedom was then spelt out in practical terms – permission to meet and serve God in private houses or places built or hired for the purpose, so long as nothing was preached against the government; the meetings to be openly held and the justices of the peace to be informed of the places chosen. This was to prevent secret meetings of the wilder antinomian sects.

Finally, the King declared that henceforth no one would be obliged to take the oaths of supremacy, allegiance, or the Tests of King Charles II's reign, before taking any office, civil or military.

It was this that roused the opposition of the ruling classes because it would allow Catholics into offices of state. It should be remembered that of all the nonconformists virtually only the Catholics included men of property and education who could aspire to such offices; the Protestant dissenters, though more numerous, were for the most part men of business and trade who had no such ambitions.

Evelyn reflected the resentment instantly felt by Anglicans when he wrote of the Declaration.

by which dissenters and Papists especialy, had publique liberty of exercising their severall ways of worship, without incurring the penalty of the many Laws and Acts of Parliament to the contrary ever since the Reformation; and this purely obtained by the Papists thinking thereby to ruine the C. of England, which now was the onely Church which so admirably and strenuously oppos'd their Superstition; There was a wonderfull concourse at the Dissenters meeting house in this parish, and the Parish-Church left exceeding thinn. . . .

It never occurred to Evelyn that it was strange to blame the papists when it was the desertion of the dissenters which left his parish church 'exceeding thinn'. The fact that this large concourse had previously filled the church because attendance was enforced by threat of fine or imprisonment does not seem to have worried him at all; nor does he seem to care what sort of support had been given to the Church's teaching and practice by such unwilling attenders.

James wrote to William on 22 April expressing satisfaction at the way the Declaration had been received. He knew this because a series of public addresses were made to him, all through the summer – some two hundred in all. They were printed in the *Gazette* for all to read and have been preserved in *Somers' Tracts*.

Evelyn happened to be at Hampton Court in the middle of June when some of these addresses were presented. 'Whilst I was in the Council-Chamber came in a formal person, with a large roll of Parchment in his hand, being an Addresse . . . of the people of Coventry.' He introduced it with a speech in which he said it came from all parties, Presbyterians, Independents and Anabaptists as well as Church of England men, above a thousand in all, full of gratitude for the Indulgence. 'To whom the K. (pulling off his hatt) sayed: That what he had don in giving liberty of conscience was, what was ever his judgment ought to be don, and that as he would preserve them in their injoyment of it during his reigne; so he would indeavour to settle it by Law, that it should never be altered by his successors.'

It was no wonder that James was encouraged by these addresses from the ordinary citizens of the nation, though they might provoke the laughter of the smart (Whig) set in town, because they came from the towns and trades, including, be it noted, from 'the combers, weavers, and other workmen in the serge manufacture about Taunton in Somersetshire' – the heart of Monmouth's support two years before. All the London companies seem to have sent in addresses, including Plumbers, Distillers and Cooks. James had, in fact, strong 'trades union' support.

One of the printed addresses was from the Quakers, presented by William Penn. The King began his reply, 'Gentlemen, I thank you heartily for your address. Some of you know (I am sure you do, Mr Penn) that it was always my principle that conscience ought not to be forced and that all men ought to have liberty of their consciences. . . .'

The reception of the Declaration was so favourable that James decided to dissolve the Coronation Parliament, which he had been proroguing for almost eighteen months, and hoped that a new one would prove amenable to the settlement. Unfortunately the methods taken to ensure a majority in favour of repeal were to alienate still further the Tory Anglicans who regarded the Test as the necessary defence of established Protestantism.

Meanwhile, in the spring William sent a special envoy to England to discuss the King's religious policy, a courtier statesman from

Utrecht whose name, Everard van Dijkvelt, caused everyone trouble; Dalrymple later fixed him as Dyckvelt. His undercover mission was to sound out the principal political lords and get written commitments from them to William of Orange as protector of the Protestant succession – no word of armed intervention as yet.

Dalrymple prints an excited letter from Sunderland's wife Anne (Digby) to the Prince, the first part written on 7 March 1687, warning him that the papists at court 'were planning to flatter Mr Dixfield with a great many fine things' – promises of 'full power' in civil and military affairs if he would declare in favour of taking off the Test, promises which would not be kept once the Catholics were free of restrictions. If the Prince agreed with the repeal it would only make him unpopular in England with the people who matter, she said; keeping the Test was the only thing that united Protestants. She was going to send this letter inside one to the Princess enclosed in another 'to Monsieur Bentick about my garden'. (Evelyn admired her gardening expertise.)

But a postscript was added a few days later; she had delayed sending it because 'Some papists the other day ... said that my Lord Sunderland did not dance in a nett ... there were dispensations from Holland as well as from Rome; and that they were sure I held a correspondence with the Princess of Orange.' Guessing that the King would ask her directly about it, she waited till he did and then was able to assure him that she 'never had any correspondence with the Princess, but about treakle water and work' and that anyway 'he must be sure that the Princess could never be capable of any thing with any body to his disservice.'

James believed the dissembling Lady Sunderland, continued to trust her slippery husband and later did not suspect his daughter Mary of any knowledge of what had been planned against him by William. He was no politician and fatally disposed to think other people as frank as himself. Surrounded by liars and traitors he went cheerfully ahead, telling William when Dijkvelt went back in May that though the envoy might have gathered some false impressions 'from persons not well affected to me ... yet I am satisfied I have not made one step but what is good for the kingdom in general, as well as for the monarchy, and have more reason every day than other to be pleased with having put out my declaration for liberty of conscience.'

[177]

William's answer survives because he kept a draft; I give Dalrymple's translation. After polite thanks for James's taking up his interests in the matter of France's annexation of Orange, he declares that

> there is no person in the world who has more aversion than I have for all sort of persecution on the score of religion, and that certainly in my life I will never put my hand to it; but at the same time that I can never resolve to do any thing contrary to the religion I profess; and that therefore I cannot concur in what your Majesty asks of me. This I hope you will not take amiss when you consider upon what foundation I do it and that in every other thing you will find no body who will be more attached to your interests, and who will serve them with more fidelity, which I wish passionately for occasions of testifying to your Majesty by effects, and that I shall be all my life with a profound respect what I ought.

James was now at Windsor and answered this smooth epistle on 16 June (old style) saying that he was 'sorry to find by it, that you cannot be for taking off all those laws, and the Tests, which are so very severe and hard upon all Dissenters from the Church of England; and since what Mr Dyckuelt said to you from me, could not alter your mind as to that, I cannot expect that a letter should prevail with you.' He ended, 'I have not time to say more now and shall always be as kind to you as you can expect.'

What would James have thought if he had known that Mr Dijkvelt had been secretly conferring not only with Whigs but with Tories and even members of his own household? For as well as the Earls of Devonshire, Bedford and Shrewsbury, and the Marquis of Halifax, there were letters to the Prince from Lord Rochester, his brother Lord Clarendon, Lord Sunderland, Lord Nottingham, the old Catholic Colonel Lord Bellasys and Lord Churchill.

Churchill wrote a high toned letter on 17 May, assuring the Prince of Orange that Princess Anne 'was resolved, by the assistance of God, to suffer all extremities, even to death itself, rather than be brought to change her religion,' and added that for himself 'my places and the King's favour I set at naught, in comparison of the being true to my religion.' He ended with a flourish, "The Princess of Denmark is safe in the trusting of me; I being resolved, although I cannot live the life of a saint, if there be occasion for it, to show the resolution of a martyr. Your Highness's most obedient servant, Churchill.'

Since Chuchill knew perfectly well that James would never try to force anyone's conscience it is a puzzle to know what induced him to join the conspiracy. Perhaps he (and/or Sarah) had decided that he would never rise further under James, who not only persisted in keeping Feversham (also a Protestant) above him, but held a disappointingly pacific foreign policy. His view, often expressed, was that war on the continent was not in England's interest; and besides, he disapproved of Christian nations fighting each other when they ought all to be united in defending Europe against the Turks. He had sent his favourite illegitimate son James FitzJames (on his return made Duke of Berwick) to fight in the Emperor's army against the Turks and the young man (not yet eighteen) had already distinguished himself in the profession his father had chosen thirty years before. Whatever Churchill's motives, he had already opted for William in preference to James before there was any question of a Catholic son and heir.

One of Dijkvelt's most important tasks in England had been (as Burnet puts it) 'to remove the ill impressions of the Prince' from the minds of his possible supporters. There were suspicions that he was 'arbitrary' and too Calvinistic a Protestant to support the Church of England. In fact William certainly was arbitrary in his ideas of kingship, witness his alarm over the proposed limitations during the Exclusion crisis. But he had early realized that to win friends in England he must always bow to the rights of Parliament, though he was careful not to rely entirely on the Whigs. His regular correspondents from England were Halifax, who had resigned his post rather than vote for the repeal of the Test, and Danby, the ex-leader of the Tories, who had not been restored to power by James, and had always been keenly Protestant.

James was so anxious to get a Parliament that would take off the Test and the penal laws that he embarked on a campaign of canvassing electors and candidates on their views. Three questions were put: (1) Whether the candidate would be in favour of repeal; (2) whether the voter would elect someone favourable to repeal; and (3) whether he was willing to live in friendly relations with those of different religious

[179]

persuasions. This canvassing by the King's agents (lord lieutenants and others) alarmed the gentlemen and burgesses concerned but a large majority answered yes to the third question, and substantial numbers yes to the others, often with the proviso of waiting to hear the debates in Parliament first. But people felt the King was trying to pack Parliament, though in fact he had no way of preventing the electors from choosing an unfavourable candidate. This was where the business of revising the charters created further odium, in trying to secure favourable electors in the boroughs. Nevertheless, it was only on this one subject of religious freedom that the King was intervening and after all the addresses of thanks he felt sure he had most of the nation (if not the ruling class) behind him.

While he was at Windsor that summer James officially received a papal nuncio, an event which swiftly became part of Whig mythology, with James on his knees delivering up England to the Pope of Rome. Because of this fantasy it is pertinent to give the account written by James Yonge in his journal. Yonge was a Plymouth man who had been a naval surgeon and was now surgeon to the newly raised regiment of the Earl of Bath (Bevil Grenvile's son); a Protestant, Yonge was a friend of James's surgeon-general Pearse, who had once given the Duke of York a tropical bird which Pepys saw at St James's.

Surgeon Yonge, who was going to attend the annual review the King had instituted, took his family to London to see the sights ('the Tower, Monument, the Abbey, Bedlam, etc') and the King's Bench prison where he saw Titus Oates, 'who seemed as fat, brisk and sportive as ever, only less superbous'.

On 3 July Yonge was at Windsor to see the Nuncio's audience.

The King and Queen went first to mass in the fine chapel, after which sitting on two chairs on the ascent at the end of the hall, the Nuntio was introduced by the Duke of Grafton . . . He spoke in Italian with his cap on to the King (both standing), to the Queen with his cap off. It lasted half an hour, then he retired under the same conduct, going backwards with his cap in his hand, and making three low bows (which was answered by their Majesties) till he came to the door, and then went off. His name was Monsignor d'Ada, a bishop of Amasa. He had thick short black hair, pale face, Roman nose, had a blue or purple mantle over his shoulders, a crucifix at his breast, and a black cap like a Jesuit's. He had been in England incognito a year.

All quite diplomatic and unsensational. Yonge watched him go, interested to see a young pale-faced Chinese convert with him, whose picture he had seen in one of the King's lodgings. The surgeon went home to Plymouth soon afterwards.

This summer Maria was planning a visit to Bath, whose waters were supposed to induce fertility, though they had failed of that effect for Queen Catherine, who had made several visits in vain. Maria had to put off hers once because she was in mourning for her mother's death. The Duchess of Modena's demise gave the Prince of Orange the opportunity to send over another envoy to bring his condolences and communicate secretly with his future supporters; this time it was his cousin (son of an illegitimate branch of the house of Nassau) Frederick van Zuylestein, like Dijkvelt an accomplished courtier. He went back with another batch of letters from Lords Nottingham, Danby, Halifax, Devonshire and Bishop Compton of London.

At last James and his Queen set off for the west, going by way of Portsmouth and Salisbury to Bath, where the Queen stayed at the Abbey House (not the one now so called but one nearer the Abbey and run by a Dr Chapman for visitors to the hot baths). James stayed over the weekend and on Sunday 21 August he went into the Abbey after service and touched for the Evil, his own priests reading the prayers. This rather annoyed Bishop Ken, who preached himself the following Sunday, no doubt to correct popish errors. But by that time the King had reached Chester.

He went by way of Gloucester, where Pepys transacted some naval business and then by Worcester, where the bibliophile Secretary for the Admiralty was diverted by the Dean's Library (one of the best in the kingdom) and got left behind, rejoining the King later at Oxford.

In Chester, James stayed with Thomas Cartwright, the new Bishop, who was a friend of Crewe of Durham and like him was promoting the Declaration. Crewe was even on good terms with Dr Leyburn, who was in Durham on a visitation of Roman Catholics, confirming about a thousand persons in that region. On Sunday 28 August the King held a levee at the Bishop's palace in Chester and then touched a crowd of people for the Evil. 'After which,' Cartwright wrote in his diary, 'he went to his devotions in the Shire Hall, and Mr Penn held forth in the Tennis Court, and I preached at the Cathedral.' Liberty of conscience in action!

Next day the King conferred with Bishop Cartwright about putting in deputy-lieutenants favourable to toleration, and he noted his own suggestions in his diary (from which, quoted in Keeton's *Lord Chancellor Jeffreys and the Stuart Cause*, I take this account). Jeffreys' relations in the district are notable by their absence; Keeton supposes because of their firmness to the Church of England's legal monopoly.

From Chester the King made a short pilgrimage to St Winefride's Well, a holy well in North Wales which had survived the Reformation; he probably prayed there for a son and perhaps vowed marital fidelity in repentance for his sins of adultery. On this progress he visited Shrewsbury, Ludlow, Newport, Lichfield, Coventry and Oxford. He was received everywhere with addresses of thanks for the Indulgence, and most towns promised to send such members to Parliament as would support it. James adds in the memoirs that he had no intention that Catholics themselves should be MPs. He did not realize till too late that the political lords and gentry suspected him of planning to put Catholics into all offices, though where he would have found them in sufficient numbers does not appear.

At Oxford James came face to face with some recalcitrant dons who were to figure in the list of Protestant martyrs compiled by the exiles in Holland. Because it became a *cause célèbre* this complex case must be outlined, briefly. The Presidency of Magdalen College was a Crown appointment. A man called Farmer was mandated by the Ecclesiastical Commission who was not only a Roman Catholic but of scandalous life. The Fellows thereupon elected their own candidate, Dr Hough, getting their Visitor, the aged Bishop of Winchester, to confirm him in office. Meanwhile, Farmer having been found incompetent, the Commission mandated Dr Parker, Bishop of Oxford and on the Foundation of Magdalen. But Parker was such a high Anglican that he was suspected of being a Romanist and he had written in defence of the King's Declaration. The Fellows of Magdalen therefore refused to have Dr Parker and insisted on keeping Dr Hough.

[182]

'The King was hugely incensed,' the memoirs relate and this loss of temper was evident to all when the dons were summoned to kneel before him on 4 September. His speech is quoted in Whiting's *Life of Crewe*. 'Is this your Church of England loyalty? . . . Get you gone, know I am your King . . . Go and admit the Bishop of Oxford, Head, Principal, what do you call it, of the College –' (someone whispered 'President') – 'I mean President of the College. Let them that refuse look to it; They shall feel the weight of their sovereign's displeasure.'

However, it was well known in Oxford that James's bark was worse than his bite – nobody was intimidated. Next afternoon the Vice Chancellor gave a banquet for the King in the Bodleian and when James asked for doctorates to be conferred on two of his chaplains and a secretary (all Catholics) the Vice Chancellor calmly said he must consult Convocation before he could give an answer. And took care not to convene Convocation for some time.

The matter was left to the Commission and dragged on for months; as the Fellows still refused to have Dr Parker they were expelled in December. When the Bishop died (Anglican to the last) the Commission appointed Bonaventure Giffard, shortly to be one of the new Catholic bishops, and a few other Catholics as Fellows. This turned the recalcitrant dons into Protestant martyrs and as such they were represented by Burnet and the pamphleteers in Holland.

Penn, an old Oxford man (he had been up with Sunderland, oddly enough) had pleaded with the Magdalen Fellows in vain, pointing out that the King's policy of toleration required the opening of university education to men of all persuasions. James had already tried to achieve this in Cambridge by asking Vice Chancellor Peachell to admit Fr Alban Francis, a Benedictine living in Cambridge, as an MA without taking the oaths. Peachell, though with great trepidation (communicated to his friend Pepys) refused, came before the Commission and was dismissed from his office. Since both universities were generally regarded as the property of the Church of England, James was accused of intruding Catholics on the Church. This misunderstanding continued right into the nineteenth century.

Meanwhile, in September 1687 James rode back to Bath, where his Queen had been bathing in the Cross Bath because it was more secluded than the King's Bath. Even so, as she went into the hot water, clothed in a voluminous yellow canvas gown, a band struck up and people watched 'from the galleries'. (After the birth of the Prince of Wales a beautiful monument was put up there, only to be destroyed in riots during the 1688 Revolution; the cherub now in a niche looking up Milsom Street is thought to be a possible survivor.)

In the afternoons the Queen went driving in the country and she received the local gentry in the largest room of the Abbey House, her graciousness and beauty much appreciated, as usual. When the King returned they went over to Bristol for the day, where they were royally received by the Mayor and the merchants, and presented with a purse of money – the custom of those days.

The King then went to London, leaving the Queen to finish her course of baths, and they met again at Windsor at the beginning of October, returning to Whitehall to celebrate their birthdays (only a few days apart) with a grand ball at court. James was fifty-four and Maria twenty-nine.

The son so much longed for and prayed for may have been conceived then and born early, but more probably he was conceived at Bath and carried full term, for he was strong enough to survive the horrendous treatments prescribed by the royal physicians and a midnight flight overseas before he was six months old. Maria said she had 'two reckonings' and her whole maternal history suggests that she suffered from irregular periods. At any rate, that autumn the child was con-ceived who was to be made one of the excuses for the deposition of his father in 1688.

5 Run-up to Revolution

William's birthday was on 4 November 1687 (he was thirty-seven) and that day a letter was published, ostensibly by the Grand Pensioner Fagel but really concocted by William and Burnet, to make known in England the Orange view of the Test Acts in such a way that William could disclaim responsibility for publication, just as he had done in the Exclusion crisis.

The Earl of Devonshire (as Lord Cavendish had now become) wrote from his Derbyshire home to the Prince of Orange:

People are in raptures to find the sentiments of your Highness and of the Princess in matters of religion, not only so equitable but so agreeable to the interest and to the taste of all the nation, except those who by a pretended liberty of conscience seek to destroy it intirely, as in effect is seen in all places where they have power to do it.

He meant in France, of course, but as James pointed out (in the memoirs) in other countries where there were Catholic rulers, in the Empire, for instance, or even in 'Rome, where the Jews are tollerated, infallibility does not oblige the forcing all others to be of the same faith: besides how rediculous it would be, for so small a party as the Catholics are' – in England. Many shared Devonshire's suspicions, however. Halifax wrote (anonymously) a pamphlet *Letter to a Dissenter* suggesting that they were being hugged now only to be squeezed later.

That November too, Mary had expressed her curiosity to know why her father had been converted to Catholicism, to his new ambassador at the Hague, the Marquis d'Albeville. (His title came from the Emperor, Orange's ally; he was an Irishman named White and much easier for William to manage that Sir Bevil Skelton.) Given this opening, James wrote her a personal account to which Mary, shutting herself up in her closet on Boxing Day, composed a lengthy reply, to the surprise and admiration of all, especially Burnet. James then sent her the papers written by her mother and her uncle King Charles, and a book: *Reflections on Differences in Religion.* Mary demolished these to her own satisfaction, writing to Anne and to Bishop Compton as well, and in February James gave up, saying he would send her no more books or papers. But he went on writing her regular letters, as affectionately as ever.

By the end of November 1687 the Queen had told Mary of her pregnancy and at Christmas the King announced it and ordered prayers to be said in all the churches in January 1688. Henry Hyde, Earl of Clarendon, attended the new church of St James in Piccadilly

[185]

on Sunday 15 January and noted that few people brought the paper of prayers with them, adding in his diary, 'It is strange to see how the Queen's great belly is ridiculed as if scarce any body believed it to be true. Good god help us.'

Clarendon's diary for this crucial year was not printed till 1765, when the Jacobite cause was lost and the 'Old Pretender', born in 1688, was dying in Rome. Clarendon was involved in an awkward lawsuit with the Queen Dowager and went to the King's levee at Whitehall on 31 January to speak to him about it. James, who took him 'into the inner room' to talk privately, was sympathetic, though he pointed out that it would not do for him to 'disoblige her' himself. Clarendon admitted that 'the king has been extremely kind to her and used her with the same respect as when the late king was living.' Catherine was always on the point of going home to Portugal but not actually going.

Clarendon attended the King's levee often in February and on 8 March he waited on the Queen who, he said, was very gracious and inquired why he did not come more to court, pressed him to do so and asked if his pension was well paid. 'I told her, yes. The King then came into the room from hunting: and so I came away.'

Princess Anne, who was pregnant again, miscarried on Easter Monday, 16 April, at about 4 a.m. Word being brought to Clarendon as soon as he was up, 'I made haste to the cockpit,' he recorded: 'I found the king with her.' This was typical of James's affectionate care for his daughter.

But by this time Anne was deep in conspiratorial correspondence with her sister Mary, in which her father figured as 'Mansell' and the Queen as 'Mansell's wife'. Her letters in 1687 had been full of spiteful remarks about the Queen, including the gossip that 'everybody believes that she presses the King to be more violent than he would be of himself, for she is a very great bigot in her way.' This slander issued in vulgar cartoons printed in Holland of the Queen beating the King. Negatively it shows that people on the spot simply did not believe in James's 'violence'.

As well as providing fuel for the pamphlet campaign mounted by the exiles, Anne backed the anti-repeal line: 'For I am wholly of your mind, that in taking away the Test and Penal Laws, they take away our religion; and if that be done, farewell to all happiness: for when once

[186]

the Papists have everything in their hands, all we poor Protestants have but dismal times to hope for.'

By 1688 she was writing her doubts on the reality of Maria's pregnancy, and her letters show how far her knowledge of the conspiracy went. On 20 March: 'I hope you will instruct Bentley what you would have your friends do if any alteration should come, as it is to be feared there will, especially if Mansell has a son, which I conclude he will, there being so much reason to believe it is a false belly.' Anne was suspicious because Maria had never made her feel her belly and had always gone into the next room to put on her smock. In consequence, 'when she is brought to bed, nobody will be convinced it is her child, except it prove a daughter. For my part, I declare I shall not, except I see the child and she parted.'

Anne went on to convey her uncle Lord Rochester's pleas for forgiveness; he had heard from Bentinck of their anger but felt his only offence had been not to see them when he went abroad. He could not, because James had given him permission so long as he did not go to Holland. He had said the same thing to Danby's son, as Danby told William on 29 March. James had said crossly that he knew 'there were those in Holland who gave themselves hopes of seeing some English lords at the head of some of their squadrons, but he would take care to prevent it.' The next day, however, the King apologized for 'speaking to him in some disorder' because he had just received some news from abroad, and told him to take no notice, 'for I dare trust you to go where you will.' But he added, 'If you go only for curiosity, you might as well satisfy that elsewhere as in Holland.'

James's suspicions of the Dutch were based on the fleet being raised there, which Van Citters, the Dutch Ambassador, assured him was in defence against France, but which he feared might portend another Dutch War, urged on by the Whig exiles. William, for his part, was telling the Dutch ministers that James had made a secret treaty with Louis to fall upon the Dutch suddenly, without declaring war; that was why he was building up the English navy and army. It was a cold war situation, each side suspecting the other of planning aggression. But James never suspected it was being planned by William specifically against himself.

In the first months of the year James had been having a prolonged

[187]

diplomatic wrangle with William about the English troops lent to Holland. He had asked for the return of the six regiments or at least enough men to make up two regiments, at first planning to lend them to France so that Louis could pay for them; as peace was still holding, this would be no threat to the Dutch. But then Louis offered to pay towards their maintenance in England, which delighted James, who was not taking a pension as Charles had done.

William wanted those regiments for his intervention in England, already in active preparation; he persuaded the Dutch States not to let them go, representing it as a religious issue; Protestants must be offered asylum in the Dutch forces, the few Catholics could go. In the event quite a number chose to return and James formed three new regiments with these veterans as a nucleus. Relations between James and William were strained by this episode but James continued his correspondence with his nephew as frankly as ever, telling him in May of his visit to Chatham and that he had ordered a third-rate to be prepared to take the Queen Dowager to Portugal.

On this visit to Chatham James ate and slept on his yacht to save the Commissioner expense. Pepys's discourse on his favourite subject of foreign salutes due to the Royal Navy was interrupted by a messenger bringing news that the Queen had been taken ill. James immediately posted back to Whitehall, where he found Maria recovering not from illness but from shock: a letter from Modena had brought news that her brother was struck down by cholera and she had fainted away. But the letter had ended by saying the Duke was recovering, and when she learned this Maria revived. James told William that they had feared a miscarriage 'but God be thanked she was very well all yesterday, and continues so now, so that I hope she will go out her full time.' He added, 'The Weather is now very seasonable, and there is like to be great store of fruit this year.' It had been an exceptionally cold spring, but now the weather had changed for the better.

By that time James had re-issued his Declaration, with an order that it should be read in the London churches on the two last Sundays of May and in the provinces on the two first of June: the usual way to make a royal declaration public to the whole nation. Apparently Bishop Cartwright had advised him that though some of the bishops might not like it, they would probably obey.

[188]

But feeling against popery was already running high in London and fears that the Declaration was designed to undermine the Protestant Church of England. On 1 April Evelyn attended the Chapel Royal for sermon and communion service, which was interrupted by 'the rude breaking in of multitudes into the Chappell, zealous to hear the second sermon' – which was preached before Princess Anne by Bishop Ken. Evelyn stayed to hear it, 'describing the Calamity of the Reformed Church of Judah, under the Babylonish persecution, for her sinns,' an obvious reference to the Huguenots in France but with overtones that could be applied to England, especially when Ken exhorted all to repentance and patience till God's providence should deliver 'the Reformed Church, where ever persecuted and insulted over'.

Evelyn had read and believed all the stories of the atrocities committed by 'the French tyrant' and had refused to pass the privy seal on James's licence to print Catholic books – another member of the Commission did it. This was the same Evelyn who had so praised James's good qualities three years earlier, the same Ken who had blessed him for declaring that black slaves ought to be baptized even if it made them free. What had happened to make them fear a Babylonish captivity, to be imposed on the powerful Protestant majority of the nation by the King, a handful of Jesuits and the small minority of Catholic gentry surviving in the country?

The answer is, not so much anything James had done as what they believed papists would do if they got the chance, on the pattern of Louis XIV and memories of the sixteenth-century Spanish Inquisition. This myth of diabolical priests torturing heretics to force them to bow the knee to idols was currently reinforced by a spate of pamphlets and cartoons, written and printed by the English exiles in Holland, smuggled over in bales and distributed widely but especially in London. The authors were those who had written similar horrifics during the Popish Plot terror; the more intellectual offerings were composed by Burnet.

On 4 April when Clarendon was at the King's levee, James 'spake much of an answer Dr Burnet had written to a pamphlet called *Parliamentum Pacificum*,' complaining of the Doctor's rudeness and insolence towards him. The pamphlet's subtitle explains Burnet's fury, for it ran: 'The Happy Union of King and People in an Healing Parliament Heartily wished for and Humbly Recommended, by a True

Protestant, and no Dissenter.' Burnet did not want a Test-abolishing Parliament called by the King; he wanted to make him out a tyrant for *not* calling a Parliament. Hence Halifax's continual guessing (to William of Orange) as to whether the King would call one or not and his conclusion that he would not, because there had not been enough conversions to enable him to carry out his 'great design' – of transforming the Church and State of England into a Catholic absolute monarchy, French-style. Since James had no such design he did not realize how his steps towards liberty of conscience and a legal but separate existence for the Catholic Church were being misinterpreted by Protestants.

James continued to believe that openness was the best policy, and so he had the three new Catholic bishops consecrated in public, Bonaventure Giffard at the Banqueting House on 22 April; Philip (Michael) Ellis, the convert son of a clergyman (known as Jolly Phil) a Benedictine who had been one of James's chaplains, at St James's Palace on 6 May; and James Smith, who had been a professor at Douay College (in Flanders) and President of it in 1683, on 13 May at Somerset House, Queen Catherine's dower house. All three were in their early forties, all English, and only one a convert.

These three bishops and Dr Leyburn, composed a joint pastoral letter to the Catholics of England, exhorting them to 'live up to the Rules prescribed' and especially of charity. Catholics might be tempted

> to insult over those who formerly abridged you of it (liberty); but it must be your care to prevent and suppress all such irregular Motions . . . a great part of the Nation, whose Persuasion in point of Religion doth differ most from yours, and which in time past hath been severe upon your Persons, is willing to enter into a friendly Correspondence with you; and if some others do repine at your being sharers in the Liberty which themselves enjoy with much greater Advantage, the most effective means to convince them of their Error, is to edifie them by your good Example.
>
> You live under a Prince of your own Religion, to whom next under God you owe this Felicity. You have his Power to protect you in the free Exercise of your Religion, and his Example to encourage your discharge of this Duty in a most edifying Manner. His Majesty's

assiduousness at the Divine Service and other Functions performed in his Chappel, notwithstanding the multitude of weighty affairs, which might frequently excuse him from such Attendance; the respectful Posture in which he performs this Religious Duty, which argues a Presence of Mind no less than of his Body, cannot but invite you, both as good Catholics and good Subjects, to a Conformity with so Eminent a Pattern.

Earnest admonitions were then given to those already in offices

so to behave themselves in them, that neither his Majestie may have occasion to repent, nor his other subjects to repine at the Choice he hath made of them. We exhort those who are not yet in public Employment to bear their Lots with Modesty and Patience, without Murmuring or Envy.

The order for the reading of the Declaration had been made in April and there had then been no protests made, formal or popular. But on 12 May, unknown to the King, a formidable protest was being organized – by Lord Clarendon, his brother-in-law. He dined at Lambeth and after the Bishops of Chester (Cartwright) and St David's had left, got the Archbishop of Canterbury and six others to agree not to read the Declaration and to petition the King against it. A draft of the petition was got out (probably by Compton) and circulated among the higher clergy in London. More meetings took place and on 16 May Clarendon noted that most of the city clergy were resolved not to read the Declaration.

On the Friday (18 May) before the first Sunday designated, the bishops took their petition to Whitehall. Bishop Lloyd of St Asaph told Clarendon about it afterwards; he also took notes for the Archbishop which survived among Sancroft's papers and were printed in 1765. Lloyd was an active talkative man with any number of bees buzzing in his bonnet; his hobby was interpreting the more recondite prophecies of the Bible to apply to Louis XIV, the Huguenots and so on. (Evelyn was quite impressed with Lloyd's prophetic powers.) Archbishop Sancroft cried off taking the petition (which he had written out himself) fearing the night air, he said.

The six bishops first sought Lord Middleton, but he was ill, so they had to apply to Lord Sunderland, suspected of being a secret Catholic. Although it was now about ten o'clock at night Sunderland, refusing to read the petition himself, took them at once to see the King in his 'closet within the Bedchamber' but did not go in with them, so that the King was alone with them.

James, though he was on the point of retiring to bed, received the bishops very graciously, according to Lloyd. They presented their petition on their knees and the King seemed pleased at first, remarking, 'This is my lord of Canterbury's own hand.' To which they replied, 'Yes, sir, it is his own hand.'

James then read that the bishops felt they could not allow the Declaration to be read in the churches because 'it was founded upon such a dispensing power as hath often been declared illegal in Parliament.' He was absolutely astounded that the bishops should take their stand with Parliament against the royal prerogative, which the Church of England had always previously upheld, preaching non-resistance to royal authority. Moreover, although Charles had withdrawn his Indulgence as a result of Parliamentary opposition, he had never conceded his right to issue them or recognized Parliament's resolutions on the subject as valid.

No wonder then that (according to Lloyd's notes) 'the King having read it over and folding it up, said thus or to this effect: This is a great surprise to me: here are strange words. I did not expect this from you; especially from some of you. This is the standard of rebellion.'

They all protested their loyalty but continued to maintain their case. When the King demanded, 'Do you question my dispensing power? Some of you here have printed and preached for it, when it was for your purpose,' the Bishop of Peterborough said, 'Sir, what we say of the dispensing power refers only to what was declared in Parliament.' Of course that was just what annoyed the King. Eventually he said, peremptorily, 'I will be obeyed in publishing my declaration.' Ken thereupon said, 'God's will be done.' 'What is that?' demanded the King and when Ken repeated it, he said, 'If I think fit to alter my mind I will send to you. God hath given me the dispensing power and I will maintain it.'

In his own accounts in the memoirs James admits to having been angry; passive obedience, so long preached by churchmen against

Parliamentary rebels, was now 'to be kept cold for a fitter season'. But he could not now withdraw his order without seeming to concede that he had no right to make the declaration in the first place.

James naturally thought the handwritten petition was private to himself. But the next morning, (Saturday 19 May) printed copies were being sold all over the town; probably Bishop Compton had seen to that. The whole dispute had been made public overnight without the King's knowledge, only the day before the first date of the pulpit reading. It was a considerable affront to royal authority to be called to account by the bishops of the Church of England in the name of Parliament.

Next day (Sunday 20 May) the Declaration was read in the Chapel Royal and at Westminster Abbey, but hardly anywhere else. Where any clergyman did attempt to read it, a large part of the congregation got up and left. It was a public demonstration against the King.

James consulted his Lord Chancellor Jeffreys (a staunch Anglican) who thought the printed petition 'tumultuary' like those presented to Charles demanding a Parliament. All the judges were summoned to Whitehall to give their opinions. But then nothing happened, except that on Monday the King went hunting, so that Clarendon could not take the old Irish Archbishop to see him in Chiffinch's lodgings, as he had arranged.

By Thursday 24 May came prompt approval from Holland for the bishops' move; Princess Mary had written to the Archbishop as well as to her uncle Clarendon. The confrontation between the King and the bishops was a godsend to the Orange cause, which was short of evidence for persecution and tyranny.

Clarendon was fifty on 2 June and noted his good health: 'God make me thankful for it and grant that laying aside the follies and ambition of this deceitful world (of which I have been too fond) I may spend the rest of my days so as to fit me for a better world.' Whether he thought he was doing this three days later when he advised the bishops on the best lawyers in town, he does not say. Then, finding they had given no thought to the question of bail, he gave them pertinent advice, so that they could use the threatened legal proceedings to the advantage of their cause. For on 28 May they had learned that they were summoned to appear before the King in Council on Friday 8 June.

[193]

Notes were again written of what passed on this occasion. The King arrived at five in the afternoon and half an hour later the bishops were called in and graciously received. The Lord Chancellor then asked the Archbishop to identify a paper as the petition written and signed by him. Sancroft took the paper but then launched into a prepared speech: 'Sir, I am called hither as a criminal, which I never was before in my life, and little thought I ever should be, especially before your majesty . . .' and went on to maintain that 'No man is obliged to answer questions, that may tend to the accusing of himself.'

'Chicanery!' said the King impatiently, and hoped he would not deny his own hand. But the Archbishop was determined not to say anything about anything, though eventually he agreed to answer if the King laid his command on them. 'His majesty said, No; I will not command you: if you will deny your own hands, I know not what to say to you.' But Jeffreys, first sending them out, persuaded the King to command them to answer and so at last they acknowledged their signatures. After another withdrawal they were told that the King was going to proceed against them for publishing a seditious libel (denying his dispensing power and right to issue the indulgence) – 'but it shall be with all fairness at Westminster Hall.' So they must now 'enter into recognisance' – give bail to appear.

Another prolonged wrangle now ensued, for the bishops, primed by Clarendon and the lawyers, refused to give bail, as they had been advised that it would be prejudicial to them as peers. Although the King assured them it would not, they would not budge. They were sent out again and the Earl of Berkeley, who had seen the Archbishop on Thursday when he had agreed to bail, tried to persuade them. (But that was before Sancroft had seen Clarendon!) All to no avail. So then, because the bishops would not give bail, they had to be sent to the Tower.

Their evening journey by the river became a demonstration against the King, for the banks were crowded with enthusiastic supporters. 'Wonderfull was the concerne of the people for them,' wrote Evelyn, 'infinite crowds of people on their knees, beging their blessing and praying for them as they passed out of their Barge, along the Tower Wharfs.' And the next day Clarendon wrote in his diary: 'Multitudes of people went to the Tower to the Bishops.' Visitors were freely admitted and the bishops, as Protestant champions, held court all day.

Their imprisonment was the best possible publicity for their cause and the worst for the King's. It was represented, at home and abroad, as an act of arbitrary persecution of Protestants by a Catholic King. In Holland it was taken up with enthusiasm by Burnet and his fellow scribblers, and the Seven Bishops became instant martyrs, their portraits issued, grouped round the Archbishop's, and the King was represented as fanatically driving against the laws of the land to destroy the Church of England – liberty of conscience was quite forgotten.

But that weekend James had other things to think about.

6 June 1688

The Queen had wanted to lie-in at Windsor, for the country air, but London was more convenient for the official witnesses to a royal birth. Whitehall was too noisy and public, so she chose to go back to her old home at St James's. But the builders were there and it seemed they would never go. At last, on Saturday 9 June, Maria declared she would go there even if she had to sleep on the boards. So she was carried across in a chair, with the King and her Chamberlain, Lord Godolphin, walking beside her.

James spent the night with her but went over to his own rooms about seven o'clock on Sunday morning, 10 June. He had only begun to dress when he received an urgent message: the Queen was in labour. Half dressed, he sent out the summons to members of the Privy Council and hurried back to the Queen's Bedchamber.

The first person to go to the Queen was Mrs Margaret Dawson, who had been a member of James's household since his first marriage and had helped to deliver all his children, Mary and Anne included. She found the Queen sitting shivering on a stool. Since the pallet bed was not aired, she persuaded her to get back into the state bed, first sending for a warming pan to warm it. This pan, which Mrs Dawson later swore on oath was full of visible hot coals, became the occasion of the most famous of the stories invented to throw doubt on the origin of the child born about two hours later.

Lady (Anne) Sunderland was fetched from church; she was not merely a Protestant but annoyed Princess Anne by making a show of it, as she had complained to her sister Mary in the spring. Just as she arrived, the King came in; he went and sat on the bed, holding his wife in his arms and comforting her; he stayed there the whole time.

The curtains at the bottom of the bed were drawn but those at the side were left open. (Mrs Dawson's evidence: Burnet said the curtains were drawn all round, nobody could see anything and only papists were allowed near the bed.) The Queen Dowager arrived soon after nine. There were eighteen members of the Privy Council present, including Lord Godolphin and Lord Chancellor Jeffreys (both Anglicans) whom James called up to the bed when the birth seemed imminent.

Maria, overcome with embarrassment at having so many men watching her, asked James to shield her face from them with his head and long periwig, which he did, still holding her all the time. Just about ten she cried out, 'I die! Oh, you kill me!' and then with a few groans the baby was delivered. 'I don't hear the child cry,' she whispered. But then its voice was heard in the first wail.

Beforehand Maria had begged that no one should say what sex the child was, for fear she could not at that critical moment support either the excitement or the disappointment. But the King had arranged a signal with Lady Sunderland; she was to put her hand to her head if it was a boy. Although she did this, James could not resist whispering to the nurse, 'What is it?' To which she replied, 'What your Majesty desires.'

'You are witnesses that a child is born,' the King said to the Councillors and told them to follow the nurse into the next room to see what it was. But there was such a crowd (about forty persons) that Lord Feversham, Queen Catherine's Chamberlain, had to clear a way, calling out, 'Room for the Prince of Wales!' There was no doubt any more that a son was born to the King.

James turned back to embrace his wife and then went into the next room to see his son, who seemed a fine child and not premature although he had arrived a fortnight earlier than expected. (This had happened with Maria's last child Charlotte, in 1682.) James then knighted the Queen's physician on the spot and gave the midwife £500 'for her breakfast'. Even these natural rewards were to give cause for suspicion. Then he gave orders for almsgiving and feasting for the poor and for the guns of the Tower to be fired in salute to a male heir.

'About two a clock we heard the Toure ordnance discharge,' wrote Evelyn, 'and the bells ringing; for the birth of a Prince of Wales; this was very surprizing, it being universally given out, that her Majestie did not look till the next moneth.' It did not see to occur to the suspicious that if the King and Queen had really been trying to pass off a spurious baby, nothing could have prevented them from arranging its arrival at the time expected.

Lord Clarendon was at church when the birth occurred.

As soon as I had dined, I went to court, and found the king shaving: I kissed his hand and wished him joy. He said, the queen was so quick in labour and he had so much company, that he had not time to dress himself till now. He bid me go and see the Prince. I went into the room which had formerly been the duchess's private bedchamber: and there my Lady Powis (who was made governess) showed me the Prince: he was asleep in his cradle and was a very fine child to look upon.

Clarendon went straight on to the Tower to visit the bishops, 'with whom was a vast concourse of people going in and out'. On Tuesday he was there again and found Lord Halifax had advised them to get three peers to stand bail; there was no need to stay in the Tower, once the demonstration of the King's tyranny had been made. Quite a low bail was accepted by the court and the bishops were out by the end of the week, refusing to pay the customary dues at the Tower. If they had given bail before, they need never have gone there. They were certainly not imprisoned till their trial, which was fixed for 29 June. (In the nineteenth century R. S. Hawker of Morwenstowe wrote his rousing verses 'And shall Trelawney Die?' which many people imagine to have been a contemporary ballad; but death was never contemplated for Bishop Trelawney and twenty thousand Cornishmen were unlikely to have marched to London to set him free, in any case.)

Meanwhile, the first scare on the baby prince's health had occurred on his very first night – 'the king was called up,' Clarendon records. James, writing to William, said, 'She (the Queen) has been very well ever since but the child was somewhat ill, this last night, of the wind; but it is now, blessed be God, very well again, and like to have no returns of it, and is a very strong boy.'

He needed to be a very strong boy, for the physicians had decided that the Queen's other children had died from taking breast milk. The Prince of Wales must be brought up by hand, fed on water-gruel made of barley flour with sugar and powdered currants added. The Papal Nuncio (d'Adda) saw him being fed and said he took his food well. But the after effects were dire and all too many 'remedies' were prescribed; a foreign ambassador was horrified at the array of medicines and the strength of them. No wonder there were frequent alarms during those first weeks of life.

On the evening of Friday 15 June Princess Anne returned from Bath. She ought to have been a witness of the birth but she had insisted on going to Bath, though the King had asked her to stay and had only given in to her plea that the physicians said it was necessary for her health to go at once. Yet it was now to be said that James had sent her away on purpose.

Mary, of course, was anxious for news from her. On 18 June Anne wrote, 'My dear sister can't imagine the concern and vexation I have been in, that I should be so unfortunate as to be out of town when the queen was brought to bed, for I shall never now be satisfied whether the child be true or false.' After repeating the old theme of never being allowed to feel the Queen's belly, she added her suspicions of the change of scene from Windsor to St James's, 'which is much the properest place to act such a cheat in'. Then she had the face to say that 'the plainest thing in the world is her being brought to bed two days after she heard of my coming (i.e. being about to come) to town, and saying the child was come at full time. . . .' She concluded that 'where one believes it a thousand do not,' and added, 'I shall ever be of the number of unbelievers.'

This was quite enough for Burnet to get to work on, and from it he concocted the scenario of the dark room, curtained bed, nobody but papists present and St James's Palace being ideal for smuggling in newborn babies, being full of dark passages and backstairs, and harbouring a colony of Portuguese friars who would no doubt lend a hand, for the good of the Holy Catholic Church. Although the scurrilous literature then disseminated now seems merely comic, it played its part by seeming to confirm all the other propaganda about the King's being just another dissembling papist who would stop at nothing to prevent his Protestant daughters from succeeding him.

William, who had planned his intervention on the pretext of religion before the child was conceived, was not yet ready to move (chiefly because he was uncertain of Louis' intentions this summer) and so had to send congratulations on the birth. But he sent them by Zuylestein, who stayed on some time in England, collecting more letters of commitment from the political lords, and insisting that Henry Sidney should get as many of their signatures as possible to a definite invitation to the Prince of Orange to come over and save England from popery and arbitrary government.

On Friday 29 June 1688 Westminster Hall was packed for the trial of the Seven Bishops. There were never less than twenty-five peers present to demonstrate the powerful temporal backing the lords spiritual had in defending the Test Acts by declaring against the royal dispensing power. Fifty or more peers turned up the next day for the verdict. For the trial lasted all day, from nine till six, when the jury withdrew, and as they took all night to agree, it ended on 30 June.

The case against the bishops was that they had published a seditious libel in the county of Middlesex and the argument was whether the petition, written at Lambeth (in Surrey) had ever been published at all, or if it had, in Middlesex. To start with, the Crown lawyers had to prove that the petition was in fact handed to the King. Since he had been alone at the time and could not be called, there was no way of proving it.

Dickensian scenes followed: Lord Sunderland, pleading a severe attack of gout, was carried into court in a chair, and said that he had certainly introduced the bishops to the King's closet and that they had a paper with them, but as he himself had not read it, he could not say if it was the petition or not. He was now at the height of his unpopularity, for he had just declared himself a Catholic – at the very worst moment for the King's interest.

Mr Pepys did his best. He had been present at the Council on 8 June and said it was understood by everybody that the paper owned there was the petition.

It was not till they got to the 'seditious libel' bit that there was any opportunity for politically slanted speeches. The two chief counsel for the bishops were Henry Pollexfen (prosecutor of the Monmouth rebels) and Heneage Finch, younger brother of Daniel Finch, Earl of Nottingham. Both were to prosper under William III. 'Mr Pollexfen and Mr Finch took no small pains to inveigh against the King's dispensing power,' wrote Robert Price to the Duke of Beaufort, in his account of the trial (printed in Macpherson's *Original Papers*, 1775). It was argued that the bishops were acting as peers, and if the dispensing power was against the law, they could not be criminals by refusing to comply with it. They quoted 'judgments in parliament and in cases in law, where the dispensing power was denied'.

The four judges divided two and two. One of them said he 'took the law to be, the King had not a dispensing power; for if he had, most part of the statute books might be dispensed with, and there would be no need of parliament.' The Chief Justice Edward Herbert, who had advised James on his rights in 1685, 'doubted, as to the proof of publishing, but took the petition to be a libel.' (This seems a fair way out of a difficult situation.)

'The jury stayed till nine this morning,' Price told the Duke of Beaufort on 30 June, 'Arnold a Brewer till then dissenting, when they brought in the bishops, Not Guilty.' Lord Clarendon, present among the fifty peers, noted, 'upon which there was a most wonderful shout, that one would have thought the hall had cracked.' The bishops were almost mobbed by their triumphant supporters as they went out. That night there were bonfires and joyful pope-burnings under the very windows of Whitehall.

That Saturday 30 June, the King was out at Hounslow where his army was again encamped for exercises. He was dining with Lieutenant-General Lord Churchill in his tent when he heard a great shout outside among the soldiers. The Commander-in-chief, Lord Feversham, himself went out to see what was the matter and came back saying it was nothing, only the soldiers cheering the bishops' acquittal. 'Do you call that nothing, my lord?' said James bluntly.

In the memoirs James recorded that his disquiet was not so much at the verdict as at the people's reaction. In Westminster Hall, he had heard, some of the bishops as they went out had cried, 'Keep your religion!' as if, he thought, 'the King had tried to invade their privileges.' And he commented wryly, 'He owned he had deprived them of one privilege, which he found went nearer their heart than he imagined, he had wrested the sword of persecution out of their hands, and it seems they enjoyed no peace if others had it too.'

Not everyone agreed with the verdict against the King, however. Several other bishops had ordered the reading of the Declaration in their dioceses, notably Durham, Chester and Hereford. And quite a number of pamphlets, before and after the trial, addressed the religious issue, not all by dissenters. One Anglican wrote: 'Is there any of our non-tested magistrates, or our unpinioned dissenters in all this freedom, has wronged our church of so much as a sprig of mint or a corn of cumminseed . . . ? Is she denied law or justice for so much as the claim of a tythe egg?' In religion, the writer said, dispensing was pardoning.

Then, since dissenters did not hesitate to point out how the Church of England had persecuted them under the Conventicle Acts of King Charles's reign, Burnet himself wrote an apology for that church. People, he said, know that 'popery cannot change its nature, and that cruelty and breach of faith to hereticks are as necessary parts of their religion, as transubstantiation and the pope's supremacy are.' But, he asserted, there was no reason to infer from our church's past errors that we are incurable. He then laid the blame for the late persecution of dissenters on the court, and so on the popish party, ignoring the fact that it was not King Charles but Parliament which had legislated against dissenters.

Princess Anne was still passing on gossip to Mary; on 9 July: 'The Prince of Wales has been ill these three or four days, and if he has been as bad as some people say, I believe it will not be long before he is an Angel in heaven.' The fireworks to celebrate his birth had been put off because of his illness, but on his recovery they were held on 17 June.

Evelyn brought his wife to town for the spectacle. 'We stood at Mr Pepys's Secretary to the Admiralty to greate advantage for the sight, and indeede they were very fine, and had cost some thousands of pounds about the pyramids and statues etc but were spent too soon, for so long a preparation.' Alas, that always seems true of firework displays.

[201]

Lord Clarendon watched them from the Duchess of Richmond's lodging after a hectic week when his only son, Lord Cornbury, had eloped with the daughter of Lady Katherine O'Bryan, sister to the late Duke of Richmond, to the disapproval of all. However, after a week of worry everything was made up and the two families watched the fireworks together; the widowed Duchess of Richmond was none other than the beautiful Frances Stuart, whose portrait as Britannia used to adorn our pennies.

In July, the weather having turned fine and hot, the Prince of Wales was sent to Richmond for the air but he did no better there on his water-gruel and powdered currants and at last the King and Queen, by then at Windsor, were told he was dying. In an agony of anxiety they took coach at once but stopped at the river till a courier met them, unable to bear the prospect of finding their son dead. But on hearing he was still alive they hurried on and found him very weak, the doctors saying they could do no more for him.

Years later, in 1712, the widowed Queen was reminded of this crisis by a proposal to found a hospital in Paris to bring up children by hand. 'The state to which I saw my son reduced by this fine experiment,' she told the nuns at Chaillot, 'would deter me from ever allowing it to be tried on the children of others.' Describing their arrival at Richmond in 1688, she recorded her momentous decision to disobey the doctors and revert to the way of nature. 'I sent into the village in quest of a wet-nurse. I gave him that nurse; he took her milk; it revived him and she has happily reared him.' The woman was a tilemaker's wife, barelegged in her cloth petticoat, but healthy. After this Maria would not be parted from either child or nurse but took them both back with her to Windsor.

Princess Anne's equerry, Colonel Sands, told a tale of going to Richmond, catching a glimpse of a dying baby in the morning and then being shown a fine healthy one by the King in the afternoon. This was later worked up by Bishop Lloyd of St Asaph into a variation on the theme of substitution: every time the baby was ill, it died, and another was put in its place.

In July, while she was still at the Cockpit, Anne was laboriously answering a long questionnaire on the circumstances of the birth, sent by her sister Mary, with a view to eliciting information which might suggest a substitution. As Anne had to get all her facts from Mrs Dawson, the result was not very satisfactory; nevertheless, she concluded: 'All that she says seems very clear; but one does not know what to think; for methinks it is wonderful, if it is no cheat, that they never took no pains to convince me of it.' And Mary, it seems, believed her.

7 William's Invitation

On 30 June, the day of the Bishops' acquittal, Henry Sidney succeeded in getting six signatures in cipher to the long letter of invitation to William of Orange which he had composed, adding his own as the seventh. 'Immortal Seven!' exclaims the eighteenth-century Whig Dalrymple, 'whose memories Britain can never sufficiently revere.' Did he think William had waited for an invitation to consider an intervention in England? All he wanted was commitment from as many powerful men as possible.

The Seven were: Shrewsbury, Devonshire, Danby, Lumley, the Bishop of London (Compton), Edward Russell and Henry Sidney. Of these the only two of real power were Devonshire and Danby, the Whig and Tory leaders in the last reign, with great estates in the north. William knew it was essential to have Tories as well as Whigs on his side and Danby had always been his supporter. These two were to raise the north for the Prince of Orange as soon as he landed, so turning an invasion into a rebellion. Lumley was to assist in this rising; he and Shrewsbury were young Protestant converts from old Catholic families. Shrewsbury, who had great charm of manner (in spite of having lost one eye) raised a large sum for William's expenses and took it over in person.

Edward Russell was a cousin of the Lord Russell executed after the Rye House Plot; a naval man, he was not a peer. Nor was Sidney a peer, but his connexions with Sunderland and Halifax gave him considerable indirect power. Bishop Compton was the only lord spiritual to sign, though there were others in sympathy. Nottingham had backed out at the last minute and Halifax was not even asked because recently he had been advising caution and delay, because things were not so bad as had been feared.

The invitation, on the other hand, began by expressing great satisfaction that William was 'so ready and willing' to give his assistance in a situation which they believed was growing worse every day. They assured him that there were 'nineteen parts of twenty, of the people throughout the kingdom, who are desirous of change' because of dissatisfaction 'in relation to their religion, liberties and properties (all of which have been greatly invaded)'. They also reckoned that 'much the greatest part of the nobility and gentry are as much dissatisfied, although it be not safe to speak to many of them beforehand' and that 'some of the most considerable' would no doubt join the Prince at his landing. (That was what William most wanted to hear.)

The letter expresses fears that if the Prince waited another year it would be too late, as changes were expected from a 'packed parliament' or if that failed 'by more violent means' (French troops to force Rome upon the English with slaughter of all recalcitrant Protestants). William was also admonished for his 'compliment upon the birth of the child (which not one in a thousand here believes to be the Queen's)' because 'the false imposing of that upon the Princess and the nation' was 'certainly one of the chief causes upon which the declaration of your entering the kingdom in a hostile manner, must be founded on your part, although many other reasons are to be given on ours.' If Mary were no longer the legitimate heir, William's armed incursion could only appear as a hostile invasion by a Dutch foreigner.

Sidney wrote a covering letter in which he emphasized the need for secrecy, 'for it is most certain, that if it be made public above a fortnight before it be put in execution, all your particular friends will be clapped up, which will . . . ruin the whole design.' In fact, nobody was clapped up by the arbitrary James; very many, however, were to be sent to the Tower on suspicion, by William and Mary.

The letters were taken over to Holland by Arthur Herbert (the brother of the Lord Chief Justice) a one-eyed buccaneering admiral who had done some shady business with slaves to make money at government expense; he was also a notorious loose-liver, admonished as such by Burnet when he had gone over to the Orange side. When

Herbert, in a closet interview with the King, told him he could not in
conscience vote to take off the Test, James lost his temper and said that
talk of conscience came ill from one 'who had put away his wife to keep
with more liberty other weomen'. Herbert retorted that he was no
worse than others he knew; at which *tu quoque* James abruptly dismissed him and he went off in a rage to join the Prince of Orange.
Disguised as an ordinary sailor he took the invitation to William, who
made him admiral of the invasion fleet.

When Sidney himself left England in August he took a draft of the
Declaration that William was to make on landing. Burnet then revised
this, using material from what was to be the *public* 'invitation' (written
by him) which was entitled *A Memorial from the English Protestants to
their Highnesses the Prince and Princess of Orange*. It begged William to
'interpose' between the King and the people of England and see that a
true and free parliament was called. It is a very long document, setting
forth in detail the illegality of the dispensing power and the King's
proceedings, which are represented as intended to bring England
under the jurisdiction of the Pope and the Roman Canon Law; James is
accused of kneeling to the Papal Nuncio at Windsor as an act of
homage for the kingdom, which we know from Surgeon Yonge's
account to be totally untrue. The *Memorial* ignores the King's promises
in his Declaration to preserve the rights of the Established Church;
promises made by a papist cannot be trusted in any case – example,
quoted *ad nauseam*, Louis XIV. In the middle of all this is a long
disquisition on the supposed passing off of a procured infant as the
Prince of Wales.

The Declaration, or Manifesto, of the Prince of Orange was a
shorter and more trenchant version of this *Memorial*, cautiously laying
everything to the charge, not of James, but of his 'evil counsellors'.
William was not coming to dethrone James (as Mary expressed his
intention in her journal) but to drive out the evil counsellors and see
that a free parliament was called – and to inquire into the royal birth.
This way of putting things was designed to reassure Protestant
legitimists till the takeover was effected. The particular charges,
transferred back to James as soon as William was in power, were to
form the preamble and basis of the Bill of Rights, looked back on for
generations as the foundation of the modern British constitution.

So James's crimes, as made out by Burnet, became the preamble to an Act of Parliament. After that, historians accepted them as facts.

When Henry Sidney left England he also took a letter for the Prince of Orange from General Lord Churchill, written after the King had left the camp at Hounslow for Windsor.

Sir, Mr Sidney will let you know how I intend to behave myself: I think it is what I owe to God and my country. My honour I take leave to put in your Royal Highness's hands, in which I think it safe. If you think there is anything else I ought to do, you have but to command me, and I shall pay an entire obedience to it, being resolved to die in that religion that it has pleased God to give you both the will and the power to protect. I am, with all respect, Sir, your Royal Highness's obedient servant, Churchill.

'Royal' was flattery; William's title was not royal. But Churchill's commitment was crucial, for he was to organize the defection of royal troops so as to prevent a battle, since if William appeared as a conqueror it would turn the English against him. In order to effect the desertion Churchill had formed a junta of disaffected officers into a secret association, sworn to assist the Prince of Orange.

One of the grievances against James (promulgated from Holland) was that he was building up a Catholic army to intimidate the Protestant citizens of London. Some colour was lent to this charge by the fact that Irish troops had recently come over and some were ordered to be received into English regiments. Six officers refused to take them and were court-martialled and cashiered. James recorded that Churchill demanded the death penalty but the King refused to impose more than the normal sentence of cashiering. Not quite so much publicity attended the persecution of the Six Officers as had glorified the Seven Bishops, but within the army it created quite a stir.

The camp at Hounslow continued into August after the King had left and the Earl of Dumbarton, a lieutenant-general, required lists of all the Roman Catholic officers and men in the regiments. In the Duke of St Albans' regiment the count was taken by Major Ambrose Norton (not a Catholic himself). His account of his experiences in the extraordinary campaign of 1688 was eventually printed in Macpherson's *Original Papers* (1775). 'The number of Roman Catholics was then very inconsiderable in our regiment,' he recorded, 'being but one lieutenant, a quarter-master and thirteen troopers.' This was not untypical. Ailesbury reckons that the King had not above eighty Catholic officers and the computations of others suggest that, even with the Irish and the Scots, there were not above 4000 men in an army totalling about 40,000. William brought over at least 4000 Catholics in his invading army, since he had no objection to employing them in miliary service; it was only James who was not supposed to do this.

Ambrose Norton continues:

This order proved of fatal consequence, and was a very great furtherance of the business of our associating officers who, daily and openly in the camp, aggravated it, with all the rancour and malice imaginable; affirming, with vollies of oaths, that it was (done) in order to turn out all the protestant officers and soldiers in the army and to have none but Roman Catholics in military employments.

Major Norton further set down what his own commanding officer, Colonel Thomas Langton, had said (also with 'vollies of oaths') under four heads: first, this purge of Protestants in the army and that the King had 'entered into a close league with France to have all protestants' throats cut in England and Scotland'. Secondly he told of a plot (authorized by King James) to murder the Prince of Orange with a poisoned waistcoat, made by his papist tailor, which was revealed by the tailor's boy 'the very morning the Prince was to have worn it'. Thirdly, the Prince had in custody 'the true mother of the Prince of Wales'. Fourthly, that King James was going to 'set up a mass in every church in England and Scotland, and he that was not a thorough papist would be hanged, quartered or burnt.' Norton added that Langton introduced some of his officers into 'the Treason-club, as it was commonly called, at the Rose Tavern in Covent Garden', where they met other named conspirators.

The principal person concerned knew nothing of all these plottings at home and abroad; his secret service was almost non-existent in comparison with William's efficient intelligence system, and his Irish ambassador at the Hague, d'Albeville, managed to be on holiday in August. Warnings did come from the French Ambassador in Holland, Comte d'Avaux, sent via Barillon, and in August King Louis sent a special envoy, M de Bonrepos, to tell James that William's preparations were intended against him and to negotiate an agreement about naval aid. A draft was actually got out but never completed because James was infuriated at the news that Comte d'Avaux had presented two memorials to the United Provinces, one designed to prevent Dutch intervention in the current German quarrels and the other announcing that any attack on the King of England would be regarded by the King of France as an act hostile to himself. This suggested just such a secret alliance as was widely rumoured but which James had taken care to avoid, and in his anger he thought the French warnings were simply a ploy to get him into alliance with France.

In the memoirs there is a passage, written later, which expresses James's view with the utmost clarity.

> Nothing rais'd the King more enemies, than this spiteful and groundless report of a League with France ... The King was too good a Christian to invade a Prince (William) he had no quarrel with, and too much an English man to engage with France against his subjects' inclinations; his intentions were to engrosse the trade of the world, while forreign states destroyed each other; but the want of wit as well as loyalty in his subjects, would not suffer them to be so happy; fear of slavery amongst the gentry and Popery amongst the Clergie, were so artificially spread, as bewitched the people, and the people were punished sufficiently for their folly and rebellion. The Dutch indeed gain'd their point, and drew in the English rather to dethrone their King, than not to have their share in an expensive and bloody war, where nothing was to be got for themselves.

After the 1688 Revolution this was belatedly realized by a large number of people in England and was the cause of the continuing strength of Jacobite sympathy all through the nineties, during King William's War.

James immediately repudiated the d'Avaux memorial and recalled Sir Bevil Skelton (who had contributed to it) from Paris in disgrace; he was sent to the Tower. All in vain; people still believed that the King was secretly in league with the French, who would come to cut all Protestant throats or, according to the circulating pamphlets, to use on them all sorts of ingenious instruments of torture (illustrated) such as the Protestant bridle, a fearsome spiked muzzle.

James did not believe the warnings against William because they all came from France, Orange's mortal enemy. The Dutch Ambassador again insisted that the Prince's military preparations were aimed against French aggression, and this was credible because Louis was massing his armies for a strike eastward, though not this time at Holland. Moreover, Sunderland always laughed off any idea of an invasion from Holland; he even fooled Barillon that this was his genuine opinion. But he had fooled Barillon all along, to the extent of extracting from him a regular pension, which James knew nothing about till Louis told him, at St Germains.

Although James did not believe William would invade him, he realized that the Prince was feeling less than friendly when he heard that prayers for the Prince of Wales had been discontinued in Mary's chapel. To his protest, Mary replied that they had 'only bin forgot'. The Queen, not appeased, wrote to her on 17 August that 'by the way you speak of my son, and the formal name you call him by . . . you have for him the last indifference.' Mary endorsed this: 'Answered, "that all the king's children shall ever find as much affection and kindness from me as can be expected from the children of the same father."' This left open the question as to whether the baby was really the child of her father.

Burnet's theory that the baby business was plotted during the summer of 1687 and linked with James's reactions to Fagel's letter setting out the determination of their Highnesses never to agree to the repeal of the Test Acts, was plausible, if James's character was discounted, which Burnet had no hesitation in doing. By 3 October (new style) Burnet was writing up his memoirs to date and put down all his enthusiasm for the project of revolution: 'the design is as just as it is great.' The Prince was 'led now to a nobler undertaking, in which if God bless him with success, and if he manages the English nation as dextrously as he hath hitherto done the Dutch, he will be the arbiter of all Europe and will very quickly bring Lewis the Great to a much humbler posture and will acquire a much juster right to the title of Great than the other has ever yet done. But I must remember that I am an historian and not a prophet.'

Burnet was lucky in that, as an historian, he was later able to omit prophecies so wide of the mark, while using his own anonymous pamphlets as evidence for facts not otherwise susceptible of proof.

At Windsor the King had seen Pepys about the naval defences; this was as far as he went in heeding the French warnings. But he was much more interested in his toleration campaign; on 24 August he gave orders for writs to be prepared, which would be issued in September, for a Parliament to be called in November. In spite of setbacks in the canvassing of electors for members who would repeal the religious penal laws, he was hopeful; there was a probable majority forecast.

James wrote to William on 17 September (27 new style) unaware that the Prince of Orange had already applied to the States General for permission to undertake his expedition to England; as Stadholder he was able to use Dutch troops without involving the United Provinces in war with Britain. But he had also secured troops from his German allies (well paid for); Bentinck had been sent in May on this errand, and to explain to the princes that he intended to force England into the League against King Louis. This was also the reason given to the Emperor and Catholic allies, and even the Pope was not averse to it; Louis XIV was a considerable nuisance to the papacy, seeming always on the point of doing a Henry VIII act and breaking off the Gallican Church from Roman control, besides starting aggressive wars in Europe when he ought to have been assisting the Emperor to fight off the Turks.

James in his letter commented on the European situation; he was very glad to hear of the taking of Belgrade, 'which, with the taking of Gradiska, will secure the Emperor's conquests in those parts. I am sorry there is so much likelihood of war upon the Reyn; nobody wishing more the peace of Christendom than myself.'

He told William he was going to London next day and then to Chatham; this he did, and the writs were issued on 19 September. The next day he was back at Whitehall, when the Queen arrived from Windsor with the three-month-old Prince of Wales. Then, late on

Sunday 23 September (3 October new style) James received an express messenger from d'Albeville which told him that the Prince of Orange was embarking his troops for an invasion of England.

8 Invasion

Next morning Clarendon, going to the King's levee, met him as he went from his Bedchamber to the Queen's. 'He told me, the Dutch were now coming to invade England in good earnest. I presumed to ask, if he really believed it? To which the king replied with warmth, do I see you, my lord?'

Now that he was convinced, James plunged at once into measures of defence. On the Friday (28 September) he issued a Proclamation on the invasion, insisting that although 'some false pretences relating to liberty, property and religion' might be given out, it was manifestly an attempt at 'absolute conquest' promoted, almost incredibly, 'by some of our own subjects being persons of wicked and restless spirits, implacable malice and desperate designs' (the exiles) who, disregarding the memory of 'former intestine distractions' (civil war) were endeavouring again 'to embroil this kingdom in blood and ruin'. He then emphasized that 'we have always declined any foreign succours, but rather have chosen (next under God) to rely upon the true and ancient courage, faith and allegiance of our own people, with whom we have often ventured our life for the honour of this nation and in whose defence against our enemies we are firmly resolved to live and die.' The Proclamation adjures people to forget their differences and unite against the invader. The King then regretfully recalled the writs he had just issued for a Parliament which he had hoped would 'quiet the minds of all our people in matters of religion.' It ended with a call to defend the country, and a prohibition, on pain of high treason, from holding any correspondence with the enemy or their accomplices.

When this Proclamation was composed, James had not yet seen William's manifesto but had some idea of the pretexts for the invasion, which he believed was instigated by the Rye House exiles, joined by

Shrewsbury, Sidney and a few others. He still had no suspicions of conspirators at home, nor did he believe Mary had any knowledge of William's intentions.

The same day (28 September) he wrote to Mary, in answer to hers telling him the Prince had just summoned her to the Hague,

> I suppose it is to inform you of his design in coming to England, which he has been so long a-contriving. I hope it will be as great a surprise to you as it was to me, when I first heard it, being sure it is not in your nature to approve so unjust an undertaking. I have been all this day so busy, to endeavour to be in some condition to defend myself from so unjust and unexpected an attempt, that I am almost tired, and so I shall say no more but that I shall always have as much kindness for you as you will give me leave to have.

Maria also wrote to say that she would never believe that Mary would come over with William, 'for I know you to be too good. I do not believe you could have such thoughts against the worst of fathers, much less to perform it against the best, who has always been so kind to you, and I do believe has loved you better than any of his children.'

On 2 October (old style) James wrote again:

> I was this morning abroad to take the air and to see some batteries I have made below Woolwich for the defence of the river. And since I came back, I have been so very busy to prepare things for the invasion intended, that I could not write till now, though tis near midnight, so that you might not wonder if my letter be short. For news, you will have it from others, for really I am very weary; so shall end, with assuring you of my continuing as kind to you as you can desire.

His last letter, on 9 October, commenting on the lack of one from her, said, 'I easily believe you may be embarrassed how to write to me now that the unjust design of the Prince of Orange invading me is so public. And though I know you are a good wife, and ought to be so, yet for the same reason I must believe you will be still as good a daughter to a father that has always loved you so tenderly and has never done the least thing to make you doubt it. . . . You shall still find me kind to you, if you desire it.' But Mary never replied.

[212]

After he got back from Woolwich on 2 October the King had a working dinner with his general officers in Chiffinch's lodgings and in the evening Lord Chancellor Jeffreys brought some of the 'old honest aldermen' to see him, on his promise to restore the Charter of the City of London. This pet plan of the Tory Jeffreys had been put into operation when Parliament was decided on, before James was convinced of the impending invasion. So were some efforts he had made towards settling Church of England grievances, which were now stepped up.

Coached by Clarendon, the bishops presented a list of ten requests on issues political as well as religious. The first demanded that government posts should go to the legally qualified (i.e. Test takers only) and another asked the King not to grant individual dispensations, and he was required to waive the dispensing power till it was settled in Parliament. But he was also asked to inhibit the four Romish Vicars General and recall the licences to Romish schools – the Jesuits had started one in London which was a great success and led, indirectly, to the foundation of new Protestant schools. He was also requested to dissolve the Ecclesiastical Commission and to fill up the vacant Anglican bishoprics, especially York, where James was suspected of planning to place Cardinal Norfolk, a Howard, resident in Rome. Finally they wanted to lay before the King reasons for his return to their communion.

It was no wonder James 'seemed displeased' but he swallowed his irritation, told them he had already decided to dissolve the Commission (Clarendon had noted this on 5 October) and to send the Bishop of Winchester to restore the Fellows of Magdalen College. He also asked the bishops to prepare prayers for the emergency.

On 14 October James was fifty-five. 'The King's Birth-day, no Gunns from the Tower, as usualy,' wrote Evelyn. 'The Sunn eclips'd at its rising: this day signal for the Victory of William the Conqueror against Harold neere Battel in Sussex: the wind (which had hitherto ben West) all this day East, wonderful expectation of the Dutch fleete.' Evelyn's modern editor points out that it could not have been a true eclipse. But the wind had certainly changed.

Now, with the invasion imminent, James decided he must do something to combat the lies about his son's birth. The baby, who had been baptized soon after his birth, was given his names (James Francis Edward) at a ceremony in the King's chapel at St James's, when Queen Catherine stood godmother and the Nuncio godfather, as proxy for the Pope. The King, on the Sunday following, called an extraordinary Council for Monday 21 October; all the peers in town were summoned, the judges, the bishops, the Mayor and Corporation of the City of London.

Although they did not know what it was for, Clarendon and Lord Nottingham decided to make a protest, so they went to the King's levee and when he had taken them into his closet, they begged to attend as ordinary peers and not as Councillors. When the King asked their reason, they told him they would no longer sit at Council with Father Petre the Jesuit. 'The King said we should see Father Petre no more at Council.' But when they complained of others 'unqualified' (probably Catholic peers) 'the king seemed a little angry and bid us go as we would, and so he went away.' So in the Council chamber they sat among the lords and not at the Board, as did the Archbishop of Canterbury.

The King introduced the proceedings himself and then evidence was given on oath by over forty witnesses who had been present at the birth of his son, beginning with Queen Catherine. In his final speech James said, 'There is none of you but will easily believe me, who have suffered so much for conscience sake, incapable of so great a villany to the prejudice of my own children; and I thank God those that know me, know very well that it is my principle to doe as I would be done by, for that is the Law and the Prophets. . . .' He was indeed always quoting this Golden Rule. The proceedings were printed.

By now James had at last begun to suspect Sunderland of being in correspondence with William of Orange and on 25 October dismissed him from office. But as he made no further move against him Sunderland was able to say that it was only because the King thought it best to take all Catholics out of office. He hung about till almost the end, but then was persuaded to flee abroad; he went to Holland, with his wife, so as to be under William's protection.

The Orange fleet had set out on 19/29 October by the east wind, but had been driven back by a sudden westerly gale, with some ships disabled and many horses lost. James had had a big weather-vane put up on the roof of the Banqueting House and astonished Barillon by joking that the wind had turned popish. Barillon was equally surprised by James's saying that he had caused the Blessed Sacrament to be carried in procession in the Royal Chapel; the French diplomat understood neither the deep faith nor the humour of the English King.

But on 28 October (old style) the wind shifted to the east again, and now it was a Protestant wind. On 31 October an agent of William's, (once an officer in an overseas English regiment), was captured with copies on him of the Orange Manifest, or Declaration, and sent to Newgate prison. Fifty thousand copies had been printed, intended for distribution on the Prince's landing. The setback of the storm had led to this premature discovery.

The Manifest gave Burnet's charges against James (or his 'evil counsellors') and declared William's expedition was 'intended for no other design but to have a free and lawful Parliament assembled as soon as possible.' But the whole document was written in the royal plural and concluded by adjuring all persons 'to come and assist us . . . that so we may prevent all those miseries which must needs follow upon the nation's being kept under arbitrary government and slavery, and that all violence and disorder which may have overturned the whole Constitution of the English government, may be fully redressed in a free and legal parliament.'

Although James naturally resented this assumption of royal authority over his subjects by a foreign prince, he was particularly struck by one sentence on William's enterprise – 'to the doing of which we are most earnestly solicited by a great many lords, both spiritual and temporal, and by many gentlemen and other subjects of all ranks.' This was the first intimation James had that William had backers in England other than the young lords who had joined him abroad. Typically, he immediately began asking any temporal or spiritual lords he could get hold of, if they had solicited William's intervention.

The first bishop he summoned was Compton, whose suspension he had just lifted. Compton came on 1 November, All Saints' Day. (On 6 November he put an account in writing, which remained in Archbishop Sancroft's papers.) The King read him the offending paragraph. 'Upon which I told him, I was confident, the rest of the bishops would as readily answer in the negative as myself,' said Compton, who had put his cipher to the invitation in June. 'And his Majesty was pleased to say he did believe us all innocent.'

James naturally expected a bishop to tell the truth. What he wanted more than private denials was a public 'abhorrence' of the Prince's intended invasion. The bishops were asked to provide this.

Next day it was Clarendon's turn to be asked the question point-blank. The King, he recorded, was satisfied with his denial 'and said he did not believe any of the nobility had invited the Prince over but those who were with him in Holland.'

Meanwhile, that very night (3 November) at eleven o'clock, the King and his Secretary of the Admiralty heard that the Dutch fleet had been sighted in the Dover Straits. Pepys went back to his office in York Buildings to send midnight messages to Lord Dartmouth (Legge) who was now Admiral in place of Sir Roger Strickland, a Catholic. The King sat on in Council, preparing to send his army towards Portsmouth.

William had at last managed to set forth on 1/11 November, and when his fleet was sighted in the Channel it seemed vast, the Dutch warships convoying the transports, with the Prince of Orange's vessel, the *Briel*, bringing up the rear, his mission emblazoned in huge letters on his sails: THE PROTESTANT RELIGION AND THE LIBERTIES OF ENGLAND. Underneath was his family motto: JE MAINTIENDRAI – 'I will maintain'. The great fleet spread so wide that it could be seen from both sides of the Channel and people on shore could hear the drums beat. That, of course, was the intention: the show of force was to encourage the English rebels and intimidate the King.

James reacted with his usual military speed.

Assoon as the King had noticed from Dover that the Enemy's fleet had passed by there, he ordered three battalions of the Guards, his own regiment of dragoons and a hundred Grenadiers on horseback to march with all expedition to Portsmouth for the further security of that place, with directions to go on towards Salisbury, if the Enemie went more Westward, which way all the rest of the Army march'd likewise, except three battalions of the Guards and Prince George's regiment of foot.

As usual James recorded all military affairs in detail.

Lord Clarendon recorded that his son, Lord Cornbury, received his orders at 3 a.m. on Sunday 4 November, to march for Portsmouth. Not long before, Clarendon had watched with pride the King review his son's regiment at Hounslow.

Now, however, Clarendon was once again involved with the bishops. Although he had not invited the Prince of Orange he did not want the bishops to put out an Abhorrence of his coming. Princess Anne lent him a copy of the Orange Declaration; it was the only copy James had left, for in a moment of irritation he had thrown the others in the fire. The Archbishop had written just such a disclaimer as James had required but he was soon dissuaded from issuing it.

The bishops had their last interview with the King on Tuesday 6 November. (Another dialogue account survived in Sancroft's papers.) When the King asked for their paper – of abhorrence – they replied they did not think it necessary: 'Since your Majesty is pleased to say you think us guiltless, we despise what all the world besides shall say.'

The King pointed out that what was necessary was something that 'should satisfy others as well as me'. Whereupon they suggested that the Declaration could not be genuine, for if the clause was true, it was unwise to disclose it prematurely, 'if false, one would not imagine a great prince would publish a manifest untruth and make it the ground of his enterprise.' No wonder the King retorted, 'What! he that can do as he does, think you he will stick at a lie?'

The bishops then declared it was a matter of state and not their business and suggested that the King should himself publish what they had said. 'No, if I should publish it, the people would not believe me,' said the King. To their shocked remonstrance that the word of a king was sacred he replied, 'They that could believe me guilty of a false son, what will they not believe of me?'

After some more wriggling the bishops told the King that the chief place to serve him was parliament, which provoked James to retort, 'My lords, this is a business of more time.' And he concluded, 'If you will not assist me as I desire, I must stand on my own legs and trust to myself and my own arms.' He had lost the last round in the battle with the bishops and he knew it. In the memoirs he records: 'The King thought when honour, Conscience and Religion were in everybody's mouth, it

[217]

should have been in some people's hearts too, which made him credit what they said, but a few days more convinced him of his errour, and that the Divines themselves were not exempt from that duplicity.'

At four that afternoon James was sitting to Sir Godfrey Kneller for a portrait commissioned by the faithful Pepys for his private collection. An express messenger arrived to inform the King that yesterday, 5 November, the Prince of Orange had landed at Torbay, unopposed. But when the painter suggested that the sitting should be ended at once, the King refused. 'I have promised my portrait to Mr Pepys,' he said, 'and he shall have it.'

9 Betrayal

Now that the King knew where the invader had landed he was able to deploy his forces; uncertain earlier, he had sent a regiment to Ipswich in case of a landing on the east coast. The total number of the royal army seems to have been about 40,000 but out of these must be counted the garrisons of the ports, so that the field army was probably not much larger than the force William had brought (about 27,000) and certainly not so experienced, for William had engaged German and Swedish mercenaries and had brought over the English and Scotch overseas regiments as well as his own Dutch Guards. Nevertheless, after the exercises at Hounslow every summer the English royal army was in much better shape than at any time since Cromwell.

At Whitehall the King held Cabinet Councils every evening, sometimes lasting far into the night. Pepys was present, transmitting orders and reports on the navy; it was a great disappointment that Dartmouth, with wind and tide against him, had been unable to get out from the Gunfleet to oppose the invasion fleet. He was now ordered to pursue and harass the enemy's ships and disrupt communications.

Pepys's opposite number for the army was Mr Blathwayt; unlike Pepys he seems to have been an undercover supporter of William's and delayed orders sent by the King to his son the Duke of Berwick, now Governor of Portsmouth, whom he wanted at Salisbury till Lord

Feversham could take command there. For Salisbury was fixed as the rallying point for the field army; three regiments were sent ahead under Lord Cornbury. Pepys, from his office, heard the artillery rattling along the Strand as they left on Saturday 10 November, under their commander, his friend Sir Henry Shere.

Meanwhile, the Prince marched to Exeter which, being unfortified, was forced to submit, reluctantly; there he issued his Declaration (new edition) and waited for the oppressed Englishmen to come in. When none did, he was heard to say, angrily, that he would go back to Holland.

James had decided to set out for Salisbury himself on Thursday 15 November. The day began well. Clarendon, who was at his levee, reported that Lord Lovelace, the first to attempt to join the Prince of Orange, had been arrested by a Militia troop at Cirencester. Next, Bishop Lamplugh of Exeter arrived to kiss the King's hand, having left his city as the Prince approached it. 'The King received him very graciously,' recorded Clarendon, 'and told him he would make him Archbishop of York,' thus rewarding a loyal bishop with the vacant see which Anglicans feared he would fill with a Romish prelate. He could do this because he had (at their request) dissolved the Ecclesiastical Commission.

But at noon the whole situation disastrously changed. From Salisbury came a messenger with news that Lord Cornbury with three regiments had deserted to the Prince of Orange.

'The express arrived just as his majesty was going to dinner,' James's memoirs record. 'His concern was too great to think of any thing but how to remedy the comfortless situation of his affairs, so calling for a piece of bread and a glass of wine, went immediately to consult what measures was fittest to be taken.'

Lord Clarendon was dining (as usual) at Lambeth when he heard the news; it was soon confirmed by his brother Lord Rochester. 'O god that my son should be a rebel!' he wrote, evidently not forewarned of this active participation in the revolution. He got permission from Lord Middleton to see the King the next afternoon, at Chiffinch's lodgings, where he fell on his knees. 'The king was very gracious to me, and said, he pitied me with all his heart and that he would still be kind to my family.'

That same day the King called together his general officers and colonels and made them a most unusual appeal.

If any amongst them were not free and willing to serve him, he gave them leave to surrender their commissions and to go wherever they pleased, but that he looked upon them as men of too much honour to follow Lord Cornbury's example and was therefore willing to spare them (if they desir'd it) the discredit of so base a desertion. They all seem'd to be moved at this discourse and vow'd they would serve him to the last drop of their blood, the Duke of Grafton and my Lord Churchill were the first that made this attestation and the first who (to their eternal infamy) broke it afterwards, as well as Kirk, Trelawney etc who were no less lavish of their promises on this occasion, though as false and treacherous as the rest, in the end.

(This Trelawney was the Bishop's brother; both went over to William.)

On Saturday 17 November, only two days later than he had intended, the King was ready to leave London. Before he did so, he made his will, which was witnessed by members of his Cabinet Council, including Pepys and Blathwayt. In the event of his death, his kingdoms went to his son, who was left in the care and regency of his mother – 'our dearest consort' – until he came of age, but she was to be assisted by the existing Privy Council, all named. This will was the only one James ever made, as it was discovered, rather to everyone's surprise, after his death thirteen years later. Probably he let it stand because it was made while he was still *de facto* as well as *de jure* King of England, even though it contained the names of many who proved unfaithful.

The same day the bishops presented a petition on which Clarendon and Rochester had been working hard, trying to get the temporal lords in town to join in asking for a Parliament; very few did. Clarendon signed but felt he could not go to court, in view of his son's desertion. He recorded that the King 'gave a very short answer to them, to this effect, that he would call a parliament as soon as it was convenient but it could not be while the invasion and rebellion lasted.'

For Cornbury's desertion had revealed to James the beginning of a rebellion: William evidently did have supporters within the country. It also made the future look so uncertain that the King decided to send the Prince of Wales to Portsmouth at once, so that if necessary he could be taken across to France for safety. Maria refused to go with her son; she would stay with her husband whatever happened. So she remained in Whitehall when the King set out that evening. He spent the night at Windsor and Pepys, who accompanied him so far, with anxious foresight wrote a statement of what was owed him, which the King signed twice, above and below. The signature was unusually shaky. He was extremely tired.

Cornbury's desertion was described by Major Ambrose Norton (printed in Macpherson's *Original Papers*, 1775) and it makes very vivid reading. Cornbury and Colonel Langton pretended they had orders to march forward and so they did almost non-stop for two days and a night. When they were near Axminster the men were told they were to 'beat up the enemy's quarters' – for William (though still in Exeter himself) had sent an advance guard to Honiton. Norton's regiment was marched into Honiton at midnight on 12 November, 'where, instead of beating them up, we were received as friends.' They had been expected for some time. Norton and some others refused to serve the Prince and were made close prisoners. They were eventually allowed to leave, but not before they had been 'plundered of all they had' by the traitor officers, who went off reviling the King and vaunting themselves as 'the first that broke the ice'.

While Norton was a prisoner, his guards were men of 'Talmash's regiment' (Tollemache) who swore they disliked being brought to fight against their own king, drank his health on their knees and said that if he would pardon them, they would gladly go over to him. This suggests very different feelings from those assisuously propagated at the time (and later) of a keenly Protestant army coming over to save England from slavery and popery, to the tune of Lillibulero. James, after Norton's report, did put out a pardon for any who came to him, but events moved so rapidly that it was unlikely the Scots ever heard of it.

When Norton's party reached Salisbury the King received them 'most extraordinary kindly', giving the officers 200 days' pay to equip themselves and £5 to each trooper, all the money received there and then. Moreover, Norton was to be made lieutenant-colonel of the reconstituted regiment, though in the event this could not be effected. Norton attended the King personally until his departure from Rochester.

James had arrived at Salisbury on Monday 19 November and stayed in the Bishop's palace – the Bishop was lying ill in London. Before Norton's return he had already heard that not all of the three regiments had deserted. Berwick had gone after the defectors and at Warminster at midnight was awakened by shouts, hastily rode out and 'rallied the fugitives' as he wrote in his memoirs, and brought them back to Salisbury. His and other estimates of the numbers involved differ but more seem to have returned to James than stayed with William. But they were hardly fit for service; most had lost their equipment and the horses which had come back were in such bad condition they could not be used for a fortnight. Worst of all, confidence had been broken; the officers suspected each other and the men their officers.

This was a crucial week for James. In fine frosty weather, just before he left London, Lord Dartmouth at last managed to sail from the Downs with the intention of attacking William's ships in Torbay. But on Sunday night, while the King was still on his way to Salisbury, the weather broke and a southwest gale began to blow, which raged for three or four days, with heavy rain, scattering the fleet and reducing the west country roads to mire. When James arrived in Salisbury, on Monday 19 November, he called a council of his chief officers the same evening, heard about the present state of the army and resolved to visit the advance posts at Warminster himself, the next day. But quite suddenly his nose began to bleed.

This was not a minor inconvenience but a severe haemorrhage. Berwick records that his nose bled 'prodigiously' and could not be stopped till a vein was 'breathed' in his arm. He had never had it before and had always led a physically active life. But in recent weeks he had been working all hours under considerable strain; he was the same age as his brother had been when he had fallen victim to a stroke and it seems likely the nose-bleeding acted as a safety valve.

James did not regard it at first as more than a nuisance and rose next morning with the intention of carrying out his inspection of the forward posts, but the bleeding came on again worse than ever and he was forced to retire to his room. This was on Tuesday 20 November, the gale and rain still continuing. Every time he tried to do anything, the bleeding would start again, though less violently, and it did not completely stop for three days. As doctors then had only one remedy for every illness – to let blood – the King was bled four times that week. He must have lost quantities of blood and it left him weak and dazed.

All this time the westerly gale raged, which he knew must be wreaking havoc with Dartmouth's ships, and now news began to come of west country gentlemen going to join the Prince of Orange, one of the first being Sir Edward Seymour, hitherto a Tory royalist. He shared the attitude of Sir John Reresby and other Tories, alienated by the Three Questions and the new deputy-lieutenants (nobody one *knew*, some even *dissenters*) and persuaded that the Prince of Orange was coming merely to settle the government back in its old ways. Disillusioned later, some became Jacobite sympathizers; Reresby, however, died just as he began to realize what was really happening. The Seymours settled into the new régime.

To James, such defections were wounding and inexplicable. Worse rumours of risings in the north began to be heard, and the dreaded spectre of another civil war loomed in menace. Lord Danby (Tory) had taken York, Lord Devonshire (Whig) was collecting troops at Nottingham. On Friday 23 November, at the end of his week of bloodletting, James held a council of war in his bedchamber at the Bishop's palace. Churchill was for marching west to meet the enemy (presumably to make his planned desertion even more effective) while Feversham was for withdrawing to the line of the Thames, to defend London. If there was a rising in the north as well as a foreign enemy in the west, it was essential to hold London. James had always believed that it was his father's inability to hold London (because he had no army there) which made it possible for Parliament to oppose him in arms and eventually win the war and destroy the monarchy. James decided to withdraw towards London.

He was influenced not only by fears of a new civil war but by the uncertainty created by Cornbury's desertion as to how far he could rely on his army, especially on his officers. Berwick and Feversham had begged him to arrest Churchill, but as they had no proof of his treachery, James refused; he could not believe that Churchill, whose career he had made and who had just sworn loyalty again, could be so base.

[223]

But in the morning he learned that during the night General Lord Churchill had deserted to the Prince of Orange, with the Duke of Grafton and such of their junior officers and soldiers as they had persuaded to go with them.

Prince George of Denmark was with his father-in-law when this news came; James, who found him as dull as did Charles, nevertheless always took him along on military affairs. It was a joke at court that his only reaction to everything during these hectic weeks was to say, '*Est-il possible?*' He said it now, probably with real feeling, for it had been planned that he should go with Churchill. Anne had written to William on 18 November with good wishes for his success, to tell him that George would join him when his friends thought proper, adding that she was not yet certain whether she 'would continue here or remove into the city' and signed herself 'Your humble servant, Anne'. Why Churchill left George behind is not known. Perhaps, like so many other people, he just could not be bothered with him.

The King reached Andover on Saturday 24 November and that evening Prince George supped with him. But during the night he made off, with the young Duke of Ormonde (grandson of the old cavalier Duke, and recently made a Knight of the Garter along with Berwick) Lord Drumlarig, Sir George Hewitt and some others, but with very few ordinary soldiers.

'*Est-il-possible?*' was James's joking reaction, and he remarked that he would have felt the loss of one good trooper more, if it were not for the distress it would cause his daughter; it never occurred to him that Anne knew all about it. George had fled so precipitately that he had left his coach and equipment behind; James thoughtfully sent it after him. This was the accepted honourable behaviour to enemies in the days of his military service on the continent. He was not to receive it himself.

The desertions had been all concerted beforehand, as Ailesbury discovered when he got home to his wife, who was half-sister to the Duchess of Ormonde. Now he knew why his wife, although pregnant, had not been anxious when he left with the King; the young Duchess had told her there would be no battle. Since Lord Cornbury was attached to Prince George's household (though he found his service so boring that he got out of it as often as he could) he must have acted with Churchill's knowledge in taking off the three regiments while

[224]

Churchill himself stayed with the King, intending to complete his confusion by carrying him off prisoner to the Prince of Orange when he went to inspect the advance posts at Warminster. Kirk, also in the conspiracy, was commanding officer there.

This plan, since it was prevented by the King's unexpected nose-bleeding, was easy to deny both then and since, but there is a good deal of evidence for it. James himself referred to it on his return to London and his son the Duke of Berwick was convinced of it. But the evidence for the plot was collected by Macpherson from the memoranda of Carte, who was at work in the time of James's son. One concerned the accounts given by Dr Sheridan (a deprived Church of England bishop) to his friend Mr Malet of Combe Florey in 1709 and 1711, sent to Carte by Malet's nephew in 1745, and relating the deathbed confession of Sir George Hewitt (made Lord Hewitt by William) who died at Chester of a sickness contracted at Dundalk camp in Ireland in 1689. Hewitt, remorseful about his treachery to King James, described a November meeting in London with Churchill, Compton, Kirk and others, when the kidnap was planned. The later note added details from which it was clear that in the event of anything going wrong, James was to be killed.

Carte's other account came from Major Ambrose Norton, who had remained in England after James had fled. At William's coronation Hewitt boasted to Norton that he and Captain Cornelius Wood were in the plot to kidnap King James and if there had been any interference from loyal officers would have 'done his business'. For 'little Wood and I, that were on horseback, were to have shot him; and if that had missed, then Lord Churchill that was provided with a pocket pistol and dagger, would have shot or stabbed him in the coach.' This conversation in April 1689, when it was known that James had gone to Ireland, fits in with Hewitt's deathbed confession made in a different tone but of the same substance, later that year.

Whether or not James's nose-bleed saved him from capture or even death, it certainly reduced his physical strength at a critical moment, just as the shock of betrayal damaged his confidence in his army and those he believed his friends. Sir Henry Shere, in command of the artillery, saw the King on his way back to London and wrote to Lord Dartmouth, 'The King is almost quite deserted.' Lamenting that the

[225]

King had been 'cursed with fools to his councillors and knaves to his bosom,' he added, 'The King is very ill, I fear, I may say dangerously so, at least in my opinion.'

In this state, just a week after his haemorrhage, James reached Whitehall about four in the afternoon of Monday 26 November, to find that his daughter Anne had fled to join the rebels at Nottingham. 'God help me! My own children have forsaken me in my distress.' Several people recorded this cry of despair and some thought the King's mind had given way, so intense was his grief.

But it was his heart that was broken, not his mind. That very evening he held a Cabinet Council which lasted till late at night. Pepys left with orders to contact Dartmouth about sending the infant Prince of Wales out of the country. The King also decided to call a Great Council – peers and lords spiritual as well as the Privy Councillors – to advise him on what course now to pursue.

When he had left London, just over a week ago, it had been in the hope that, in spite of Cornbury's desertion, he could still lead an English army to meet a largely foreign invading force. But now, with one of his chief generals and many staff officers gone to join the Prince of Orange, with two great lords in the north in arms for the same cause, and every hour bringing news of fresh defections, there was no possibility of making a fight for it without involving the country in another civil war.

Almost everyone seems to consider that at this point James lost his nerve, if not his wits, panicked, or suffered some kind of mental or moral collapse. No surviving contemporary records suggest this. But he had to make some very difficult decisions in an entirely new situation – new to him, though not to those who had engineered it and now had the whip hand.

10 Escapes

Anne had fled at night from the Cockpit. A backstair (still extant) had been constructed and down this she went with Sarah Churchill, to be met by Bishop Compton, who had reverted to his military youth, equipped with boots and pistols. They drove away to Nottingham where Anne made herself conspicuous as an Orangist, heading an Association in defence of William and against the hated papists. In one of the cartoons printed in Holland William and Mary are represented as hurrying to the rescue of Anne, who has chains on her wrists!

There was a great outcry when she was discovered to be missing; 'Her nurse and my lady Clarendon run about like people out of their sences, crying out, The Papists had murther'd her.' So the memoirs, and indignation is expressed at the danger to the Queen in consequence of these mob-rousing allegations.

A letter was printed which was said to have been left on Anne's table for the Queen, 'but no such letter was found, or at least delivered to her.' In the printed letter Anne insisted that Prince George 'did not leave the king with any other design than to use all possible means for his preservation,' which caused James to comment ironically on 'the pretence of preserving the king by rising up in arms against him.' He added, 'and now that conscientiousness was grown so much the fassion, my lord Churchill thought fit to explain the tenderness of his too.' It was all done for religion. Yet, as James pointed out, he had begun to remedy the (minor, after all) religious grievances before William had left Holland. So true was this that Burnet was forced to add a paragraph to the Orange Declaration (second edition) insisting that the King's promises, made out of fear, would never be kept if the threat were removed.

James was still taking Catholics out of employment; on the day of his return he requested Sir Edward Hales (his convert test case for dispensation) to give up the Governorship of the Tower to his erstwhile prisoner Sir Bevil Skelton, whose warnings had proved so fatally justified. James was so amused at someone's witty remark that he had committed Skelton to the Tower only to commit the Tower to him, that he repeated it in the memoirs.

But although he could see the ridiculous side of all this, the desertions of Churchill and of his daughter Anne were deeply wounding. '"O if my enemys only had curs'd me I could have borne it,"' he wrote in the memoirs, 'but it was an unexpressible grief to see those he had favour'd Cherish'd and exalted, nay his own children, rise thus in opposition to him; this was what required a more than natural force to support; those strokes had been less sencible, had they come from hands less dear to him.'

In spite of these emotional shocks the Great Council was summoned for Tuesday 27 November, the day after his return from Salisbury. There were nine spiritual and between thirty and forty temporal lords in town; no Catholics came, having been asked not to attend. There were actually few left in London, for the Earl of Powis was with the Prince of Wales, Lord Dover (Jermyn) at Portsmouth, and Father Petre had already left the country before James went to Salisbury, with Lord Waldegrave, the new ambassador to France in place of Skelton. (Waldegrave had been ennobled when he married James's daughter by Arabella Churchill, Berwick's sister Henrietta.)

At the Council the King's two Secretaries of State, the Scottish peers Lord Middleton and Lord Preston (both Anglican) sat one each side of him, 'a little backwards from his chair,' as Clarendon put it in his account. The King opened proceedings by asking their advice; he said there had been no time to deal with the petition for an immediate Parliament before he left, but he now realized that the desire for it was pretty general in the country.

After a little silence the Earl of Oxford suggested that the lords who had signed the petition should speak first, so Rochester led off, saying Parliament was the only remedy, though no one could tell if it would have the desired effect. Lord Chancellor Jeffreys and Lord Godolphin followed and then Clarendon suddenly burst into a violent tirade, blaming the King for everything, 'laying open most of the late mis-carriages' as he said himself, particularly the raising of a regiment under the Earl of Stafford into which none but papists were to be admitted. 'I pressed this so earnestly that the King called out and said,

[228]

it was not true, there were no directions for admitting none but papists: but I went on. . . .' In the memoirs James recorded: 'my lord Clarendon flew out into an indiscreet and seditious railing, declameing against Popery, exaggerating fears and jealousies (suspicions) and blameing the King's conduct, so that nobody wonder'd at his going a day or two after to meet the Prince of Orange.' He does not say it was a poor return for his kindness to Clarendon at his son's desertion, but it was so.

Halifax spoke next 'very flatteringly' remarked Clarendon sourly – tactfully, most people thought. A Parliament seemed impracticable at present but he would never be against one, said the eloquent Trimmer, and perhaps some concessions might be made to the Prince of Orange to secure its meeting; sometimes things were prudent which at other times might be thought complying. Then Lord Nottingham 'endeavoured to cut a feather, and spake much in Lord Halifax's sense,' grumbled Clarendon.

The debate was serious and 'warm' at times. The King spoke of the defections from his army and of Churchill's kidnap plot, foiled by the providential nosebleed. 'The king further said that it would appear that the Prince of Orange came for the Crown, whatever he pretended; but that he would not see himself deposed; that he had read the story of King Richard II.' Richard, after allowing himself to be deposed by Bolingbroke (Henry IV), died in confinement; most people thought he had been quietly put out of the way.

At the end of the debate the King said, 'My lords, I have heard you all: you have spoken with great freedom and I do not take it ill of any of you. I may tell you I will call a Parliament, but for the other things you have proposed, they are of great importance and you will not wonder if I take a night's time to consider them.'

The next day the Chancellor had orders to issue writs for a Parliament to meet on 15 January 1689. The King also summoned Halifax for private consultation; if anyone could manage a compromise it was surely the Trimmer. He persuaded James that it would be necessary to treat with the Prince of Orange, whereupon the King appointed him his Commissioner, along with Nottingham and Godolphin. 'He pretended not to be pleased with the employment,' commented Clarendon sourly, when Halifax told him this on Friday 30 November.

[229]

The Commissoners had to wait for passports to come from the Prince but Clarendon, regarding the treaty as agreed, set off early on the Saturday morning, with his brother-in-law Sir Henry Capel (brother of the suicide Earl of Essex) as a passenger, so nervous of pursuit that he made Clarendon get up at 3 a.m. on the way. They reached Salisbury on Monday 3 December and there met the Dutch Ambassador Van Citters who was, not surprisingly, already in touch with William of Orange and told them where to find him.

Clarendon's journal for this jaunt (not printed till 1765) traces his gradual disillusionment, from an initial belief in the Prince's Declaration that he had come to call a free Parliament to the realization that William had indeed come for the Crown. He was well received by the Prince and congratulated on his son's timely desertion. It was in private interviews with Burnet that he began to guess the real object of the enterprise. When he said that the King had agreed to hold a Parliament, Burnet burst out, 'How can a parliament meet, now the kingdom is in this confusion: all the west being possessed by the Prince's forces, and all the north being in arms for him?' And when Clarendon quoted the Prince's Declaration, 'The Doctor, with his usual warmth answered, it is impossible; there can be no parliament, there must be no parliament, it is impossible.' It was plain that a Tory Parliament called by the King was not wanted.

Clarendon next ran into Churchill, who asked him when the Princess had left the Cockpit and was surprised it was not sooner; this showed that Anne was in the conspiracy and explained to her uncle her uncooperative behaviour in the last few weeks, detailed in his journal, joking about the baby prince's birth and refusing to speak to her father in favour of his old Tory friends. Later he met Prince George and was shocked still more to hear that Anne was not pregnant – her constant excuse in matters concerning the birth of her brother. 'Good god bless us: Nothing but lying and dissimulation in this world,' he lamented. In fact, though Anne was not pregnant when she said she was, she must have conceived soon afterwards, for her son was to be born on 24 July 1689 – and because of her lie was thought to be dangerously overdue!

By this time William was in Salisbury, which he entered on horseback, through gaping crowds. 'As he passed them, he put off his hat and said, thank you good people; I am come to secure the protestant religion and free you from popery.'

No popery was all right for the populace, but Clarendon saw Wildman and Ferguson the Plotter in the Prince's train, and other republicans and 'fanatics' abhorred by 'honest men'. Supping with some of the Whig exiles he found them grumbling at a Parliament's being called before they had time to work up their interest, 'as if it could not be a good parliament in case those gentlemen were not in it.' Clarendon said sharply that some of them would need pardons first. Whereupon Mr Harbord (Pepys's old enemy) boasted that 'he had drawn his sword against the king; that he had no need of his pardon but they would bring the king to ask pardon of them, for the wrongs he had done.'

Meanwhile, Burnet had been lecturing Clarendon on losing the Prince's favour and told him that Rochester must not expect to be employed – suggesting that the Prince expected soon to be appointing ministers of state. Clarendon pompously replied that if God blessed the treaty between the King and the Prince, all would be well. 'Upon which the doctor interrupted me, saying in great heat, what treaty? How can there be a treaty? The sword is drawn: there is a supposititious child which must be enquired into. He was thus walking about the room in a wonderful warmth, when somebody knocked at the door . . . and so I left him. Good god, what are we like to come to, if this man speaks the prince's sense? We shall have a fine reformation.' Reformation was what Clarendon wanted; Revolution was what he was to get.

William now left Salisbury and proceeded on his way, calling at country houses and admiring the pictures (particularly the Van Dycks at Wilton) and was at the Bear Inn at Hungerford when the King's Commissioners at last tracked him down. Clarendon was summoned to his bedchamber at nine on Saturday morning 8 December and the King's letter was read to the assembled company. 'It was in French: upon which he said (and I thought it came with tenderness from him) this was the first letter he ever had from the king in French: that he was always used to write to him in English and in his own hand.' It almost seems that William had not till then realized the personal implications of his invasion of his uncle's kingdom. Clarendon pointed out that in

[231]

the circumstances a formal letter written in French by a secretary was the correct procedure.

William then set the English lords to hammer out a reply and himself moved to Littlecote House (Parliamentary in the Civil War) for quiet – where his bedchamber can still be seen. The main argument was over the writs for Parliament, the Whigs wanting them superseded; they did not want a house with a Tory majority. They won, but when the answer was taken to William he struck out the cancellation clause, and when Capel objected he replied, 'By your favour, Sir Harry: we may drive away the king, but perhaps we may not know how easily to come by parliament.' The significance of the phrase on driving away the king Clarendon only realized later, but he as well as William knew that only the king could lawfully call a Parliament, and his hopes revived when the Prince eventually won the writs battle, after a Sunday spent quarrelling about it.

Although James did not know what was going on at Hungerford he was able to make a shrewder guess at William's intentions than was Clarendon. He knew the Prince of Orange would not risk an armed intervention in England merely to secure a Parliamentary settlement which would leave James, however circumscribed in power, still king, with his son as heir to the throne. No; William must intend to take power himself and with the wealth of England behind him, challenge the might of France.

Believing this, James could not see much future in the present negotiations. As long as William was there with his army to back up the disaffected peers, the King was bound to be forced by Parliament to give up the royal dispensing power, cancel his Declaration on Liberty of Conscience and perhaps be put under a regency of William and Mary, as had been suggested during the Exclusion crisis – if he was not simply deposed and sent to end his days in some remote castle. So, though he had sent the Commissioners to negotiate, he spent the intervening days trying to make sure of the safety of his son and heir. 'Tis my son they aim at, and tis my son I must endeavour to preserve, whatever becomes of me,' he wrote to Dartmouth, pressing him to get the child away to France as soon as he could. On 30 November he gave orders to Pepys for the yachts *Anne* and *Isabella* to fall down the river to Erith. The *Mary* yacht was already at Portsmouth.

But a few days later he received an anguished letter from Dartmouth, saying it would be treason to send the Prince of Wales out of England. He could not give the real reason, that he was no longer in control of the navy; it had been corrupted weeks ago by the Duke of Grafton and others, and now some of the associating officers were patrolling the bay, intent on capturing the baby prince and handing him over to Orange.

But James became aware of the disaffection in the navy when he received, on 2 December, an address from the fleet, glad to hear the King was going to treat with the Prince of Orange, desiring that a Parliament should be called, and declaring their resolve to stand by the Protestant Religion – 'but not one word of standing by the King,' wrote James in the memoirs. And the address was brought by two of 'the most factious and disaffected officers of the Navy'.

Scarce anything ever went nearer the King's heart than to see the English Mariners, so famed for a brave and loyal race of people, prove false to a Prince who had encouraged, cherished and promoted that profession, more than any King since the Conquest; who had been all his life a model and example as well as a spectator and praiser of their courage: he gloryd in nothing more, than that he had shar'd with them in the hardships and dangers of defending the dominion of the seas.

Soon afterwards he got another agonized letter from Dartmouth (who was personally loyal) trying to justify his signing the address about the treaty. He also warned the King that the advance troops of Orange's army would soon be between Portsmouth and London. At that news James immediately sent orders for the prince to be brought back at once and began to plan a new escape for him with the Queen, by way of the river.

The baby, in the care of Lord and Lady Powis, had a narrow escape on the way back. By chance the escort learned from a local man that there were soldiers on the road through the forest of Beare and he directed them to a skirting road so that they managed to evade the enemy. Even so, the Irish troops sent by the King to meet them were pelted by angry Protestant mobs and the infant prince was actually carried under the cloak of St Victor, a young Frenchman whose father's life had once been saved in battle by James. St Victor had come over with the Comte de Lauzun to offer service to the King. Lauzun was the same age as James and had known him in their youth; he had spent ten years imprisoned by King Louis for daring to aspire to the hand of Mademoiselle, who had secured his release by endowing Louis' favourite bastard, the Duc de Maine, with some of her estates. James decided that Lauzun was just the man to conduct his wife and son to France.

But at first the Queen absolutely refused to leave the King; she could bear anything, even imprisonment, so long as she was with him. Because she was later blamed for having persuaded the King to flee too, it is expressly stated in the *Life* that she did not seek to persuade James to leave but to let her stay. But when she discovered that he had already begun to think of escaping himself, then she said she would go if he promised to follow her within twenty-four hours. And James did make her that promise.

So on Sunday 9 December the King and Queen retired to bed at ten with the usual ceremony but afterwards got up again. Maria put on her disguise; she was to pass as a laundress, with the baby as a bundle of washing. The King then handed her over to Lauzun and with one last silent farewell look at James she went across the stone gallery and out through the privy garden to a carriage borrowed from the Tuscan Ambassador, the Florentine Terriesi.

In this, with the baby and his two nurses, she was driven to the Horseferry, crossed the river in storm and darkness to Lambeth stairs and then had to wait under the lee of a small church while the Frenchmen went to look for the next coach, which was to be waiting at the Swan Inn. Maria always remembered how she had stared back at the lights of Whitehall across the dark water, trying to pick out the room where James would be.

Even when they were in the travelling coach they were not safe away, for a mob out hunting fleeing papists shouted that here were some. Mercifully they did not manage to stop the coach and the Queen was able to go on board the vessel waiting in the Thames off Gravesend, where her lifelong Italian friend, Donna Vittoria Montecuccoli Davia, and some other ladies, were already embarked. She made a very

[234]

uncomfortable crossing below decks, sick herself and with sick nurses. But they got safely to the French coast and the baby only began to squall when he woke up hungry in the morning and the wet nurse was too ill to feed him.

St Victor had gone back at once from Gravesend to Whitehall to tell the King that the Queen and the Prince were safely embarked.

That day, Monday 10 December, James wrote to Dartmouth:

Things having so very bad an aspect, I would no longer defer securing the Queen and my son, which I hope I have done; and that by tomorrow by noon they will be out of reach of my enemies. I am at ease now I have sent them away. I have not heard this day as I expected from my commissioners with the Prince of Orange; who, I believe, will hardly be prevailed with to stop his march; so that I am in no good condition, nay, in as bad a one as it is possible.

He added that the Duke of Berwick would bring Dartmouth his instructions, either to take the fleet to Tyrconnel in Ireland or, if there was too much disaffection, to stay at sea as long as possible.

James then went ahead with preparations for his own escape.

11 Capture

When he wrote to Dartmouth James had not yet heard from his Commissioners but in the memoirs he gives the Prince of Orange's answer 'which he received that night'; it was couched in the royal plural throughout, as if William considered himself already king. The only thing he agreed to was that both armies should be kept forty miles from London during the sitting of Parliament. Otherwise William demanded that all papists should be disarmed and removed from offices civil and military, any proclamations 'which reflect on us or any who have come in to us be recalled', and any persons arrested be freed (none had been); the custody of the Tower and of Tilbury fort to be put into the hands of the City; public revenue provided to pay the Prince's army and that, to prevent a French landing, Portsmouth was to be put into hands approved by the Prince.

In the memoirs James says that 'he saw plainly what was aim'd at' in these proposals. 'He was too well acquainted with the ambitious views of that prince to immagin (as many did) that all this undertaking was out of pangs of conscience for the Religion and Liberties of the people; that in those arrogant demands he assumed in a manner already the Regal authority.' So James was confirmed in his resolution to follow the Queen abroad.

It seemed to James that only by escaping abroad could he retain freedom of action. If he stayed in England he would be the virtual if not the actual prisoner of William, forced to agree to all his demands, a mere cipher, as he called it, made to do 'mean things' and to submit to the direction of a Parliament which seemed likely to pursue the old policy of Exclusion in a new form. He was sure he still had some support in the country but his friends would be powerless to help him. Whereas if he could get away, uncompromised, there was every chance that when circumstances changed he would be welcomed back – for he did not think the English would appreciate William's rule. 'You will find him another Cromwell,' he had already told Clarendon.

His flight was to be put down entirely to fear for his own life, and his father's fate was certainly in his mind. But the examples he quotes in the memoirs are of kings, caught in an impossible situation at home, who fled abroad, to return at a more favourable time and regain the throne. Edward IV did this; so did James's own brother Charles, escaping after his defeat at Worcester to return nine years later at the Restoration. James's flight is comparable to that of heads of state during the last war in Europe, who fled when their countries were overrun rather than collaborate with the conquerors, knowing that many of their compatriots would do just that.

So James decided to make his escape from the net thrown round him but he would do his best to queer the pitch for William first. He wrote to Feversham, telling him of his intention to 'withdraw' and ordering him to disband the army. 'If I could have rely'd upon all my troops I might not have been put to this extremity I am in, and would at least have had one blow for it; but though I know there are many loyal and brave men amongst you, yet you know, you yourself and several of the General

Officers tould me it was no ways advisable to venter myself at their head: there remains nothing more for me to do but to thank you, and all those officers and soldiers, who have stuck to me and been truly loyal. . . .' and he hoped they would keep themselves free from 'associations and such pernicious things. . . .'

When Feversham read this message to the troops it drew tears. He then disbanded the army; the men had all been paid to within a week or two. James recorded with satisfaction that this was 'no small disappointment to the Prince of Orange (as appeared afterwards by his resentment at what had been done) who had already fram'd to himself great prospects of advantages from these troops in further prosecution of his designs against France.' For 'before he was master of them they had dwindled away to a very small number.' Many of these men later went overseas to offer their services to James again.

In the memoirs James records that he thought it necessary 'to perplex his enemys also in the Civil as he had done in their military affairs, by recalling the writs for assembling the Parliament, which he knew would disconcert the measures and malice of those who sought his ruin, and retard at least the injurys they design'd him.' He sent for the writs and burnt them himself in his inner room. William, who had refused to let the Whigs supersede the writs, would have understood very well what he was doing. He wanted a lawful Parliament to declare him the lawful king, James being excluded for his Catholic profession; but James prevented that. The ultimate changeover was strictly illegal.

Only the King could summon a lawful Parliament and only acts signed with the Great Seal carried the authority of law. James had already taken the Great Seal from the Chancellor and he took it with him, dropping it in the Thames on his way over. An account preserved in the Stuart Papers, which James wrote on 20 February 1693, gives his motives in destroying the Seal – 'lest our rebel subjects joined with the Usurper the Prince of Orange might by virtue thereof have made use of our own authority against our person. . . .' Straight away in January 1689 he caused 'one Rothier to make one, which we carried with us into our kingdom of Ireland.' This seal was 'not so beautiful as the old' and so, in 1693, he caused it to be broken and a new one made. James, who was sixty later that year, had still not given up his claim.

Five months after his escape the original seal was dredged up by a fisherman. By then Parliament (or rather the Convention unlawfully assembled) had settled the new form of government in England without it, and made William king.

James meant to keep his departure secret but he was never good at dissembling and rumours were already going about. Ailesbury heard them and relates in his memoirs (written long afterwards) how, alone with the King in his inner room, he begged him not to go. James tried to put him off, calling it a coffee-house rumour. But Ailesbury persisted, suggesting that the army could be re-formed and with the King at its head could march on Nottingham, where it would soon disperse the 'whishtail militia' collected by Lord Devonshire.

It was an impracticable proposal, setting English against English in a new civil war, and even if James had won, what sort of reign could he have had after such bloodshed? Nor was he at all likely to win against William's trained army. But Ailesbury continued to believe, to the end of his long life, that the King ought not to have left England.

This first flight was certainly undertaken in haste; James had always been impetuous in action, but the sequel was to show that he had not misjudged the situation. He put off the faithful Ailesbury as he had put off the sheriffs of the City of London, with vague promises to see them next day.

That evening he sent for Terriesi, the Tuscan ambassador, and entrusted a strongbox to his care, so heavy that it was thought to contain treasure, possibly even the Crown Jewels. In fact, though James put in about £3000 in cash, it held all his journals and papers, from which the memoirs and the *Life* were compiled. The box made a circuitous and hazardous journey but eventually arrived safely in Paris.

As on the previous night James officially retired to bed but soon got up again and put on a suit of ordinary plain clothes and the inevitable black periwig, which seems to have been his only idea of disguise. 'And then betwixt 12 and 1 on Munday night the 10th December he left his Pallace of Whitehall.' He took a Hackney coach to the Horseferry and when he had crossed the river, set out on Bay Ailesbury, the horse given him either by Thomas or his father, with the loyal convert Sir Edward Hales, his quartermaster and a guide, for the fifty-mile ride down into Kent.

They crossed the river Medway at about seven in the morning of 11

December and were met by James's equerry and friend Ralph Sheldon, with a relay of horses. By ten they had reached Elmley Ferry near Faversham, where a Custom House hoy (small coastal sailing vessel) had been hired to take them to the ship which would transport them to France. The wind was strong and the captain said he must take in ballast, which James (in his capacity as old tarpaulin) recognized as necessary. But in getting it in they missed the tide and were grounded for the best part of the day.

Just as they were on the point of getting afloat once more there came alongside three boats with fifty or sixty men, out 'priest-codding' – hunting escaping priests for gain. They swarmed on board and down into the cabin. Sir Edward Hales, whose estates were in Kent, was recognized at once, as a notorious convert to Rome. James, in his sober suit and black wig, was taken for his Jesuit chaplain. Hales tried bribery and did get a promise from the ringleader, Ames, who, distrusting his comrades while he was away securing a coach, induced the prisoners to hand over their watches and money for safe-keeping, actually giving them a receipt, which James put in his pocket.

Ames was right to doubt his friends, for after making such a noise all night that no one could get any rest, some of them came below at early dawn 'and fell to searching their pockets and opening their breeches felt all about in a very rude manner, and the more because they found nothing.' So runs the account in the memoirs. James had slipped his coronation ring and a diamond bodkin of his wife's inside his drawers for safety. 'But at last one of them, feeling about the king's knees, got hould of the diamond bodkin and cry'd out he had found a prize, but the King faced him down he was in a mistake, that he had several things in his pocket, as sizers (scissors) a toothpick case and little keys, and that perhaps it was one of these he felt; at which the man thrusting his hand suddenly into the king's pocket lost hould of the diamond and finding those things the king had mentioned remained satisfied it was so, by which means the bodkin and the ring were preserved.' James added that they were so ignorant about jewels that 'finding a pare of diamond buckles lap'd in a paper in the king's pocket they took them for glass and gave them him again.'

When it was broad day a coach was brought to the shoreside but it was not to assist their escape; instead, Hales was told he must appear before the Mayor. So they were driven to Faversham, still escorted by the rabble, and taken into an inn (*The Arms of England*, appropriately enough) 'where as the king went upstairs notwithstanding his disguise and black periwig, he perceived several people knew him; so he took no more pains to conceal who he was.'

James now took what steps he could to proceed with his escape. He sent Ralph Sheldon to the master of the hoy, to arrange for him to wait some distance from the town, and to get horses to carry him there. He also sent a message to Lord Winchelsea (the Lord Lieutenant) which was preserved in his family, 'copied exactly' by J. Cryke on 10 January 1727 and included as the sixth and last appendix to the *Life*, as printed in 1816. It deserves quotation, to show that James was not in the state of mental collapse some accounts have represented him to be.

> Feversham, December 12 1688
> I am just now come in here, having been last night seased by some of this towne, who telling me you were to be here this day, I would not make myself known to them, thinking to have found you here, but that not being, I desire you would come hether to me, and that as privatly as you could do, that I might advise with you concerning my safty, hoping you have that true Loyalty in you, as you will do what you can to secure me from my Enemys, of which you shall find me as sensible as you can desire.
>
> James R.

But his intention was suspected and the rabble so beset the inn 'that it was impossible for the King to get away, much less assist others taken on the way to Dover.' There were afterwards accusations that he had done nothing to save anyone but himself. In fact he had sent Father Petre and others out of the country already.

Among the fugitives caught at that time were the Catholic bishops, Leyburn and Giffard, who were thrown into prison, in the Tower and Newgate respectively. Leyburn, released in 1690, coped with the London district in poverty and hardship till he died in 1702 at the age of eighty-six. Giffard was then transferred to London where he stayed till his death at the age of ninety in 1734. His last years were spent in the convent at Hammersmith belonging to Mary Ward's Institute of the Blessed Virgin Mary, whose nuns wore secular dress to conceal their illegal existence. (It was in James's reign that the famous Bar Convent of the same order was founded at York in 1686; it managed to survive, building a 'priesthole' in the new Georgian chapel for emergency hiding, and has just celebrated its tercentenary, though with no thanks to King James, as far as I know.)

'By close of evening' on 12 December Lord Winchelsea arrived, but attended by only two gentlemen. James says he resolved to lodge at the Mayor's house but as he 'went down staires the rabble were very rude to him, so that he had much adoe to force his way through . . . ,' one reason being their fear that Sir Edward Hales might escape, 'and at that very time the people of the country were plundering his house and killing his deer; and he being sencible how odious he was to them, prudently stayed at the inne and would not follow the King, least his company might draw a greater inconvenience upon him.' (Hales later escaped and joined the King at St Germains.)

At this point James was recognized by some of his old seamen, 'who as he went along cry'd out that a hair of his head should not be touched, but still kept a strickt eye upon him that he might not escape, and when he cam to his lodging, they made his withdrawing room a sorte of corps de guard.' So another night was spent without much opportunity for rest and none of escape.

The next day, 13 December, Sir Basil Dixwell and Sir James Oxenden came to Faversham with their two Militia troops 'under pretence of securing the King from the Rabble, but indeed to secure him to themselves and to make a merit of it to the Prince of Orange' – to whom they sent off a messenger post-haste. 'In the meantime those two gents kept a very strict guard upon the King, and had the impudence to find fault with him for sending away a letter for mony, cloaths etc, without shewing it them before he seal'd it.' They set the seamen to watch him, commanded, unfortunately, by 'an ill looking, ill-natured fellow, one Hunt' who was 'Exceeding rude' to his prisoner.

At this point James's story is interrupted to tell what was happening in London, and his account can be checked and amplified from George Hilton Jones' book *Charles Middleton: the Life and Times of a Restoration Politician* (1967), where he quotes from State Papers and from a letter

[241]

written in February 1689 by Francis Turner, Bishop of Ely, to defend his conduct the previous December.

A Council of Regency was called the morning after the King's flight, at which Archbishop Sancroft presided; this was clearly the Tory Anglican response to the situation. They ordered Feversham and Dartmouth to avoid engagement with the Dutch forces and sent a delegation (including Turner) to take an address to the Prince of Orange. They adjourned at eleven at night, and although a principal object had been to keep order in the capital, they signally failed to do so, for that night the mob got loose. As they had already smashed up and burned down any Catholic chapels they could find, they now attacked the residences of Catholic ambassadors. Barillon had prudently got a guard for the French Embassy, so it was left alone, but the Spanish Embassy was looted and burned – ironically, since Spain was Orange's ally and people in the Spanish Netherlands were praying for his success. But they were all papists to the mob. 'No king! no law!' the rioters were heard shouting in the streets.

Next morning the Council of Regency met in the new council chamber (designed by Wren) at Whitehall and Halifax, as the only Marquis present, took the chair; he was now acting for the Prince of Orange. Orders were sent out, but Middleton, who was present, signed nothing.

That night occurred the extraordinary panic known as Irish Night. A rumour ran about that Irish soldiers were coming to cut all Protestant throats; drums beat in the streets, candles were set in windows and men marched about in bands. The panic was not confined to London but spread widely into the country. It was later discovered to have been started by Speke, one of William's agents. The resulting chaos created an appearance of emergency which could be used to justify an intervention by William to restore order, the disorders being blamed on the King's 'deserting the government'. If he had been still at Whitehall no doubt it would have been said that he was now incapable of keeping order and must be taken into custody for his own safety. (William's excuse soon afterwards.)

William, who had heard with relief of James's flight, was at Henley when the delegation from the Council of Regency arrived. He was pleased with the address from the City but not with that from the lords

– presumably because of the Regency label, which seemed to pre-empt the sovereignty which William desired.

'Somebody told the Prince how Lord Feversham had disbanded the army,' wrote Lord Clarendon, 'and that the soldiers were all running up and down not knowing what course to take; at which the Prince seemed very angry at Lord Feversham and said, I am not thus to be dealt with.'

Clarendon, admitting that by now he was 'weary of my company', got the Bishop of Ely to his lodging and 'told him, all was naught'. He had realized that the Prince of Orange was not going to play the part designed for him by the honest men of the Church of England.

This Thursday 13 December the news of the King's capture came to the Regency Council in London, first brought by a servant of the Archbishop's, from Canterbury, and later by a seaman, Robert Clinton, who had to wait long at the door before he was admitted. His tale of the King's being in the hands of the rabble finally moved the lords to take measures to rescue him; Feversham was to go down with a detachment of guards next day; Ailesbury rode off at once.

Ailesbury remembered his ride as a nightmare journey, struggling through drunken mobs still caught in 'Irish' panic, bent on cutting down the wooden bridge over the Medway, sure that London was burning. Ailesbury managed to convince them it was not but he got little sleep and arrived at Faversham after noon on Friday 14 December, worn out. The Mayor's house had 'a pretty large hall' which was full of people chattering as if at a market. The King was sitting in a chair with his hat on and his beard had grown in the last five days: with a shock, Ailesbury was reminded of the picture of his father on trial.

James answered Ailesbury's greeting by saying something like 'You were all kings when I left London.' (No king, no law!) Ailesbury, offended, protested, 'Sir, I expected another sort of welcome after the great dangers I ran last night by repairing to you.' At this typical exaggeration from the tall young but unmartial nobleman (the King's dangers were after all much greater) James's 'countenance became more serene, and he told me he was glad to see me.'

Ailesbury insisted on serving the King his dinner on bended knee, partly to impress the chattering throng with his dignity, and it had the desired effect of quietening them. Soon the royal servants began to arrive and 'gushed out their tears for joy to see their king', as Ailesbury put it. Many of James's devoted household were to follow him into exile. They had brought him clean shirts and clothes, which were especially welcome, as in the company of the rabble he had picked up some of their lice – Ailesbury had noticed him shifting uneasily at dinner.

While Ailesbury was eating his own dinner, 'the King went into the hall to take leave of those faithful seamen who had lain there night and day. "Honest friends," said the King, "you will not know me presently." And indeed, after shaving and dressing, and with a good periwig, he had not the same countenance.' Ailesbury noted that before he left the next day, James 'rewarded well those loyal seamen'.

By this time Middleton and other lords had arrived and James seems to have accepted the fact that he must stay in England, since he had been sent for by the remnant of peers in London. Still King, whether going or staying, he continued to act as king as long as he was allowed to do so. The next week's events were to be crucial, showing what was really happening in the Revolution, which is no doubt why they were compressed and passed over when its history came to be written.

12 Last Days in London

The King left Faversham on Saturday 15 December, Ailesbury and the other lords riding in the coach with him. James noted sardonically that the news that he was returning to London 'troubled hugely those seditious Kentish gents, who had projected to themselves mighty advantages from their rude and rebellious carriage to their Sovereign.' This had included reading the Prince of Orange's Declaration under his window.

At Sittingbourne they met Lord Feversham and his troop of guards, who greeted the King with cheers, kneeling in the road, 'with tears of joy running down their faces', says Ailesbury. Escorted by these Royal

Horse Guards James proceeded to Rochester, where he stayed the night in the house of Sir Richard Head.

The first thing he did was to write an official letter to William, 'wherein he tould him, he would be glad to see him at London on munday, to endeavour by a personal conference to settle the distracted Nation, that he had order'd St James's to be prepared for him.' He entrusted this letter to Lord Feversham, who left that very night. By sending this invitation James resumed the initiative and threw upon William the necessity of showing whether he meant what he said in his Declaration.

On the way to London next day (Sunday 16 December) the King was met by some loyal officers who told him that the guards at Whitehall had declared for Orange; therefore he gave up the idea of going by water, so as to keep his loyal guards with him. Then, when they reached Blackheath they found many gentlemen and citizens on horseback had come out to meet him and Ailesbury says that two eminent merchants came to the coach side to beg the King to pass through the City. He agreed, and at about four in the afternoon the coach started on the long drive from St George's Southwark to Whitehall and all that way 'there was scarce room for the coaches to pass through, and the balconies and windows besides were thronged, with loud acclamations. . . .'

James recorded that

he was hugely surprized with the unexpected testimonys of the peoples affection to him, it is not to be imagined what acclamations were made, and what joy the people express'd at his Majesty's return, such bonefires, ringing of bells, and all imaginable markes of love and esteem, as made it look liker a day of tryumph than humiliation and this was so universall amongst all ranks of people, that the King, nor none that were with him, had ever seen the like before, the same crowds of people and crys of joy accompanying him to Whitehall and even to his Bedchamber door itself.

It was a typical English reaction – betrayed by his own generals and forced to flee from a foreign army, James had become the underdog and as such commanded sympathy, reviving memories of Old Jemmy, the hero of the navy, so long admired.

[245]

The account in the memoirs goes straight on that no sooner was the King within his Bedchamber than 'the scene began to change' with the arrival of Zuylestein bearing a letter from the Prince of Orange which demanded that the King should remain at Rochester. James told Zuylestein that if the letter had reached him at Rochester he would have stayed there but 'now he hoped the Prince of Orange would come next day to St James's' for a conference. The envoy was just leaving when the King was told that the Prince, who was now at Windsor, had arrested Lord Feversham.

Instantly recalling Zuylestein, James denounced this act as 'against the law of nations and the universal practice, to detain a publick minister', and demanded his release. Feversham had gone as his envoy with the invitation to a conference, but even as his chief general he ought to have been immune from such treatment. William not only ignored this complaint, leaving Feversham incarcerated at Windsor when he moved on to Sion House, but never answered James's invitation to a conference or made any further communication direct to him. 'So he threw off the mask before the end of the first scene,' commented James, 'For hithertoo the pretence of the Expedition had been only to bring the King to reason, in reference to the Laws, Liberties and Religion, and to engage him in a League against France, the one to Satisfy (or rather bubble) the people, the other his Foreign Allys.' But 'now that the King sends message after message to him to desire a personal conference in order to rectify and settle whatever was amiss . . . the Prince of Orange dreaded nothing now so much as what he gave out to be the only motive of his Expedition.'

As it was Sunday James decided to hear mass in his own Royal Chapel; kings were allowed the privilege of a mass celebrated after noon. Then, asserting his royal right once more, he proceeded to sup in public. Evelyn, who was present, noted that a Jesuit said grace. There were quite a number of spectators, though few attendant lords (so many had gone off to join William). Dartmouth's son (who afterwards made such acid comments on Burnet's *History*) was then a boy of fourteen and a page in waiting; he recorded that while the King dined he recounted his adventures in Kent, as if they had happened to another person; it was James the memorializer talking.

'Wee have now turn upon luck,' Burnet wrote to Admiral Arthur

Herbert, 'the foolish men of Feversham by stopping the King at first time have thrown us into an uneasy aftergame.' They certainly had, and William called a meeting at Windsor of the peers who had joined him, to decide what to do with the unwanted King; Clarendon was commanded to attend. He had been shown James's letter to the Prince by Bentinck, who was lodged, appropriately, in the Duchess of Portsmouth's apartments. Discussing this later with Burnet and Bishop Lloyd of St Asaph Clarendon was shocked when Burnet merely laughed at Feversham's arrest and Lloyd said that 'the King by going away had made a cession.' This was what the lawyer Pollexfen had said too, asserting that the Prince at the head of his army had only to declare himself king 'according to Cromwell's model; which he said was a far more equal way than the old constitution. Good god bless me!' Clarendon exclaimed, horrified at this blasphemy against royalist ideals.

On Monday 17 December, the day after James's unexpectedly popular return, Clarendon was summoned to the meeting of peers at Windsor, chaired by Lord Halifax, to decide the fate of the King. Arriving rather late, he found everything had been settled already. The King was to be advised to leave Whitehall and go to Ham House – the Duchess of Lauderdale's house on the Thames near Richmond. When Clarendon ventured to ask why the King could not go to one of his own houses, 'Lord Delamere very angrily (a little thing puts him in a passion) said, he did not look upon him as his king, and he would never more pay him obedience and that he ought not to be like a king in one of his own houses.' (In the Convention Delamere said that he had been in favour of sending the King to the Tower.)

The Prince had come in before this outburst; he approved of Ham and enjoined secrecy; he then insisted that the order must be carried out by the English lords and named Halifax, Shrewsbury and Delamere. Then he gave orders for an early march on London and for the Dutch Guards to go ahead and take over the posts at Whitehall. Finally, James must be out of the capital before William entered it.

Clarendon left Windsor soon after. 'I thought it was the most melancholy day in my whole life,' he recorded. Too late he realized that he had helped to bring about a revolution.

That Monday 17 December, while the traitor lords were deciding

[247]

what to do with the King, was a strange day at Whitehall. Present at the King's levee were Colin Lindsay, Earl of Balcarres and John Graham of Claverhouse, recently created Viscount Dundee by James at Salisbury, where they had joined him with advance troops from Scotland. (Lindsay's descendant wrote an account taken from family papers which was used by Agnes Strickland.)

James announced that as it was a fine day, he would take a walk; Balcarres and Dundee went with him and reaffirmed their loyalty. James made them give him their hands 'as men of honour' rather than kissing his as subjects, and then told them that he could not remain in England as a cipher or a prisoner, and intended to 'go for France immediately'. He gave Balcarres a commission for civil affairs in Scotland and Dundee one to command the troops.

Back in the palace at Whitehall James held a Council, though there were only eight Privy Councillors left to attend. (One was the extraordinary Colonel Titus; when James had made him a Privy Councillor all the Tories were shocked.) Several orders were made but were not obeyed; one seems to have been for the release of the Catholic bishops.

James also wrote a letter to Louis XIV which he gave to Barillon to deliver.

Sir, and my Brother, As I hope that the queen, my wife, and my son, have last week landed in one of your ports, I hope you will do me the favour of protecting them. Unless I had been unfortunately stopped by the way, I should have been with you to ask the same for myself as well as for them. Your ambassador will give you an account of the bad state of my affairs, and assure you, also, that I have done nothing contrary to the friendship that subsists between us. I am very sincerely, sir, my brother, Your good brother, James R. At Whitehall this 27/17 Dec 1688.

At some time during this strange day Ames and some of his priest-codders turned up to return the King's watch and to assure him that had he known who he was, he would have behaved himself very differently. James took his watch back and handed Ames his receipt, much to the man's amazement. Then the King gave him ten pounds 'to drink his health' and they parted in good humour.

It was the last money the King had about him and when he touched a motley crowd for the Evil he had to borrow a hundred gold sovereigns from Godolphin, to bind one on the arm of each. It was typical of James to find time for this sacred royal service to the sick on this the last day of his actual reign.

It was the day he had fixed for his meeting with the Prince of Orange but neither he nor any messenger arrived. At last the King retired to his Bedchamber. 'At eleven a clock my Lord Craven came to acquaint his Majesty just as he was going to bed that Count de Solms was in the parke with three battalions of the Prince's footguards and some hors, and said he had orders to take the postes in and about Whitehall.'

Lord Craven was eighty, an indomitable old royalist; Solms was a cousin of William's and his general. The King sent for Solms and told him his guards must be for St James's Palace, for the Prince. Solms showed his orders for Whitehall and the King had to order Craven to withdraw and allow the Dutch to take over the posts. Craven went down on his knees, begging the King to allow him to fight the Dutchman. But James could not allow such useless bloodshed. He raised the old man, praising his courage and loyalty, but insisted that he should obey this last order. So the Dutch Blue Guards marched in and took up their positions at the gates and entrances of Whitehall, even at the Bedchamber doors.

'Things now began to have a gloomy aspect,' the memoirs continue, 'his majesty saw no hopes of a conference, much less of an accommodation, he perceived he was absolutely the Prince of Orange's prisoner and at his mercy.' Nevertheless, when some of his attendants questioned whether he should venture to sleep with the Dutch guards at the doors, he brushed the doubt aside and 'went to bed at his usual time and slept with as much tranquillity as he ever did in his life.' Like his brother Charles, James had the ability to sleep at night whatever the stresses and noise of his surroundings. At Salisbury someone had suggested that old Lord Peterborough, who coughed badly, should be told not to sleep in his room. 'I sleep sound and do not hear him,' said James, unwilling to offend his old friend.

Tonight, however, he was woken out of his first deep sleep at some time after midnight. The description is vivid and it should be remembered that Lord Middleton, who was then in waiting and 'lay by the

[249]

king', later joined James in exile. Middleton was called up to find three lords at the Bedchamber doors: Lord Shrewsbury, who had recently taken Bristol for the Prince of Orange; the violent-tempered Lord Delamere (Booth) and Lord Halifax. They said they must see the King immediately.

> When my Lord Middleton would have had them stay till the King was awake in the morning, they answered that their business would admit of no delay: There was no arguing with men who were Masters, so my Lord Middleton went to the King's bedside and found him so fast asleep, that puting by the curtaine did not wake him, till kneeling down he spoke pretty loud in his ear, by which his Majesty was at first a little surprized but immediatly composing himself asked what was the business? which when my Lord Middleton tould him, he ordered them to be call'd in.

The three lords then brusquely told the King that the Prince required him to retire to Ham House and to be ready to leave by nine in the morning, as the Prince intended to enter London about noon. James was being treated as a defeated enemy and he was shown the Prince's orders, addressed not to him but to his traitor lords. This was confirmation of James's assessment of his predicament and he told them he was willing to leave London but that Ham was 'a very ill winter house and unfurnished', and that he would rather go back to Rochester.

At first they would not hear of it; Delamere was rude, Halifax argued every point – only Shrewsbury was civil and promised to represent his wishes to the Prince, who was now at Sion House. But James must still be ready to leave at nine and he was not to go through the city. William agreed to the change of place; he was anxious to facilitate James's escape, especially since his triumphal return through the city, which had shown how much sympathy there was still for him among the people. Therefore his removal must take place as quietly as possible, by water, and under armed guard.

But when the news got about that the King had been taken from his own palace a prisoner under foreign guard it caused another upsurge of compassion for him and resentment at the incoming Dutch which was to form the basis of the Jacobite movement. And it showed that James had been right to reckon that he could only keep freedom of action by escaping abroad.

James was ready to leave at the appointed time but the Dutch Guards, in unfamiliar surroundings, took so long embarking that they did not start till about eleven. This gave time for the foreign ambassadors and remaining courtiers to come and take farewell of the King (some in tears) and for a small crowd of sympathetic observers to collect on the bank. It was raining, of course; a cold wet midwinter day, Tuesday 18 December, 1688. So King James II left his palace of Whitehall and his city of London, a prisoner under armed guard, rowed down the river in the rain.

13 Into 1689

Because of the Dutchmen's delay in embarking, the little flotilla of boats missed the tide and could not get under London Bridge. Hanging about, the King sent a lunch basket over to the Dutch captain with his compliments. Someone with him protested that he would rather throw the Dutchman in the river. James rebuked him; the Dutch soldiers were only doing their duty.

But in consequence of the delay they did not reach Gravesend till seven in the evening, when it was pitch dark. So although coaches had been sent to carry them on, they had to stay overnight. James noted that he was strictly guarded at Gravesend. William did not want him escaping till he was well outside London.

William at last entered London about four in the afternoon; he did not risk going through the city, disappointing his supporters who had been waiting two hours in the rain to welcome him. Instead he drove by back ways to Westminster and so into Whitehall on that murky December evening, an entry later put down to modesty rather than apprehension. But when they heard he had arrived, people crowded to court to see him. Evelyn recorded, 'He is very stately, serious and reserved.' Very soon this was to change to 'morose'.

[251]

Next day Clarendon wrote, 'It is not to be imagined, what a damp there was upon all sorts of men throughout the town. The treatment the king has met with from the Prince of Orange, and the manner of his being driven, as it were, from Whitehall, with such circumstances, moved compassion even in those who were not very fond of him.'

One of these, curiously enough, was Gilbert Burnet. In his letter to Admiral Herbert, written on Christmas Day (Foxcroft's *Supplement*) he says,

> Compassion has begun to work, especially since the Prince sent him word to leave Whitehall . . . Your reflections on the poor King's misfortunes are worthy of you. I could hardly have thought that anything relating to him could have given me so much compassion as I find his condition has done . . . but wee must now shut our mouths for there is discontent enough already . . . and you know wee have not the arts of cajolery.

He meant William, who he believed was already designing an expedition into France for the summer. That, of course, was his object in coming to England.

Compassion for the King did not move his daughter Anne; she drove into town that Wednesday, covered in orange ribbons and favours, in great good humour, and was seen at the theatre shortly afterwards.

Meanwhile, that same day James arrived at Rochester, again staying with Sir Richard Head, to whom he gave a ring as the only gift he could make. (His descendants showed it to Agnes Strickland.) The King was attended by his four Bedchamber Lords and several general officers, among them Sir John Fenwick, who surrendered his commission rather than be forced to serve the Prince of Orange. The same thing was done by officers of the Earl of Bath's regiment, which was at Rochester, while so many ordinary soldiers deserted that next day only about 150 out of some 420 marched out. More guards came from Dover, and the officers waited on the King.

During the few days James remained at Rochester he 'had advice from London either by letters or by peoples coming down to tell how matters went in town.' One of these was Lord Middleton, whom he had ordered to stay in town for William's entry and then come and advise him. After much discussion Middleton admitted that it would be dangerous to stay, but that if he went, 'the door would immediately be shut upon him.'

James had already written to two loyal aldermen, Sir Thomas Lewis and Sir Thomas Stampe, offering to put himself in their hands till 'he had given full satisfaction to his people' but they replied that they could not guarantee his security, since the Common Council had been influenced by Orange's agents to obstruct any accommodation. James made this offer to two of the bishops as well, but they gave the same answer, they could not promise him security.

Because he did not know what the meeting of peers called by the Prince might produce, and because he heard that the Common Council had been ordered by William not to take the usual oaths on St Thomas' Day, 21 December (which he regarded as an assumption of royal power) James felt it would be madness not to get away as soon as he could. He realized that if he stayed it would have embarrassed the Prince and his party 'how to dethrone a prince, who by the Law could do no wrong, and was so willing to give full satisfaction to his people,' but he also saw that 'if he had crossed the Prince's arm therein, it would have been in his power to find a shorter way of removing that obstacle. . . .'

Orange's admirers absolve him from any such intention but James had some excuse for suspicion because William was generally thought to have connived at the murder of the de Witt brothers on his way to power in Holland. If James, shut up at Ham or elsewhere, had conveniently died (of an ague or a fit), William could not be blamed for it. What he would actually have done, no one can know; perhaps sent his father-in-law overseas to 'honourable confinement' in Holland, which to James would have been a fate almost as final as death.

The events of the last week, however, had impressed on James the necessity of making public his reasons for flight; so now he wrote a letter which he asked Middleton to publish after he had gone. He was careful to leave it for Middleton, not give it direct, so as not to implicate him in his escape.

The letter is very personal, written with simplicity and feeling and beginning abruptly, 'The world cannot wonder at my withdrawing myself now this second time; I might have expected somewhat better usage after what I had written to the Prince of Orange' – his invitation to a conference. But all he got was the arrest of Feversham, the takeover of Whitehall by Dutch Guards, the midnight order and enforced removal next morning, and all this done by one who had invaded his kingdom without just cause but had cast on him 'the greatest aspersion that malice could invent' – concerning his son.

James felt strongly on this subject. 'I appeal to all that know me, nay even to himself, that in their consciences neither he nor they can believe me in the least capable of so unnatural a Villany, nor of so little Common Sence, as to be imposed on in a thing of such a nature as that; What had I then to expect from one who by all artes had taken such pains, to make me appear as black as Hell to my own people, as well as to all the world besides. . . .'

The last part of the letter gives his reasons for leaving the country.

I was born free and desire to continue so; and though I have venter'd my life very frankly on several occasions for the good and honour of my country, and am as free to do it again (and which I hope I shall yet do, as old as I am, to redeem it from the slavery it is like to fall under) yet I think it not convenient to expose myself to be secur'd so as not to be at libertie to efect it, and for that reason do withdraw, but so as to be within call when the Nation's eyes shall be opened, so as to see how they have been abused and imposed upon, by the specious pretences of Religion and propertie; I hope it will pleas God to touch their hearts out of his infinite mercy, and to make them sencible of the ill condition they are in, and bring them to such a temper that a legal parliament may be call'd, and that amongst other things that may be necessary to be done they will agree to a libertie of conscience for all Protestant dissenters; and that those of my own perswasion may be so far considered and have such a share in it, as they may live peaceably and quietly as Englishmen and Christians ought to doe and not be obliged to transport themselves, which would be very grievous, especially to such as love their Country; and I appeal to all who are considering men and have had experience, whether any thing can make this Nation so great and florishing as Libertie of Conscience, some of our Neighbours dread it; I would add much more to confirme all I have said, but now is not the proper time.

This letter was written on Saturday 22 December. He had reached Rochester on the nineteenth, and the next day the Captain of the Dutch Guards 'and near half the soldiers' came to hear mass with him; they were Catholics, as were about 4000 of William's army. Besides being Catholics the Dutch officers had evidently been instructed to relax their watch on the royal prisoner for they left the back of the house unguarded, and the garden ran down to the river. So it was easy for the King to arrange with a Captain Trevanion to have a shallop (rowing boat) ready on the river to carry him to the smack (fishing boat) that would be lying 'without the foot of Sheerness'.

James had sent orders to his son the Duke of Berwick to surrender Portsmouth and come to him at Rochester; till the young man arrived (he was only eighteen) he was in some anxiety. In the propaganda Berwick had been designated to be made 'king of Ireland' by his bigoted father, and might now be in danger.

The King had to tell the Earl of Lichfield (his niece Charlotte's husband) that he was going, and eventually Ailesbury too, as he had asked to lie in the Bedchamber that night. This led to another touching scene, recalled by Ailesbury in old age. When his last pleas for the King to stay had failed and it came to the final farewell, 'he was pleased to embrace me tenderly, as in French "à Dieu."' Such moments of feeling (which James never records) show the devotion he inspired in so many friends and servants, and in both his wives. Forthright in expressing his opinions, James was so reticent of his feelings that some people thought he had none and called him impassive.

'His Majesty went to bed at his usual houre, and when the company was gone, got up again, went out by a back pair of stairs and so through the garding . . .' to the boat. He took only his son Berwick, a Mr Biddulph and his valet Labadie. Nobody this time prevented him.

James wrote a detailed account of his escape by sea, which proved quite hazardous. The weather, as usual, was atrocious. First 'it blew so hard right ahead, and the tyde of ebb being down before they got to the salt pans, it was almost 6 in the morning before they could get to the Swale' – where the earlier escape had run aground. Here they had to wait, on another ship, for the tide, when they saw the smack and transferred to her. On Sunday they had to anchor off the Essex shore to ride out the gale, which only slackened in the evening, so that after sailing out, they had to anchor again off the Buoy of the Nore till next morning. 'It began to snow about Six, the wind continuing still easterly; but about ealeven it cleared up, and then they saw the high land of France . . . and so came to anchor before Ambleteuse . . . and so went on shore to that village about three on Tuesday morning, being Christmas day, old stile.'

In the memoirs a story is added which Berwick also told, of how

> it was the cause of some mirth to him (James), when growing very hungry and dry, Captain Travanion went to fry his Majesty some bacon but by misfortune the frying pan having a hole in it, he was forced to stop it with a pitched rag, and to ty an old furr'd can about with cord to make it hould the drink they put in it; however the King never eat or drank more heartily in his life.

It was obviously a tremendous relief to James to have got away from his impossible position in England; gales, snow and adverse winds in a small boat were things he could cheerfully cope with, in comparison with treacherous lords and scheming invaders. Far from being in hopeless depression he felt he was now free to take action. But first he must journey on to Paris to find his wife and child again. He sent Berwick riding ahead and followed himself by coach.

It was 4 January 1689 (new style) when the King landed in France and the country was snowbound. It had been already snowbound when the Queen arrived at Calais; she was persuaded to move to Boulogne and was there when she heard of the King's capture by the rabble. She could hardly be prevented from rushing back to England to share whatever fate might be in store for him. But the King of France sent a train of carriages and a small army of men to shovel away the snow, and himself drove out from Paris to meet her, descending from his coach to take the baby Prince of Wales in his arms and make speeches of welcome to the royal fugitives. By this time they had heard that James had escaped again and had landed safely – news which had sent Maria into hysterics of relief when she heard it.

With royal magnificence Louis was handing over the palace of Saint-Germain-en-Laye (known to Jacobites as St Germains), the ancient château where he had been born, recently restored, with gardens and fountains designed in the seventies by Le Nôtre. It stood above the Seine and its terraces commanded a wide view, with Paris (then) in the distance. Louis himself escorted Maria to her apartments, where everything possible had been done for her comfort, even to a casket containing a present of money left discreetly on her dressing table.

The same night the Duke of Berwick arrived, saying his father hoped to be there next day, 7 January (28 December, old style). So at six in the evening of that day Louis came again and sat on the bed where Maria had spent the day resting, talking to her in a friendly way until James arrived, when he went down to the hall to meet him.

Sharp-eyed French courtiers were standing round ready to note every detail of this encounter between the royal cousins, who had not met for about thirty years. Louis was then at the height of his power, a dignified, somewhat portly man of fifty, who inspired awe, admiration and exasperation all over Europe and who had devoted his considerable talents to the advancement of his country in every field. James, five years his senior, was taller and leaner; the French onlookers thought he looked old and tired – no wonder, after his recent experiences. He came into the hall slowly and bowed so low he almost went down on his knee, but Louis took him by the arms and embraced him as an equal, and then led him aside for some private conversation.

It was so long since James had been speaking French and his stammer was so noticeable that he gave the impression of being stupid to people used to elegant and eloquent conversation. They expected him to make emotional speeches on his misfortunes and the wickedness of the Prince of Orange, and when he did not they immediately voted him insensible to his sufferings.

Louis then took James upstairs to the Bedchamber, saying as he entered, 'Madame, I bring you a gentleman you will be very glad to see.' Maria, tears springing to her eyes, gave a cry of joy and James went straight to the bed and took her in his arms, much to the surprise of the watching courtiers. 'The King of England remained long in the arms of his wife,' wrote Dangeau, the court chronicler. Evidently he was not insensible in this respect. Presently Louis took James to see his son in his nursery and then brought him back to his wife and left them together.

[257]

Kind Louis might be, but he was a stickler for etiquette, which he had used to build up the royal supremacy over the nobility; he was determined not to have another Fronde. James and his Queen were caught up at once in the complex court ritual. The precedence of the French royal and semi-royal ladies was rigidly established and they were all jealous of Maria because, there being no Queen of France, she, as a queen, took first place. Louis' Spanish wife was dead and as he had plenty of legitimate male descendants he did not make a second state marriage but was secretly married to Madame de Maintenon (once governess to his illegitimate children) who had a good deal of influence behind the scenes. Louis was enchanted by Maria; he said she was his ideal of a queen and he treated her always in the grandest style. But because she was tactful as well as beautiful, Maria managed to make friends, rather than enemies, among the royal ladies, from the start of her exile.

James found the etiquette of the French court tiresome. He made his formal call at Versailles, but when Louis came to return it, he said, 'After this, let's have no more ceremony between us.' But that did not meet with the approval of the Grand Monarque and so the exiled King of England had to conform. But when he discovered that Lady Powis could not even sit on a stool in the presence of royalty because she was not of sufficiently high rank, he immediately made the Earl of Powis a Duke. Maria's faithful friend Donna Vittoria Montecuccoli was made Countess of Almond, so as to have the right to a folding stool. In later years James sometimes sat on a *tabouret* (solid stool) himself, instead of a chair, so as not to make too much distinction between his own royalty and his grand, but not crowned, visitors from Versailles. Louis would not have approved.

However, on his first brief sojourn in France James hardly had time to learn the rules of court etiquette. He was immediately involved in planning his next moves. A few days after his arrival on 2/12 January, he wrote to the Earl of Tyrconnel, his Deputy in Ireland, hoping he would be able to hold it 'till summer at least'. He added, 'all I can get this King to doe, is to send 7 or 8000 muskets, he not being willing to venter more arms or any men till he knows the condition you are in. . . .' Just before he left Rochester he had had a letter from Tyrconnel 'which tould me all was quiet with you, and I hope is so still, and that the P of O

[258]

has sent over no force to invade you yet.' He added that the bearer would give 'an account how wee all got away and how kindly I have been received here.'

Two days later, 4/14 January, only a week after he had reached St Germains, James wrote an official letter to Lord Preston, which he desired to be read to the Privy Council. Although couched in more formal language, it was essentially the same as his letter left at Rochester, pointing out that he had been ready, and still was ready, to call a Parliament to settle the grievances of the nation. He sent this letter by the hand of his equerry Ralph Sheldon, who was also to ask for the King's personal equipage – coach, horses, guns, dogs and clothes – to be sent after him; something he had done for Prince George at Salisbury, as he reminded Lord Dartmouth when writing to him about it.

Sheldon arrived in London on the night of 18/28 January. 'Pretty early' next morning Preston called on Clarendon, who doubted whether the letter was legal, not having the Great Seal; he also thought the Prince of Orange would not suffer the King's board to meet. The letter was quashed. The illegal Convention began a few days later.

However, James made a second attempt to communicate with the councils of state in England. On 2/12 February, a Saturday, Lord Halifax (who, of course, was chairing the session of peers) said a letter had been put into his hands, but after a lot of discussion managed to put off reading it till Monday, when it was dismissed unread 'as the letter of a private man'.

By these two formal letters James had tried to put his case before the Privy Council and the Convention at the very earliest opportunity. Both were suppressed, so that he was condemned unheard, as he complained in the memoirs; his father had at least stood trial.

The letters are given verbatim in the *Life*. The one to the Privy Council, which was re-issued with that to the Convention, pointed out that the King had issued writs for a Parliament before the invasion began and that further efforts at agreement had been frustrated by the Prince of Orange's 'laying a restraint upon our royal person'. So, first making it clear that his flight was to freedom, not from sovereignty, the King affirmed that he desired 'nothing more than to return and hould a free parliament'.

Commenting on the suppression of this first letter the King renewed his promise of settling the religious question through Parliament, and so to 'heal all divisions, cover with oblivion all past faults, and restore the happynesse of our people, which never can be efectually done by any other power.' But as James remarked in the memoirs, 'The Prince of Orange was too jealous to suffer, and Master enough to prevent, the publication of these letters.'

Clarendon's journal reveals something of the manoeuvres going on in England, in which the peers at first played a leading part, though after a substitute for a House of Commons was assembled (mainly of members of Charles II's last – Exclusionist – Parliament) the Lords began to find themselves waiting for Commons decisions – something that had never happened before, Clarendon peevishly recorded. The real arguments began when the Convention was called in January, as to whether the King had abdicated or deserted the government and whether, in consequence, the throne was 'vacant'. Clarendon and the Tories maintained that in an hereditary monarchy the throne could never be vacant, and so they argued for a regency.

William, who had once told Bentinck that he wished everything did not have to be left to Parliament, had managed to make his views known through intermediaries; he was not interested in any form of regency, nor did he want to be his wife's gentleman usher or hold the Crown by apron-strings; he would be King himself. When the regency party lost the final vote in the Lords (by a narrow margin) it was then soon settled that William and Mary were to be joint sovereigns, he holding the rule and continuing to do so if she died before him; Anne was thus persuaded to give up her place in the (new) succession, to her uncle Clarendon's annoyance.

The decision was made on 6 February 1689, just four years after Charles II's death. 'I think this was the most dismal day I ever saw in my life,' wrote Clarendon. 'God help us; we are certainly a miserable undone people.' In his view the Revolution had destroyed the traditional English monarchy. He soon decided to go no more to the House of Lords and retired to the country before his niece Mary arrived, on 12 February.

On 13 February, Ash Wednesday, a very wet day, William and Mary were formally offered the Crown in the Banqueting House at Whitehall. It was graciously accepted.

John Evelyn thought the Princess ought at least to have showed 'some reluctancy, of assuming her Father's Crowne and made some Apologie, testifying her regret, that he should by his misgovernment necessitate the Nation to so extraordinary a proceeding . . . But nothing of all this appeared; she came into W-hall as to a wedding, riant and jolly, so as seeming quite Transported. . . .' The very first morning she got up early and 'in her undresse' went round looking at the rooms and furniture, took over the Queen's bed (now on show in Kensington Palace) 'and within a night or two sate down to play at Basset, as the Q. her predecessor us'd to do. . . .'

And it was not as if Evelyn disapproved of the change of government. He went on to criticize the bishops who, after contributing to the Prince's expedition, now began to 'boggle and raise scrupuls and such as created much division among people, greatly rejoicing the old Courtiers and Papists especially.' The bishops, as James would have said, had been well and truly bubbled by the Orangist conspirators, not expecting that William would make himself King. Sancroft's scruples led him to refuse to crown the new sovereigns or to take oaths to them, while the King he had crowned and sworn loyalty to, still lived. He was eventually deprived of his see and all its temporalities (something the papist tyrant James had not done to any) and retired to a cottage in the country, where he prayed every day for the true royal family till he died in 1693. Several other bishops followed his lead, including Ken, who found a refuge at Longleat in Wiltshire. So many clergy (about 400) became 'non-jurors' as almost to split the Church of England and some of their congregations followed them into the wilderness.

Evelyn also noted, 'Another objection was the invalidity of what was don, by a Convention only, and the as yet unabrogated Laws: which made them on the 22, make themselves a parliament, the new King passing the Act with the Crowne on his head' – though William had not yet been crowned. As a matter of fact he thought coronation a load of old popish superstition, but he had to go through with it, or the English people would not regard him as really a King. The date was fixed for 11 April.

But before William was crowned (by Bishop Compton) the news was out that King James was in Ireland, once more ruling in a kingdom which had remained loyal to him.

14 Ireland

James spent barely two months in France and began at once to make plans for Ireland. Already in mid-January he had raised the subject with Louis, at Marly. To be invited to this royal country house was a special favour. Madame de Sévigné wrote that King Louis 'said the other day that this king was the best fellow in the world, that he should hunt with him, that he should come to Marly and Trianon and that the courtiers would have to get used to it.' Although it suited French policy to support James against William, it is clear that Louis himself genuinely liked his cousin and admired Maria, quite envying James for her wifely devotion. On public occasions and at Racine's plays, she was always placed between the two kings.

Maria wrote to Charlotte, Lady Lichfield, on 21 January (new style) saying that she was very well 'and have the satisfaction to see my poor child grow visibly every day, and the King look better than he has done this great while.' James had remarkable resilience, quickly recovering from the strain of the last two months in England.

He wrote letters to several European rulers, the principal one to the Emperor, reproaching him for allowing his ally the Prince of Orange to dethrone a Catholic King. The Emperor wrote a polite but insulting reply, addressing James as Serene Highness and not as 'your Majesty' and telling him it was all his own fault for not joining in the League against France – 'as if England were a feudatory of the Empire,' commented James in disgust.

He had also kept in touch with his Protestant cousin Sophia, Electress of Hanover, who had been shocked by William's invasion. She wrote to a female relative (who had called William a second Joshua) that he might have begun by defending the Protestants in France rather than those in England, where the persecuted Huguenots had been granted asylum, and she hoped William would not emulate Joshua by hanging kings. Although when William was crowned she wrote formal congratulations, she said to his face, 'but I lament King James, who has honoured me with his friendship.'

It was when James heard of the bare majority vote in the illegal Convention to offer the Crown to William and Mary, that he decided to go to Ireland himself and at once. King Louis gave him a great send off, presenting him with his own sword, and saying that though the best wish he could offer was that he would never see him again, yet he would always be glad to welcome him back.

Maria could hardly bear the parting and clung to James, weeping and half fainting, till he gave her in charge of her ladies. The Frenchwomen watching rather disapproved such emotion; the Frenchmen, headed by King Louis, were full of admiration. Before he left, James had taken Maria to the Visitation Convent at Chaillot, founded by his mother (and where her heart was enshrined) telling the nuns he was glad his wife would be able to visit them while he was away. She soon became a devoted friend of the senior nuns and Chaillot was to be her haven in the long years of her widowhood.

James drove off for the coast, and though he was delayed by a series of accidents, he sailed on 6 March (new style) and landed at Kinsale on the twelfth. When William heard this news he was so angry that he took the mean little revenge of cancelling the order for James's equipage to be sent to France. Luckily the Queen's had already gone and so her coach with the coachman (who had once driven for Cromwell), her clothes and personal effects, arrived safely at St Germains.

It is plain that when William allowed James to escape he never expected him to be so active once he had left England. At fifty-five James was regarded as an old man and William must have thought he would settle down as a pensioner at the court of France. There is a story (printed in Dalrymple) that on the very day of their coronation Mary received a letter from her father, saying that till now he had thought her carried along by her husband but that it was in her power to refuse to be crowned in her father's lifetime and if she persisted, she would call down on herself a parental curse rather than a blessing. Gossip had it that Mary turned on William and said it was all his fault for letting the King go; while he retorted that she had known and gone along with all he had done. When this got round to James, he said he felt as if his own daughter was saying, 'Away with him from the face of the earth.'

It was Mary's and Anne's turning against him which hurt most deeply.

Rizzini, the Modenese envoy, arrived from England before James left France and he wrote to Maria's brother, the Duke of Modena, noting the French opinion that James was insensitive. 'But whoever understands his imperturbable nature is well aware that, however inured he is grown to suffering, so that he is never accustomed to show pain, he is not on that account exempt from severest inward wounds, which are so much the more painful as they are concealed and deep.' Rizzini had known James ever since his marriage to Maria; he knew them both well.

Donna Vittoria also wrote to Modena, saying that the King's departure was the only thing painful to the Queen; otherwise she enjoyed their present peace and quiet; as for the King, 'he accommodates himself very contentedly to a private life.' This ability to adapt to circumstances was to stand James in good stead in the years to come. But just now he was taking up the role of King again – King in Ireland.

James landed at Kinsale but it was in Cork that he met his old friend Tyrconnel; he greeted him with a fraternal embrace and made him a Duke. When, towards the end of March, he made his entry into Dublin, Tyrconnel rode before him, carrying the sword of state. The King, attended by his lords, rode into his Irish capital on horseback, wearing a plain suit of cinnamon colour and a black slouch hat, the royal blue riband of the Garter over his shoulder. He was the first English king to visit Ireland since Richard II.

James II was greeted with enthusiasm, bells ringing, Irish girls in white strewing flowers in his way, the gentry coming out in their coaches, the Corporation and guilds on foot, and the Catholic clergy carrying the Host in a monstrance. James dismounted to kneel before the Holy Sacrament.

He took up residence in Dublin Castle, then somewhat dilapidated but with a block of modern state apartments built by the old Duke of Ormonde towards the end of his long term as Viceroy. Here James lived as King, with his ministers of state and a small court. Thus he had very quickly re-established himself in his own kingdom, showing that he regarded the Convention as illegal and William as a usurper – among the Jacobites he remained always the Prince of Orange.

Because James never did regain his throne in England, later generations are apt to write him off from the moment he left London, but his contemporaries did not make that mistake. For over a year the true King of Great Britain was actually in power in one of his kingdoms and it was quite on the cards that he might make a successful return to the other two. This made a considerable difference to the attitude of the most powerful men in England, as William was well aware. Although he declared war on France in May 1689, he was not able to leave England to command his armies on the continent himself, as he had planned.

Even before the Convention had concluded its business pamphlets were beginning to appear, suggesting that some of the charges against King James were false; once William and Mary were crowned the opposition, instead of subsiding, grew more vociferous. Burnet retaliated by reprinting all the propaganda on the pretended Prince of Wales, but it was impossible to keep up the legend of the secret league with France to cut all Protestant throats when Sunderland publicly denied it, in a defence of himself which he published in March. He and his wife had both written to William from Holland, (where Sunderland had been reconverted to Protestantism by one of Mary's chaplains), Sunderland lamenting that he had not been in England to vote for William at the Convention. Although his name was excepted from the amnesty, he soon returned privately to England, and was pardoned, kissing William's hand in 1690; thereafter he advised him behind the scenes.

With Sunderland mysteriously reinstated and Father Petre living quietly abroad as Rector of the college at St Omers, the Orange party had to make do with Jeffreys, who had tried to escape, disguised as a seaman but was recognized and sent to the Tower. Already a sick man, afflicted with kidney stones, he died soon afterwards, Anglican to the last, receiving communion with devotion. Dead, he became the immediate villain of the Bloody Assizes. But as far as James was concerned, the slanderers had an uphill task against the rising Jacobite reaction.

James was aware of this reaction in England. One of his correspondents was Catherine Sedley, who figures in Clarendon's journal and in Ailesbury's memoirs as boldly anti-Orange. When Mary tried to snub

[265]

her father's notorious mistress, Catherine retorted that if she had broken one commandment with the King, Mary had broken another against him. In this first year as Queen, Mary behaved with unsuitable frivolity and tactlessness. Finding that James had banned *The Spanish Friar*, she had the play put on, only to discover that it was about an old king put in prison by his daughter. Everyone in the theatre kept turning to stare at her, while she sat back in her box, embarrassed and flirting her fan to hide her face. At another play about the Cavaliers, the audience cheered the line about the King enjoying his own again. Then Jacobites like Sir John Fenwick insulted Mary by not taking off their hats when they passed her in the park. Trivialities, but they showed which way the wind was blowing, and so soon after the Revolution, too.

However, James was also facing difficulties in Ireland. The most immediate was the resistance of Protestants in the north, at Coleraine and Derry. Then Tyrconnel had collected an army said to number 100,000 men but they were untrained and largely unarmed. Louvois, the French war minister, had insisted on sending French generals and officers to take command and King Louis, while providing arms and money, had also loaded James with what was to prove one of his heaviest burdens, Comte d'Avaux as ambassador.

D'Avaux, whose warnings from Holland had gone unheeded, had a low opinion of James's ability and hated Ireland, sending home a stream of criticism, starting with 'His Britannic Majesty speaks of everything before all the world.' As the King of France's representative d'Avaux was given a grand reception at Dublin Castle and sat on the King's Council, along with the Duke of Tyrconnel (Ireland) and the Earl of Melfort (Scotland) who did not get on with each other either. D'Avaux had no idea of the differences between the three kingdoms or of James's duty to his Protestant subjects, regarded as expendable by the French.

James issued a Declaration on the first day of April 1689, which he sent to his other two kingdoms too, outlining his intentions for the future and offering terms to the rebels, with promises to protect their religion and property. He now heard from Scotland that his supporters had managed to get his official letters read at the Convention in Edinburgh but then, finding that there would be a majority for the Prince of Orange, they left it to organize resistance. James sent two

Scots officers with commissions to raise men; he hoped to send more effective help soon and even to go there himself.

But he had already discovered that the rebels in the north were more numerous than he had been led to suppose; he also found there was practically no viable artillery in Ireland and had to set men to work *making* it. He lost no time in trying to put the offensive on a more efficient footing, sending the best of the newly equipped regiments under the French commander Pusignan to assist Hamilton against Coleraine. He decided that 100,000 barefoot enthusiasts were not an army and ordered Tyrconnel to reduce numbers, and he sent urgently south for arms to be hurried north. Then, only a few days later, he went north himself.

The rebels were defeated at Coleraine and everyone was optimistic that Derry would now surrender; indeed, James was on his way back to Dublin when he heard that the Mayor had opened negotiations. He immediately rode the thirty miles back to his army, with only a few hours' sleep in his clothes, only to find that the French General Rosen had deployed his troops much nearer the town than he thought advisable. James went up on a small hill in full view of Derry and sent a trumpeter for an answer to his summons to come out and discuss terms. None came; instead, cannon and musket shot were fired towards him and an officer next to him was killed. For all that James remained outside the town on horseback for hours in the pouring rain, hoping for negotiations.

In fact Derry had just received a reinforcement from the loch and the militants in the town had persuaded the rest on 'No surrender'. Since the defenders were numerous and better armed than the besiegers and could easily be relieved by sea, it was not a foolhardy decision. It was only the inefficiency of the English ships in coming to their relief that eventually reduced the besieged to starvation rations.

On the way back to Dublin James received the surrender of two rebel strongholds and was able to demonstrate his good faith by insisting on the observance of the pledges on life and property given in his declaration.

On 26 April he reached Dublin once more, 'where he found the Duke of Tyrconnel not returned from visiting the troops; the arms not arrived from Cork, Kinsale or Waterford; and that in the arsenal

[267]

nothing had been done for preparing of tools, which obliged him to renew his orders on those two heads,' as he wrote tersely in the memoirs. And when Tyrconnel did come back it turned out he had not had the heart to disband as many men as James had wished, so that the untrained force was still too large. What was worse, those who were turned off began to live like bandits in the countryside, so that the King had to institute provost marshals to try to keep order; needless to say, order was not always kept.

In May James opened a Parliament, the first held in Ireland since 1666, to which Protestant bishops, not Catholic, were summoned; some attended. So did some members, though quite a number of Protestant gentlemen had fled to England, where Clarendon had failed to interest William in their affairs. In his opening speech James declared: 'I have always been for Liberty of Conscience and against invadeing any man's right or libertie; haveing still in mind the saying of holy writ, Doe as you would be done too, for this is the Law and the Profets ... wheresoever I am Master, I design, God willing, to establish it by Law, and have no other test or distinction but that of Loyalty.'

But the Catholics of Ireland were more interested in property than liberty, still resenting the Act of Settlement after the Restoration, which had allowed even appropriations under Cromwell to continue in Protestant hands. During the debates on the Act of Attainder (against absent rebels) the King was only stopped by d'Avaux from going to the house in his ordinary clothes to reprimand the over-active legislators. Instead he prorogued the Parliament in July, just after he had received the news that the long expected invasion from England was on the way.

By then Derry had been relieved by Kirk from the sea and the siege had to be given up – not before an unfortunate incident when the French General Rosen had ordered the country people to be driven under the walls, to starve or be taken in by the then nearly starving defenders. James immediately sent countermanding orders and privately said he would have liked to hang Rosen – but of course he had to write to him politely, saying that he could not have read the royal declaration.

And then came the tragic news from Scotland that Dundee, in the hour of his success at Killiecrankie, had fallen mortally wounded. After his death the Highland army melted away and the opportunity was lost for effective opposition to William in Scotland.

On 12 August 1689 the English fleet appeared off County Down and during the next few days the Huguenot General Schomberg (whom James had fought *with*, in the continental wars of his youth) landed his forces and equipment; but it took him nine days to reduce Carrick-fergus. The King arrived on 26 August and in September himself took command and did his utmost to bring Schomberg to battle, but that wary old commander (he was about eighty) refused to be drawn and dug himself in at Dundalk; his men, especially the English, were already succumbing to disease in alarming numbers.

In vain did James draw out his army, marching in the head of the first and second line within less than a cannon shot of the enemy, his soldiers shouting defiance and daring them to come on. Schomberg was not to be drawn and they had to retire, James remaining in the rear (nearest the enemy) till the last. It was just his luck that he was not able to fight what might have been a successful battle now, but at least Schomberg was stopped from doing anything but retire into winter quarters at Belfast, whence he sent a stream of complaints to William, on the inadequate equipment and supplies, the illness and other difficulties he had to contend with. The year's campaigning had ended in uncertainty but not too badly for King James.

It was the winter that really did for him, for it was impossible to feed the army during those long months. A great many had to be sent home and some lived off what they could pick up from other people's property. In Dublin those still under arms got into continual quarrels with the French. D'Avaux thought every erring Irishman ought to be strung up at once and was incensed to see them on their feet and swaggering after a court martial; he thought the King weak for sparing them.

When a Protestant uprising threatened, d'Avaux advised a reprisal after the manner of St Bartholomew's Eve, with a seizure of Protestant property to follow. The first time he suggested it the King did not answer; pressed again, he replied briefly that he was not going to cut his subjects' throats – to which d'Avaux retorted that then they would certainly cut his.

Of course some of the Protestants thought that was just what James was aiming to do, in spite of his declaration. Yet the *Stuart Papers* are full of pardons issued to merchants, in an attempt to keep the balance. But because of an acute shortage of cash the King had been forced to coin copper and brass money and this debased coinage affected his Protestant subjects worst, since they had more both of money and goods. Back in St Germains the Queen was pawning her jewels for cash, but there were still not enough arms coming from France. 'The King's affairs looked like the primitive Cahos,' wrote James gloomily in the memoirs.

Even his Council were at loggerheads. Nobody (except James) could get on with the Earl of Melfort, John Drummond, the Scots convert who had so annoyed the English Protestant Lords; the King had to send him to France in August 1689, whence the Queen sent him on to Rome, his expenses paid by King Louis. D'Avaux criticized Melfort for taking long walks with his beautiful wife; Melfort (from Paris) criticized Tyrconnel's wife – none other than the once lovely Frances Jennings unsuccessfully pursued by James some twenty-five years ago. It was her connexion with her sister Sarah Churchill (now Countess of Marlborough) which caused suspicion.

James's own little court at Dublin Castle was accused of immorality by the Dean of St Patrick's, imprisoned in the Castle after the abortive Protestant rising. He survived (like all James's 'victims') to write as scurrilously against the King as Dr Burnet, now Bishop of Salisbury. Yet on coming to Dublin James had only taken over Christ Church, where he went regularly to mass in state; the other old churches were all left in the hands of the Protestant clergy.

Somehow the King struggled through to the spring of 1690, when there was a general shake-up. Rosen was recalled and Lauzun sent instead. James liked Lauzun but though brave, the little Gascon was not the world's greatest general and had besides been given strict orders by Louvois not to endanger French lives but to rely on delaying action to prevent William engaging his full forces against France. There were now more French lives to endanger, for James had been persuaded, much against his will, to send some thousands of Irish under his best Irish general, Mountcashel, over to France to be trained and incorporated in the French army, in exchange for 4000 experienced French troops.

But best of the changes, d'Avaux had gone, though not before he had presented James with a memorial of criticisms. The King listened patiently but resented it so much that he wrote to King Louis, who tactfully recalled d'Avaux, sending him as ambassador to Sweden, an assignment much more to his taste.

William at last decided that he must go to Ireland himself but he did not get there till June 1690. He left Mary in charge as Queen regnant, assisted by a Council of nine peers headed by the Marquis of Carmarthen (Danby). William had no opinion of women's powers and it was quite a surprise to him when Mary turned out rather better at presiding in England than he was – a surprise to her too. Her letters to him (which he kept) are full of remarks about the nine lords and the progress of Kensington Palace as well as of current political problems, and always ended with declarations of heartfelt devotion.

James was forced to watch the English navy bring over William and his army (largely of foreign troops); he had now no ships of his own and had been unable to persuade the French fleet to intercept the convoys. As a matter of fact, the day before James was losing his battle at the Boyne, Admiral de Tourville was winning his at Beachy Head, against the combined English and Dutch fleets; it was James's fate that everything always happened at the wrong time for him, through no fault of his own.

James knew he would be criticized for fighting at the Boyne, since his army was inferior to William's both in number and experience. He decided to fight there because he felt it would demoralize his native troops to retreat and lose Dublin without striking a blow for it.

The battle has been described many times from the scanty records and experts still argue over the exact moves, but James's army made quite a fight for it (Berwick distinguishing himself) and they were not routed but made an orderly retreat, covered by the French; only some of the raw Irish recruits threw down their arms and ran, which started the legend of a rout. James himself was certainly not the first to flee, nor the first to reach Dublin, as the story was later told against him. He went on the advice of Lauzun, who urged him to go back to France and get more assistance there. Once in Dublin, which he reached about sunset on the day of the battle (1 July), Tyrconnel advised the same.

In Dublin James found letters from the Queen telling him of the

French victory over Prince Waldeck and the allies at Fleurus in Flanders, which encouraged him to hope that he might persuade Louis to assist him in a descent on England while William was out of it. William could not return at once to England since he had failed to follow up his victory by cutting off the retreat, and in fact he was so slow in moving that the Jacobites were able to retire and reorganize behind the Shannon, as Tyrconnel had told James they would.

James stayed only one night in Dublin and was afterwards bitterly criticized for deserting Ireland in the hour of defeat. But he went away on the advice of all his Council, consulting the members singly; leaving orders that Dublin should not offer resistance to the enemy, so that it would not suffer sack and looting, and handing over all remaining funds to Tyrconnel. As he was going with the aim of promoting a rapid counter-invasion of England, speed was essential, but as usual with James's quick reactions it was misconstrued as a cowardly flight from defeat, always remembered as such in Ireland.

When he reached the coast the King took ship for Brest, where he heard of Tourville's victory at Beachy Head. He was more than ever convinced that now the way back to England lay open.

15 St Germains

With his usual bad luck James arrived back in Paris just as the people were celebrating with bonfires the supposed death of William of Orange – in fact, he had received a slight wound from a stray bullet just before the battle of the Boyne. (It was old Schomberg who was shot dead crossing the river.) Into this misplaced rejoicing James came with the news of his own defeat. The only person pleased was the Queen, happy to know he was safe before she heard the battle was lost. It was sixteen months since she had seen him, the longest separation of their married life; his letters to her, anxiously awaited and joyfully received, which she often mentioned to the nuns at Chaillot, seem not to have survived. The Prince of Wales, whom James had left a baby in arms, was now a two-year-old child, running about in his tartan frock and able to ask his father's blessing. It was a happy reunion. No doubt the dogs were pleased too.

But nobody else was pleased; Jacobites as well as the French criticized James for leaving so abruptly after the battle. And when King Louis called, kind as ever, he nevertheless put off James's eager proposals for an immediate crossing to England and whenever James tried to see him at Versailles he pleaded indisposition, till the opportunity had gone by.

In the memoirs James recorded that nothing had ever tried his patience more; he had never come nearer to despair. He begged to be allowed even one ship to take him across the Channel, sure that his English sailors would not fight against him. It was no good. Louis had been persuaded by Louvois that James was not worth further backing; Ireland was lost and nothing could come of another expedition.

But Ireland was not lost. The Jacobites had retreated to Limerick, where the walls were so dilapidated that Lauzun said they could have been knocked down with toasted apples; he had withdrawn the French troops before the siege began. But William's artillery was still on the way when Patrick Sarsfield executed a cutting-out operation, up-ended the guns into the ground and blew them up. So William, bereft of technological superiority, found himself beaten by ferocious Irish, hurling stones when their ammunition ran out. And it rained and rained. Eventually he was forced to raise the siege and, leaving an army to winter in Ireland under the Dutch General Ginkel, he returned belatedly to England in October, to the celebrations Mary had been organizing and having to put off again and again since the Boyne. This failure of William's to follow up his victory rather altered Louis' outlook, but by then it was too late.

James was only too well aware that he was now despised as a coward, he whose courage had been praised by Turenne and Condé when William was in the nursery. This bitter humiliation added to his frustration in being unable to seize the advantage of William's absence from England to make a bold attempt to recover his kingdom – which might well have succeeded to judge by the evidence which has survived of widespread disillusion there.

Dissatisfaction among the people was caused by the war, which William had declared (in May 1689) without consulting Parliament or

[273]

his English ministers, and then sent English troops overseas, under Churchill, which suffered heavy casualties in the indecisive campaign. Dissatisfaction was increased by the favouring of Dutch ships and trade above English and by the fact that though the hated chimney tax was taken off, a poll tax was imposed which came harder on the poor. Then William himself was not only foreign but 'morose'; he would not dine in public, he was bored with plays and with music (except for military bands) and disapproved of it in church; he loathed Whitehall, felt ill in its foggy damp atmosphere and moved out to Hampton Court, which was considered inaccessible for a working monarch. It was a very different style of monarchy from the Restoration.

Dissatisfaction among the politicians was caused by William's re-lying so much on Dutchmen, rewarding them with estates and English titles; his Dutch generals dined with him but Churchill was left standing. Although he had been made Earl of Marlborough things were so different from what he had imagined that Sarah was soon calling William 'the Dutch Abortion' and they began to turn Anne against her sister, so that quarrels became endemic. The Whigs were disgusted to find their old enemy Danby (now Marquis of Carmarthen) highest in favour and Tories like Nottingham in power, with Godolphin and others of James's government; even Sunderland was back – to Evelyn's astonishment. The Whigs felt they had made the Revolution and were not getting their due reward.

If William was a disappointment to the Parliament men, he was still more so to the religious Protestants, the Presbyterians in particular, who shared his theology and had hoped for a Measure of Comprehension which would allow them back into the Church of England, reversing 1662; but this was not carried by a Parliament of Anglicans. By the new Toleration Act (1689) Protestant dissenters were allowed freedom of worship but had to register with the bishops and everyone still had to pay tithe to the Established Church. Nor could dissenters hold any civil office unless they took the Test oaths and the Sacrament in Church. As for Catholics, there was nothing for them, except that they were no longer prosecuted for treason, since William had to keep up his reputation for tolerance with his Catholic allies.

Yet although the Church of England had managed to retain its legal supremacy, the Revolution effected a lasting alteration in its internal balance. First there were the non-jurors, who maintained a High Church underground for years; then in their places Mary (to whom William left church affairs) appointed Latitudinarians whose doctrine (or lack of it) shocked the traditionalists. Burnet was made Bishop of Salisbury, to Clarendon's disgust, though he was (by his own account) a hard-working preaching and teaching bishop. He reckoned he ought to have had Durham but the Prince had promised it to Compton; then, rather than let Compton have it, Crewe came back from Holland to vote for William and kept his see till long after all the royal family were dead, dying himself in 1721 aged eighty-eight. His Dean, Denis Granville, shocked at this compromise, went into exile and died at Paris in 1703. Bishop Cartwright also chose exile and went with James to Ireland, but died there soon after.

The oaths presented a problem to laymen too, especially peers, though they had been discreetly altered to leave out the words 'rightful and lawful'. Ailesbury decided they had thus become 'garrison oaths' – to the present defenders of the nation – and took them, while remaining loyal in his heart to his rightful king. Clarendon, however, refused them and his near relationship to Mary did not save him from being arrested on suspicion in the summer of 1690 and sent to the Tower, along with many others. On a lower social level, Pepys resigned and paid double taxes rather than serve William. The dissatisfaction with William's rule was so general that even Burnet wrote a letter of remonstrance to him which so annoyed him that he refused for months to see the man who had done so much to prepare the way for him. (This letter seems to me the one printed by Dalrymple as probably written by a peer; no peer could have dared such a bold lecture, which is much in Burnet's ebullient style.) Even Trimmer Halifax was saying that if King James would give assurances about religion he would be welcomed back at once.

James, who had never stopped giving assurances, knew this, and it was desperately frustrating not to be able to convince King Louis of it, before the chance passed. He was saved from sinking into utter despair by his old friend Marshal Bellefonds (whom he calls Belford) who in November 1690 took him to visit the monastery of La Trappe in a remote part of Normandy.

La Trappe was a community of Cistercians, reformed by the Abbot

[275]

Armand Jean de Rancé, once a court Abbé much in need of reform himself. These were the first Trappists, vowed to silence and penance, living on a vegetarian diet, cultivating their own land and reciting all the monastic offices, including Matins in what to most people is the middle of the night. This austere life attracted men of the world, ex-courtiers and soldiers, and it appealed to James so strongly that he told the Abbot he wished he could retire from the world and find peace as a penitent there.

Of course he could do no such thing but Abbot de Rancé taught him how to submit his will to the will of God, accept all his misfortunes as penance for his sins and thus live in the spirit of La Trappe even when in the world. The Abbot continued to advise him and some of his letters survive in the *Stuart Papers*; in the first, on 21 December 1690, he wrote, 'Your Majesty knows so perfectly what God has done for you and the impressions you preserve of it are so lively and so deep that one cannot doubt that you will have all the protection you need.'

He understood the King's problems very well. James was anxious to rebut the imputations of cowardice by taking part in the French war and was frustrated again by Louis' refusal; the Abbot tactfully told him King Louis must preserve the life of his guest and again counselled patience and submission. Another inquiry on whether it was consonant with Christian penitence to keep up a royal equipage, drew the answer that while royal state was necessary to a king's station, all extravagance and waste should be avoided. James had always practised economy and even now contrived to manage his pension from Louis so carefully that he paid all his dependants regularly and even saved money for charity.

After this first visit James went into retreat at La Trappe every year, eating with the monks and attending their offices in the church; he was not only saved from despair but given a positive pattern, psychological and spiritual, for his life in exile. Once he took Maria to stay in the guest house at La Trappe, and she called it 'a terrestrial paradise'. Her own place of retreat was at Chaillot, nearer home if her children were suddenly taken ill. (Or her husband: she once dashed back to nurse James through a bad attack of boils – to his grateful surprise.) At St Germains every day started with mass and they attended all the feasts and devotions at the parish church, James taking his turn watching before the Blessed Sacrament when there was Exposition. They drove into Paris for Lenten sermons or to visit religious houses. The French court considered all this piety rather overdone but ordinary people respected them for it.

James even composed a prayer thanking God for making him aware of his sins by allowing the loss of his three kingdoms (the personal aspect of this loss). Yet he did not give up hope of return, though as the years passed restoration was seen as more for his son's sake than his own. Jacobite attempts continued all the time.

The battle of the Boyne is generally regarded as having finished off James but it did not look like that to William. For the duration of his war with France, nearly the whole of his reign, he lived under the threat of a repetition of his own coup in reverse: a Jacobite invasion from across the Channel, supported by risings in England. And it was not till after James's return from Ireland that the first Jacobite plot for bringing him back was discovered. It was entirely a Protestant plot, implicating Lord Clarendon, the Bishop of Ely (Francis Turner) and William Penn the Quaker, among others. Letters from them were captured with Lord Preston and Mr Ashton, as they were trying to slip off to France in a fishing smack on the last day of the year 1690.

Clarendon, who had written to urge James to take the first opportunity of coming over when William went across to Holland, assured him he would now have wide support. He was immediately arrested and sent to the Tower for the second time. William then left Mary to cope with the conspiracy and set off amid winter gales in January 1691 for the Hague, where he received a tremendous welcome as King-Stadholder, with bonfires, triumphal arches and banquets laid on, surprising the English lords in his train by appearing comparatively genial. The truth was he hated England and only wanted it to back up his military campaigns against France. From now on he was to spend the major part of every year out of England, not merely on campaign in Flanders but enjoying long hunting holidays with his men friends at his country palaces in Holland.

Left to herself, Mary became a stern suppressor of Jacobites on William's behalf. Mr Ashton, giving nothing away, was executed for treason before the end of January, although he had played with Mary at Richmond in their childhood. He was the first to suffer as a traitor for loyalty to his lawful king and James was shocked and grieved to the heart.

Lord Preston lost his nerve and bought his reprieve by giving away his associates; there are many references to this in the private correspondence of the time and fears as to what had been disclosed. Preston was kept in prison till William's brief visit to England in the spring, when he implicated Lord Marlborough (Churchill), Godolphin and others supposedly of the new government party. As there was no other evidence available William decided not to proceed against them, but he gave no further command to Marlborough. As to Clarendon, it was decided not to put him on trial and he was eventually released on condition of retiring from public life; it was felt that fear would keep him (and the Bishop and Penn) from any new intrigue. Clarendon never took the oaths but lived in the country editing his father's *History of the Great Rebellion* which he was able to publish in the first year of the reign of his niece Queen Anne. But Bishop Turner went over to join the loyal Anglican exiles in Paris. They included Edward Herbert, the ex-Lord Chief Justice, supported by a pension from his brother the Admiral, who had been made Earl of Torrington by William but soon fell out of favour for alleged non-cooperation with the Dutch fleet at Beachy Head.

Churchill (never called Marlborough among the Jacobites) was certainly in correspondence with the exiles; he told a Jacobite agent he could neither eat nor drink for thinking of his treachery and begged for James's forgiveness and a written pardon. James, surprised and a little suspicious, nevertheless complied and sent one for Godolphin too, who cherished a sentimental admiration for Maria, whose Chamberlain he had been. Although these traitors of 1688 were probably only hedging their bets in case James should return, the fact that they did it argues a strong general expectation of a restoration. Incidentally, in the autumn of 1690 Churchill had got William's permission to carry out raids on Cork and Kinsale, taking both and thereby disrupting Jacobite communications with France. On this raid the Duke of Grafton, son of Charles II and Barbara, who had deserted James in 1688, was killed, but left a son to inherit the title and Arlington's Euston estates, which continue to his descendants.

The war in Ireland was more or less ended a year after the Boyne by

[278]

the battle of Aughrim on 12 July 1691; the Dutch General Ginkel went on to take Limerick, which this time surrendered on terms – afterwards broken, for the penal laws were imposed on Ireland in all their rigour. The surrendering soldiers were offered the choice of enlisting with William or going overseas; most of them chose to go, and offered their service to James, who formed them into regiments and gave the command to the Duke of Berwick and Patrick Sarsfield, whom he had made Earl of Lucan. These regiments were paid by the King of France and were in much the same position as the English regiments in William's service before the 1688 Revolution. Tyrconnel, who had been in poor health for several years, collapsed and died in August 1691, and so a chapter in Irish history was closed.

In December 1691 Anne wrote a contrite letter to her father: 'If wishes could recall what is past, I had long since redeem'd my fault,' and more to the same effect. It did not reach James till the following spring and may have been intercepted by William's spies, for early in 1692 Marlborough was suddenly deprived of all his court offices (worth £12,000) just after handing King William his shirt at the royal levee. No reason was given, though at the last session of Parliament he had moved that all foreigners should be sent out of England. He had also been instrumental in securing for Princess Anne from Parliament an income of £50,000 when William had proposed cutting James's grant of £30,000 to a mere £5000. But this was hardly sufficient to explain why he was sent to the Tower in May, when a Jacobite invasion was expected. Since there was insufficient evidence for a treason trial, however, he was eventually released, though he remained under a cloud for years.

Meanwhile, a major quarrel had developed between Mary and Anne over the dismissal of Lady Marlborough. Sarah represented this as a merely personal affair but of course Mary had good reason for demanding the dismissal, though she could not make it public. Anne, still passionately devoted to Sarah ('Mrs Freeman' to her 'Mrs Morley') refused; rather than give her up she retired to Sion House, which became the rallying point for Protestant English disaffected from Dutch William. He retaliated by having her guards removed. Mary made a final appeal and then dropped all relations with her sister, though she continued to see Anne's son, William, Duke of Gloucester, a lively and intelligent child but delicate and hydrocephalous. He was, however, the only heir any of them were likely to have.

Churchill had promised assistance to the proposed Jacobite expedition; so had Admiral Edward Russell (who had signed the Invitation), in the negative sense that he would keep the English fleet out of the way; he too was disillusioned with William. The new Jacobite expedition was very well organized. Louvois had died in the summer of 1691 and Louis was now ready to help his cousin once more. The French navy was to transport James and his army (mainly the recently re-formed Irish regiments) but Admiral de Tourville was ordered not to get into action with the English. William was in Flanders and it was hoped that Mary would not resist her father in arms. (A false hope, for Mary behaved 'like a second Queen Elizabeth' cheering on the fleet and the garrisons to meet what was represented as a French and popish threat to the nation.)

It was James's old enemy, the weather, which defeated him this time. Contrary winds delayed embarkation so long that the Dutch fleet effected a conjunction with the English, so that Russell was unable to keep out of sight, as planned. And when the combined fleets appeared off the coast of Normandy, nothing would stop Tourville, though inferior in numbers, from sailing out to give battle. It was a fatal move.

In the misty days of late May the French ships were driven inshore and James, standing on the cliffs of La Hogue, was forced to watch his hopes destroyed by his own English sailors. Yet seeing them swarm up the sides of a French vessel to fire her, patriotic pride overcame all other feelings and he was heard to exclaim, 'Oh, none but my brave English could do so brave an action!'

James was barely persuaded to leave his post of vantage before shot from the burning ship fell on the very place where he had been standing. It was still some time before he could be got to leave the coast and go back to St Germains, where the Queen was expecting another child, and impatient for his return.

James was present at the birth of this last child, a daughter, who was born on 28 June 1692 (new style) four years after the Prince of Wales. It was James himself who carried the baby, washed and swaddled, to his wife, saying, 'See what God has sent us for our consolation.' Louise Marie, *la consolatrice*, lived up to the name her father had given her; she was indeed a solace in their exile, a lovely and lively child, adoring and adored by all her family.

Maria was thirty-three when her daughter was born; James was fifty-eight. They had been married for nearly nineteen years and now he was as devoted to her as she was to him. The Prince of Wales turned out an intelligent and charming little boy; Jacobites called him the Blackbird, because of his dark hair and eyes, but he was fair skinned, as his father had been, not swarthy like Charles II. Pictures of him and pictures of all the royal family (with dogs) were soon circulating in England and Scotland. The Prince was not only obviously a Stuart but a boy everyone could be proud of as a future king, unlike Anne's poor little William, with his big head and unsteady gait.

The disappointment at La Hogue did not discourage James's English supporters, especially as William's campaign that year was unsuccessful and many English soldiers lost their lives in it. 'Will should have knotted and Mall gone to Flanders,' was the comment in England. (Mary had taken up knotting, a kind of crochet, to calm her nerves.) In fact the Jacobite cause took a new lease of life when Lord Middleton, imprisoned in the Tower but eventually released for lack of evidence, went over to France in 1693, where he soon became James's Secretary of State, more popular and more shrewd than Melfort, and not a Catholic. Middleton kept in close touch with the moderate Protestant supporters in England and his good sense and humour come out even in the Jacobite correspondence, which was increasing all the time, as were the pamphlets promoting the cause.

Another visitor at St Germains in 1693 was Lord Ailesbury, who took elaborate precautions to keep his visit secret, having himself carried into the castle in a curtained sedan chair. He had his own plan for a return and spent about three hours discussing it with James, who seemed to him little changed from what he had been five years ago at Whitehall. Before he left, the King sent for the little Prince of Wales and told him to embrace a very loyal and valued subject; Ailesbury was deeply moved. But when he talked of the King's coming over, he noted that James said abruptly, 'Over? Over? You know I cannot.'

Transport depended on King Louis and so Ailesbury sought an audience at Versailles; although they failed to agree on the viability of

[281]

the plan, Louis was impressed by Ailesbury's rank, riches and importance and did not realize that he was not one of the political hierarchy
who held the real power in England. In fact, Ailesbury disliked such
men, even Middleton, whom he suspected of dealings with Sunderland; he much preferred Lord Melfort (hated by everybody else) who
lent him a comfortable private chaise for his journey back to the coast
and thoughtfully stocked it with good wine, since the wine at French
inns was so bad.

In October this year (1693) James was sixty and although he felt it his
duty to be ready to return to England he left it to others to make the
plans and draft the declarations. His son Berwick said it became more
difficult to interest him in the details. Then too the Jacobites were
divided among themselves as to the best methods to pursue. 'The King
now perceived that the fewer friends he had left, the harder it was to
content them,' he wrote in the memoirs, '. . . there was no making a step
which did not displease many.' This is recognizably James's own style,
but in the later part of the *Life* the narrative is shaped more by the
compilers, who comment on the King's propensity for trusting the
untrustworthy and on his over-hasty decisions, as well as praising his
Christian resignation and refusal to allow any denigration of his
enemies in his presence.

La Hogue did not throw James into gloom and dejection, as some
have imagined. After that disaster, when he and Maria visited Chaillot,
the Mother Superior said how sorry she was that their prayers for his
success had not been granted. When James did not reply she thought
he had not heard and began to repeat it. 'Madame,' said James, 'I heard
very well what you said, and the reason why I made no reply was
because I was unwilling to contradict you, and be obliged to let you see I
am not of your opinion, who seem to think that what you ask'd was
better than what it pleased God to doe; whereas I think what he orders
is best and that indeed nothing is well done but what is done by him.'
He had learned resignation to the will of God at La Trappe and this
gave him an inner peace which no external events could shake.

The sudden death of his daughter Mary in December 1694, though
it revived the hopes of the Jacobites, was to James only a cause of
sorrow. He found it 'an additional affliction' that she seemed to have
died unrepentant. He had to see 'a child he had loved so tenderly

persever to her death in such a signal state of disobedience and disloyalty, and to hear her extoll'd and set out for it in the brightest colours, as the highest vertue, by the mercenary flatterers of those times,' who persuaded her it was her duty to sacrifice her parents to her religion. 'Thus she was cannonised for a sort of Paricide by usurpeing her Father's throne and sending him togather with the Queen and the Prince her brother to be vagabons in the world.' Because Mary had persisted in her usurpation to her death, James could not allow official mourning for her at St Germains, but privately he did mourn the sad end of the daughter he had loved so much.

Mary had not been a happy woman. The expedition to take over the throne of England had drawn William close to her but once he got back to Holland and his continental wars he returned to his old ways, accepting her devotion but showing emotional fondness only for his male friends; young Keppel was now the rising favourite. Although Mary had begun to realize that her action against her father had been widely blamed, her determination to stick to William was reinforced by an 'assassination plot' in August 1692, supposed to be arranged with the consent of King James, when a young French officer called Grandval was caught in William's camp, summarily tried, and executed by the *English* penalty for *treason* – hanging, disembowelling and quartering. (William actually had a medal struck depicting Grandval *in extremis*, to the disgust of the Victorian Agnes Strickland, who saw one.) Mary believed in her father's guilt and was deeply ashamed, imagining everyone was staring at her as the daughter of a murderer. As for James himself, to him this was just one more attempt to blacken his character; he never countenanced any such underhand attacks.

In the year 1693 Sunderland had persuaded William to turn to the Whigs, if he wanted Parliamentary support for his war; this had resulted in Mary's losing Lord Nottingham, on whom she had much relied, and having two Whigs put on her Council. In the spring of 1694 William doled out dukedoms to Shrewsbury, the Earl of Devonshire and the old Earl of Bedford in recognition of his son, the executed Lord Russell, hero of the Whigs. Mary could not get on with all this Whiggery and when William came back in the autumn he seemed to disapprove of everything she had done. That year he had succeeded rather better in the war and in consequence of his passing the Triennial

[283]

Bill, Parliament voted him all the supplies he needed for the next year's campaign.

Mary had been feeling ill for some time, on and off, but that December, after staying up late destroying papers, she collapsed and took to her bed. Small pox was diagnosed; in a week the dread disease ravaged her and she died in the small hours on the morning of Friday 28 December 1694. William astonished everyone by the depth of his grief; he shut himself up in his rooms and would see no one but Keppel.

As London was gripped in the worst winter for years, Mary's body was embalmed and the funeral had to wait till March; even then the roads were still snowbound when her body was borne, to the strange and ominous music for sackbuts (trombones) composed by Henry Purcell, to Westminster Abbey, where his beautiful mourning elegies were sung – 'Man that is born of woman hath but a short time to live.' (The composer died eight months later, only thirty-six, and the same music was performed for him.)

After Mary's death Sunderland persuaded William to make up the quarrel with Anne, whom many regarded as the true heir; her son William was certainly the Protestant successor. Anne, like her sister, had put on weight and she suffered from gout; she had to be carried into Kensington Palace in a chair, but the meeting was successful, both of them in tears for Mary whom neither had treated very well in life. William gave Anne Mary's jewels and St James's Palace, and took an active interest in his namesake's upbringing, though it was not till 1698 that he settled his education, appointing Marlborough his governor and Bishop Burnet as his religious instructor. By then peace had at last been concluded and France had officially recognized William III as King of England; so it was safe to give this court appointment to Marlborough. But in spite of this recognition of King William, the late King James was still living at St Germains.

16 The End of Exile

The last attempt to restore James before peace was made was planned for the beginning of the year 1696; a rising in England was to be concerted with the landing of the King and his forces from France. The insurrection was to be organized and commanded by Sir John Fenwick, the ex-general who had remained loyal to James.

Sir George Berkeley (or Barclay) was sent over with a commission from King James to raise men and at the last minute the Duke of Berwick crossed the channel to try to get the English Jacobites to rise before the French ships set out, according to King Louis' wishes. Berwick soon realized that this was impracticable; they dared not expose themselves to annihilation before ever King James landed. Berwick also discovered that Sir George Berkeley had become involved in an unauthorized sub-plot to kidnap William on his return from hunting, at Turnham Green. This plot, involving forty men who were to set upon William's guards, appeared rash and dangerous to Berwick but as he could not prevent it he crossed the Channel again and was driving to warn his father when his chaise broke down at Clermont. Here he found James himself, on his way to the coast. Alarmed at the news, James sent Berwick to Louis and himself went on to Calais to await developments.

Meanwhile, the kidnap plot was betrayed by Pendergast and La Rue (who were probably *agents provocateurs*); so William did not go hunting that day, many of the plotters were arrested (though Sir George Berkeley got away) and the government made the maximum capital out of the Assassination Plot, as they called it, and issued proclamations of those wanted for treason – with Berwick's name heading the list.

James waited at Calais till he received Louis' request to return and that was the end of the last attempt on England in his lifetime. He had not commissioned any assassination or kidnap plot and cashiered Sir George Berkeley when he turned up at St Germains. 'It was a more than usual trouble to the King,' he wrote in the memoirs, 'to see his

[285]

project broke, his hopes blasted and his friends ruin'd, by their pursuing methods contrary to his judgment and without his consent.'

Included in the *Life* is a relation by Sir George Berkeley, giving the King's actual commission 'to make war' on the usurper. When in England he was persuaded that to attack the Prince of Orange with his guards about him was allowable; he ends, 'Now I declare I never saw la Rue or Pendergast so as to know them.' He wrote this out and signed it at Paris, 4 August 1697.

At St Germains it was suspected that the whole episode was a 'contrivance' such as the Prince of Orange had 'ever found the best expedient to ward himself from the displeasure of the people'. This is certainly suggested by the enormous publicity given to something that never actually happened, and to the trials, which were pushed on so that the accused could be condemned before a new act became law which required more witnesses in treason cases. The trials were publicized, with portraits of the conspirators, in the German states which were William's allies.

Finally, there was the relentless pursuit of Sir John Fenwick, who was captured just as he was on the point of leaving the country. Although he had nothing to do with the Assassination Plot, he was accused of treason and when evidence failed he was attainted in Parliament – the last man to be so judicially murdered in England. During his incarceration in the Tower Fenwick had tried to delay his trial and condemnation (a foregone conclusion, as he warned his loving wife in letters which have survived) by naming Marlborough, Godolphin and others in correspondence with St Germains as privy to the insurrection plan. When the attainder was moved against Fenwick, Marlborough voted for his death. Godolphin absented himself.

Sir John Fenwick went to the scaffold on 28 January 1697, attended by Thomas White the non-juring Bishop of Peterborough, Anglican and loyal to King James to the last. (At Dunster Castle in Somerset there is, or was a few years ago, a portrait of his wife, Lady Mary – a Howard by birth – sadly holding up a miniature of Sir John, in remembrance.)

The Assassination Plot thus served William well. He got rid of several enemies and the English public was so shocked by this revelation of 'the late King James's' turpitude that William became, for a short time, almost popular. Especially when it appeared that he was at last willing to make peace with King Louis.

The peace negotiations were long drawn out but the treaty was finally ratified at Ryswick in the autumn of 1697. The news came to Fontainebleau just as James and Maria arrived for their annual visit, to the vexation of Louis XIV who, James felt, minded it more than he did. For the King of France, though he had recognized William as King of England, was determined this should make no difference to his friendship with King James.

During the negotiations James had felt it his duty to make a formal protest and try to secure an amnesty for his supporters. He also claimed Maria's 'appanage' as Queen; she had brought a large dowry and he argued that as he was treated as dead, she ought at least to have the jointure of a Queen Dowager. (Charles II's Queen Catherine, after staying several more years in England – on bad terms with Mary – had at last gone back to Portugal, where she ended her career, surprisingly, as Regent.)

James failed on all counts. As soon as peace was made William got a measure passed in Parliament against suspected Jacobites, including any who had merely gone to France during the war to see the late King. Ailesbury saw he would suffer if he stayed in England; he had already spent a year in the Tower and he had lost his wife. To save his considerable estates for his son he left England before the deadline and eventually settled in Brussels, where he married a Catholic and became a Catholic himself, living to a ripe old age and writing his memoirs nearly forty years after the Revolution.

Poorer Jacobites congregated round St Germains and became an increasing burden on the limited resources of the exiled King. He used to summon them to his closet (painted in green picked out with gold), talk to them about their families and affairs and as they left present them with a paper packet containing money. To one woman who came back in tears to thank him, he said it was nothing to what he owed her husband, wounded and invalided in his service.

His inability to help his followers was what caused James the most distress. Once he met some of his Scots officers who, knowing he could no longer support them, were enlisting in the French army as ordinary soldiers. James wrote down all their names in his pocket book, hoping

[287]

that one day he would be able to do something for them and then took off his hat to salute them with a low bow. Turning to leave, he was overcome once more and turned back to bow to them again – by this time, everyone was in tears.

As to Maria's appanage, it was actually voted to her by Parliament but William simply appropriated it to his own use; he did this in retaliation for Louis' refusal to banish James from France. In 1698 Bentinck (now Earl of Portland) was sent over as ambassador with a splendid train to impress the French with William's greatness. The French courtiers were duly impressed; success always impresses worldly people, just as failure draws scorn and belittlement – as the philosopher Leibnitz observed to Electress Sophia in 1690, apropos James's reputation. The first thing Bentinck mentioned in his first private audience with King Louis was the banishment of James, if not from France, at least from St Germains, which was too near England for comfort.

Bentinck wrote to William on 4 February 1698: 'He said that he could not imagine why I asked that he should remove King James; that he was so near a relation, that he was grieved for his misfortune, that he had liked him for so long, and that in honour he could not send him away.' And that was that.

Bentinck was annoyed to find that James was still treated as a King at the court of France. Twice the ambassador had to give up his intention of hunting because he was told 'the King of England' might be there; James had a standing invitation to hunt with the royal hounds and often did. The late King (as he was now called in England) further annoyed Bentinck by seeming not in the least embarrassed by his presence; on one occasion he sent the Prince of Wales over to talk to Bentinck's son. In fact he harboured no resentment against Bentinck, whom he regarded as William's subject, bound to be loyal to his master.

In Lord Portland's train had come a number of English Whigs who stared at the late King with hostile eyes, calling him old, lean and shrunken – he was then nearly sixty-five – and rejoiced that he was no longer in England. But nobody could help admiring the young Prince of Wales, then ten years old and a fine looking boy with fine manners, who might have become their king.

So even after the Peace of Ryswick James stayed on at St Germains. He became godfather to French royal infants and he and Maria assisted at the wedding of Louis' grandson; their children too were presented at court and much admired.

Bentinck went back to England, where he became increasingly alienated from the master he had served so devotedly. It was not so much that he was jealous of young Keppel, now made Earl of Albemarle (shades of Monck!) as that he was shocked at William's compromising his reputation – in Holland as well as in England – by allowing Keppel's familiarities. William maintained that there was 'no crime' but he refused to give up the young man's company and in the end Bentinck retired from court, married again and had a second English family; he outlived William by seven years, leaving large estates and heirs in both countries.

William had now achieved all the objects at which he had aimed in 1688, but only after a nine-year war which had ended with the situation much the same as when he had started it. Louis had given up the Flemish towns he had taken and had even agreed with William on a partition of the Spanish inheritance between the Bourbon and Habsburg heirs, when the childless and invalid King Carlos II of Spain should die. William had secretly arranged this, by-passing his old allies the Emperor and the Spanish government and ignoring his English ministers till all was settled with France – which caused great indignation in Parliament when it was discovered. But as soon as the Peace of Ryswick was made, Parliament had voted that King William must disband his huge 'standing army' and send away his Dutch Guards, although he had just changed their uniform from blue to English red. 'If I had a son, they would not use me so,' said William. But it was James who had the son.

In July 1700 James's grandson William, Duke of Gloucester died suddenly at the age of eleven. This loss of the Protestant hope for the future prompted William to make a secret proposal to adopt the Prince of Wales as his heir, provided he was sent over to England to be brought up there.

Many Jacobites then and later thought that James ought to have accepted this offer, to restore the legitimate line. But James believed in hereditary monarchy; the Prince could only lawfully succeed his father; to be adopted by the usurper was to owe his throne not to God but to Parliament, which had made itself the arbiter of the monarchy in

[289]

England. On this score James had refused the elective monarchy of Poland, which was offered to him in 1696; it was an honour, but he had no ambition for mere power. The English Crown was his by right and he had a responsibility for that traditional kingship. Besides this ideological reason, however, James had more personal objections. His son was only twelve; how could he hand him over to William and the treacherous makers of the Revolution? He refused.

That autumn he took his son to Fontainebleau for the first time; the young Prince enjoyed himself and charmed the French court with his liveliness and excellent manners. Maria told the nuns at Chaillot that she had never felt so well. 'The king my husband has also been perfectly well. He has been hunting almost every day and is growing fat. We have had the most beautiful weather in the world.'

James was then in much better health than William, so that there was open speculation as to whether his nephew might not be the first to die. If that were to happen James said he would go over to England at once, even if he went alone. It would be to claim the crown for his son rather than himself, for he felt his own life was drawing to a close.

'My life has been a sea of tempests and storms,' he had written in the papers he left for his son's guidance. The image is significant; the sea, with its storms and sudden changes, had dominated his working life and he had always drawn metaphors from it to describe the moral and political vicissitudes he had passed through. But now as the century turned there was a short stretch of calm weather before the last voyage.

In those papers James had left advice on the government of the three kingdoms of Great Britain, and he was one of the few kings who had actually lived and ruled in all three and knew the peoples and customs of each at first hand. He was very sure that the Scots and the Irish ought to keep their own Parliaments and that his own system of two Secretaries of State, alternating between London and their own capital cities, was the best. His attitude to Ireland is perhaps typically English in thinking that its development would have to come from England, but since he was determined that it too should enjoy freedom of religion, the improvements would benefit everybody.

James's warnings to his son on sexual sinfulness in princes (in themselves full of common sense, pointing out the rapacity and selfishness of most royal mistresses) have been more noticed than his advice on government and are mocked as obsessive by those who think he should have been repenting tyranny, bigotry, etc. But as his letters and memoirs show, James thought he had acted on principle, kept his word once given, and ruled in accordance with the laws of England as they then stood; even in suspending the religious penal laws he believed he was exercising the royal prerogative justly. But he had always known that adultery was a sin and he had continued to commit it after his conversion to the Catholic Church; therefore his repentance in old age and his anxiety for his son's future were quite natural. In fact, James III seems to have lived up to the standards set for him by his parents.

So did the Duke of Berwick, after starting rather as James had done, by marrying for love in 1695 the young widow of Patrick Sarsfield, Lord Lucan; she had been Honora de Burgh, daughter of Lord Clanricarde. James, who had wanted a greater match for Berwick, was at first displeased but was soon won over by the charm of his daughter-in-law. Honora already had a small son by Sarsfield; she had another by Berwick (afterward Duke of Liria) but then fell ill and died early in 1698, to his great grief. Two years later he married again, another exile, Anne Bulkeley, and they had a large family. James had hoped to get Berwick's brother Henry (known as the Grand Prior) into a naval career, but he was an unsatisfactory youth, quarrelsome and profligate, no good for anything; he died the year after his father, leaving a daughter by his marriage to a French lady.

James's plan for the education of his legitimate son has been criticized as too rigorous and over-supervised; he was never to be without an attendant. But this was essential for his safety and he was allowed to play with the children of the exiles. He visited his parents every morning and evening and his mother watched over his well-being devotedly, as her letters to Chaillot show. His Governor was the Earl of Perth, James Drummond, much better liked than his brother the Earl of Melfort. Stories were told of his generosity to poor Jacobites when quite a small child, for instance his giving all the money in his purse to some veterans he met when out for his drive. In the early portraits young James looks smiling and happy; it is sad to think of the long life ahead of him, full of frustration and disappointment.

Little Louise looks bright and happy too; everyone loved her. James

[291]

had a picture painted of her sitting beside him when she was really too small to sit, propped up like a little doll. Louise was a blessing to his old age, after the misery of his betrayal by his elder daughters, equally beloved as children.

Agnes Strickland tells a charming story of James and the child of one of the exiles. When she was naughty this little girl had been shut in a lobby by her mother, who did not realize there was an internal window which looked down into the king's closet. From his desk James saw a pathetic tearful face, fetched her down and kept her playing at his knee till her mother was sent for. When this had happened more than once, the puzzled mother wondered how it was that every time her daughter was shut up for naughtiness she found her with the King. Whereupon James smiled and nodded towards the window.

Stories of this kind show that at St Germains James was not plunged in gloomy resentment and religious melancholy, as he has often been represented. Nor did he make a parade of his penitence; Maria once caught sight of a discipline accidentally left out (a form of penance then still in use but usually only for monks) and recorded that she had never seen him so embarrassed.

Life at St Germains was orderly and economically managed, but it was still royal. That gossip, Anthony Hamilton, thought it gloomy, but even he remarked in a letter on the bevy of lovely girls growing up there, who amused themselves with picnics and mild entertainments. There were visits to Versailles, to Saint Cloud, Marly, and Fontainebleau; James went hunting still and to the *carrousels*, or military reviews, which Louis held – though now he was inclined to shake his head over the vanity of human ambitions and wars. Masses were said every year for Charles; James and Maria often talked of his kindness with affection. Maria kept in touch with Charlotte, Lady Lichfield and other English friends. The old English servants were kept on and regularly paid; the valet Dupuy outlived the master he had followed on land and sea from early youth; Maria mentions the good old man in a letter.

So the last years of the century passed quietly for James, though with an undertone of sadness for the loss of England, the country he had loved so much, and worked so hard for, all his life. And then on Friday 4 March 1701, the King was in the chapel at St Germains listening to the 'Lamentations of Jeremias the Prophet', when he heard the words (sung in Latin): *Remember, Lord, what is come upon us: consider and behold our reproach. Our inheritance is turned to strangers, our house to aliens.* He fell forward in a dead faint and though after a few hours he seemed to have recovered, a week later, while he was dressing, he had a stroke which affected his right hand and side.

He was devotedly cared for by his loving wife and recovered enough to be sent to the baths at Bourbon, at Louis' insistence, in the summer. They spent several weeks there and James's condition improved a good deal. On the way home they visited Paray-le-Monial, the Visitation Convent where Sister Marguerite Marie had her vision of the Sacred Heart. Maria took part in the Corpus Christi procession, carrying a lighted candle; James could only watch from a balcony.

At last they got home, eager to see the beloved children again, who had written to them while they were away. Young James was just thirteen, Louise was nine. For the rest of the summer James seemed to be recovering; he was able to walk on the terraces, holding his wife's arm, dragging his right leg a little. Sometimes he even got on horseback again. But he did not feel equal to going to Fontainebleau that autumn, though he wanted Maria to go and take the Prince of Wales. As if she would have left him!

Then on Friday 2 September James once more fell in a faint in the chapel. The next day he seemed better but on the Sunday he had a bad fit and vomited a quantity of blood. The Prince of Wales was brought in and burst into tears at the sight of him. 'The king with a sort of contentedness in his looks stretched forth his arms to embrace him.' James began talking to his son so vehemently that people tried to stop him, but he pleaded, 'Do not take away my son till I have given him my blessing at least.' He thought, and everyone else thought, that he was already dying. When the Blessed Sacrament was carried in, to give him Viaticum, 'he cry'd out, the happy day is come at last.'

This is the account in the *Life*, which adds, 'All this while the poor queen, not able to support herself, was shrunk down on the ground by the bedside, in much greater anguish and in as little sign of life as he; the King was sensibly touched to see her in such excessive grief and seem'd to suffer more on her account than any other; he sayd what he could to comfort her, and to be as resigned in that as she was in all other things to the will of God.' But she only recovered a little when she

[293]

began to hope, by his passing a good night, that he might not be going to die after all.

King Louis came to visit his cousin, descending from his coach at the gate to avoid disturbing him with noise. Madame of Orléans (Liselotte, daughter of James's cousin the Prince Palatine, Rupert's elder brother) also came and wrote on 8 September: 'I found King James in a piteous state. His voice, it is true, was still as strong as usual, and he recognized people; but he looks very bad and has a beard like a Capuchin.'

Soon even the Queen's hopes vanished as James grew weaker. She was beside his bed 'in a sort of agonie too, which the King perceiving was concern'd of and notwithstanding his weak condition sayd, Madam, do not afflict yourself; I am going (I hope) to be happy. To which the Queen reply'd, Sir, I doubt it not, and therefore it is not your condition I lament, it is my own.' She was ready to faint away and the King told those present to carry her from the room.

James took a fortnight to die. On Tuesday 13 September King Louis came again and announced that he would recognize James's son as King of England. Everybody burst into tears and cries of gratitude; there was so much noise that James's now feeble voice could not be heard.

Next day, rallying again, he embraced the Prince and told him he had sent Lord Middleton to Marly to thank the King of France. Louis' gesture meant that James could die knowing that his son's claim would be supported by the powerful King of France, and his family cared for. Incidentally the sceptical, humorous Lord Middleton was so impressed by what James said to him on his deathbed that he later made a retreat and became a Catholic, in spite of fearing (rightly) that it would do no good to the Jacobite cause in England.

Because he knew he was dying James was anxious that the two principals of those who had most injured him should know that he had forgiven them: the Emperor and William of Orange. They were to be written to and told. So was the Princess Anne; Maria promised to write to her and the letter, dated 27 September 1701, is printed in the *Life*. In it she recorded that James

some few days before his death, bid me find means to let you know that he forgave you from the bottom of his heart, and prayed God to do so too; that he gave you his last blessing, and prayed God to convert your heart, and confirm you in the resolution of repairing to his son the wrongs done to himself; to which I shall only add, that I join my prayers to his herein, with all my heart, and that I shall make it my business to inspire into the young man who is left in my care the sentiments of his father, for better no man can have.

James was now sinking every day but remained attentive for the mass, which was said daily in his room. He had reaffirmed his faith, received the Last Sacraments, and sank slowly and quietly into unconsciousness. The tempests and storms were over and gone, for now he was going to the safe harbour of Christ, whose call had cost him almost all he had and the crown of three kingdoms, but who had given him back love in hundredfold from wife and children, servants and friends, and would now receive him into the kingdom that has no end.

At last, on Friday 16 September 1701, at three in the afternoon, the hour of the Lord's death, at which he had been accustomed to pray for a happy death himself, he died in silence and peace.

Afterwards

William lived only six months longer than James. He died after falling from his horse (said to have been Sir John Fenwick's horse, Sorrel) and breaking his collar bone, but his health had been extremely bad for a long time. The day before he died he signed the Act of Attainder and Abjuration against the son of James II, which meant that the boy was liable to the death penalty if he ever set foot in England. He had already been excluded from the throne by the Act of Succession in 1701, which secured the Crown, after Anne, to the next Protestant heir, Sophia Electress of Hanover (youngest daughter of Elizabeth, the Winter Queen) and her son George, cutting out all Catholics.

Anne became Queen in 1702 without any trouble and indeed with some rejoicing from those who had always disliked being ruled by Dutch William. But William's foreign policy was followed, so that England was soon committed to a second war with France, the war of the Spanish Succession, in which Marlborough at last came into his own, winning a series of victories which ensured his fame, though the Allies did not succeed in ousting Louis XIV's grandson Philip from the throne of Spain, thanks largely to the generalship of Marlborough's nephew, James's son the Duke of Berwick, who became a great Marshal of France and a peer of Spain.

The younger James made an unsuccessful attempt on Scotland in 1708 when he was barely twenty and after it joined in the European war as the Chevalier de St George. Considerable Jacobite traffic was still going on with England when the Peace of Utrecht was made in 1713 and James was forced to leave France; the ageing King Louis, broken by the deaths of his son and grandson, which left him with an infant as heir, could no longer support the claims of the Pretender.

In England Queen Anne had at last rebelled against the intolerable arrogance of Sarah, Duchess of Marlborough, the Marlboroughs went out of favour and the Jacobites began to hope that the younger James might succeed her after all, but the plans were bungled as usual and

[296]

when the Queen died in 1714, Marlborough and Shrewsbury were able to bring in George of Hanover without any difficulty.

Louis XIV died in 1715 and the Regent Philippe of Orléans (son of Monsieur and Liselotte) was not prepared to support the Stuart cause. Partly in consequence the restoration attempt of that year (the Fifteen) was a failure and the third James, after some wanderings, settled down in Rome for the rest of his long life – he did not die till new year's day 1766, an old man of seventy-seven. His mother had stayed on in France, retiring to Chaillot. Her daughter Louise Marie died at nineteen in 1712. Maria never met her son's wife, Clementina Sobieski, or saw her grandsons, Charles Edward and Henry (afterwards Cardinal of York and the last of the family to die, in 1807) for she died herself in 1718 at the age of sixty. Madame (Liselotte) used to visit her at Chaillot and missed her quietly cheerful company; chastened by the years, she thought Maria more of a saint than James (whom she had laughed at in 1689 for his stammer), though she now acknowledged his goodness too, because he had borne his misfortunes so patiently.

James's body had been embalmed and stood coffined but not buried in the church of the English Benedictines in the Rue St Jacques, awaiting a funeral in Westminster Abbey which never happened. Instead, at the French Revolution, the mob broke into the church, smashing and desecrating statues and tombs alike. It was reported that they opened the coffin of the old King of England, dead nearly a hundred years, and found his body incorrupt, with a long white beard. Earlier generations of the Parisian people, who had treated it as the shrine of a saint, would have been confirmed in their veneration, but to the revolutionaries kings and saints alike were hated and James's body disappeared, so that no one knows where his mortal remains ended. He would not have minded that, since he had deliberately chosen to sacrifice all that he had in this world for the sake of the kingdom of heaven.

As James II and VII never returned to England and as his son never succeeded in regaining the throne, the history of the Revolution of 1688 was written by those who made it, and in order to justify themselves James's intentions and acts were misrepresented and exaggerated and, as the generation which knew him died out, his character was traduced and slandered till he became indeed 'black

[297]

as hell' as he had complained in his farewell letter of December 1688.

This tradition of the bigot and tyrant, cruel, stupid and humourless, received considerable reinforcement in the heyday of Parliamentary government and expanding empire at the hands of Lord Macaulay, so favourite an historian among the Victorians.

But now that Catholics and Protestants are rediscovering their common Christianity in a secular and sceptical world, is it too much to hope that, three hundred years after his brief reign, justice might be done to the first ruler of Britain to bring in Liberty of Conscience for all?

Notes on Sources

All the sources used in this biography are printed, though many are not readily available, since no modern editions have been published. Fortunately I found them all in the Bath Reference Library and my thanks are due to the Librarians, who allowed me easy access to them and to the volumes of the Historical Manuscripts Commission, Stuart State Papers, Somers' Tracts and other collections, and the modern editions of Evelyn's and Pepys's Diaries.

The Life of James II, edited by James Stanier Clarke, 1816. Clarke was the Prince Regent's Librarian (the same who corresponded with Jane Austen) and in his preface gives a full account of how the manuscript *Life* came into the Regent's hands in the course of the Napoleonic Wars, after the death of Henry Stuart, Cardinal of York, in 1807. The *Life* itself was compiled after James's death (1701) by one or more of his secretaries (Dicconson is usually credited) under the supervision of the widowed Queen and her son. It was based on James's own memoirs 'writ in his own hand' and much of it, especially the earlier part, is a straight transcription. James kept journals, or records of his experiences, from 1652 when he first took service in the French army under Marshal Turenne. Some time after the Restoration his first wife, Anne Hyde, copied them out, putting them into a more historical form. This early journal received unexpected authentication in 1954 when David Randall of Indiana University discovered in France a manuscript volume of these campaigns *'tirées mot pour mot des mémoires de Jacques Stuart'*. The preface was written by Cardinal de Bouillon, a nephew of Henri de la Tour d'Auvergne, Vicomte de Turenne, the great Marshal. The Cardinal told how he had met King James in 1695 at Saint-Germain-en-Laye and after hearing his reminiscences, begged him to record them; whereupon James said he had already done so and would get his secretaries to extract the relevant parts and translate them into

[299]

French. This was done and the resulting volume was presented to the Cardinal in January 1696, on condition it was not published during the King's lifetime. Although a curtailed and altered version was published in 1735 in Andrew Ramsay's *Vie de Turenne*, the original manuscript remained forgotten in the family archives till its discovery in 1954, when its sale paid for repairing the roof of the château. It was then translated and edited by A. Lytton Sells, who collated it with the *Life* and found it corresponded so closely that much of it could be printed in the *Life*'s version, in James's own English. As the French version is written in the first person, perhaps the third person narrative (*his R.H.* etc) is the creation of the compilers of the *Life*.

This discovery changed the attitude of historians to the *Life*, which had previously been pronounced spurious by Whig writers who thought James too stupid to have written memoirs himself. Suspicion is still cast on the later parts, though the compilers put '*Mems*' in the margin, with quotation marks, and the style is recognizable to anyone who has read many of the extant letters. James's style is blunt, natural, even colloquial, with touches of ironic humour and characteristic phrases. In quoting these passages I have referred to them as 'in the memoirs'.

The original memoirs 'writ in his own hand' were bound into nine volumes and lodged for safety at the Scots College in Paris (a seminary for Catholic students for the priesthood, during penal times). Here they were seen by James Macpherson, who published in 1775 a collection of *Original Papers*, taken from papers preserved by Nairne, one of the secretaries at St Germains, and others collected in the earlier part of the eighteenth century by Carte. Both Carte and Macpherson saw original memoirs and papers written by James and made extracts from them. Macpherson added some papers he had found at Oxford, mostly concerning the affair of the Fellows of Magdalen College. During the French Revolution the nine volumes were taken to St Omers (a school for English Catholics) to be transported to safety, but it seems that they were burned, in a panic, by a Frenchwoman. Therefore, so far as we know, all that remains of them is in the *Life* (and/or Macpherson's *Original Papers*) but that is sufficient to give James's own view of the many crises of his eventful life.

Before Macpherson published the papers, there was printed in 1765 the diary of Henry Hyde, second Earl of Clarendon (and James's brother-in-law) for the years just before and after 1688; together with some of his correspondence and some papers belonging to Archbishop Sancroft, with notes on crucial interviews between the bishops and the King. Clarendon's own dealings with William of Orange throw a good deal of light on what was going on in 1688.

In 1771 Sir John Dalrymple, a Scots Whig, published a history dealing with the period 1660–92. It was no sooner done than new sources were opened to him from the royal archives, including the strong-box containing King William's private papers, among which were a great many letters from James. Dalrymple published these (and other letters to William) in 1773 in a much larger volume as an Appendix to his history; hence the references in nineteenth-century books to 'Dalrymple's Appendix'. He also included many despatches of the French Ambassador Barillon, with translations which I have used in quotations as they are nearer in style to the English of the period. But Dalrymple 'modernized' the seventeenth-century spelling in (for instance) James's letters.

Fifty-four Letters from James, Duke of York to William, Prince of Orange from October 1678 to November 1679 are printed by the *Historical Manuscripts Commission* (15th Report, Appendix Part V, Savile Foljambe Mss, 1897) and these are given in the original spelling. Another publication of the Historical MSS Commission (1897) (15th Report, Appendix Part VIII) contains 109 letters from James to the Earl of Queensberry, from June 1682 to July 1685, the few after his accession written in the same personal style as before it. As well as showing his interest in Scottish affairs they contain comments on the Rye House–Monmouth Plot, much as those written to William, but even more bluntly expressed. James's letters to his niece Charlotte, Countess of Lichfield are printed in Volume 58 of *Archaeologia*. (Both these last sources I owe to Mary O'Regan, Law Librarian to the City of Leeds, who has listed all the sources for James's letters.)

The Stuart Papers: the Calendar of State Papers from which I have taken James's account of the Great Seal (1693), his warrants, etc issued in Dublin, letters to foreign courts during his last exile and some letters from Abbot de Rancé of La Trappe.

Mary of Modena (Maria Beatrice d'Este): her letters and her

reminiscences to the nuns at Chaillot are taken from *The Lives of the Queens of England* by Agnes Strickland (revised edition 1883) also useful for Mary and Anne (Volumes 4–6). Strickland consulted archives in France, England and Scotland and has some amusing footnotes reprimanding Lord Macaulay for his omissions in this respect. Quotations from Maria's letters to Modena and from her secretaries etc are taken from Carola Oman's biography, *Mary of Modena* (1962).

Gilbert Burnet's *History of his Own Time*, published after his death in 1715, is not reliable, since he was politically involved in the 1688 Revolution and often changes his presentation of events as the situation changed around him. For this reason the unpublished parts of his writings are of particular interest; they were edited by H. C. Foxcroft in 1902 as *A Supplement to Burnet's History of His Own Time*.

Somers' Tracts: This was a collection made by John Somers (Baron Somers 1697) a lawyer who became Lord Chancellor in William's reign and continued to be important in Anne's, of pamphlets of the period, which were edited by Walter Scott (who also advised J. S. Clarke on the *Life*). Volumes 9, 10 and 11, in particular contain a mass of writings on political and religious controversies showing how people at the time thought about the issues and the persons concerned in the 1688 Revolution. Unfortunately they are too verbose to be quoted extensively.

More information about the politicians of William's reign than I could well use is to be found in *The Correspondence of Charles Talbot, Duke of Shrewsbury*, edited by William Coxe, Archdeacon of Wilts, published in 1821.

The pastoral letter of the Roman Catholic bishops in 1688 is taken (together with information on Catholic ecclesiastical affairs and persons) from Dom Basil Hemphill's *The Early Vicars Apostolic of England* (1954).

The Enigma of James II by Malcolm V. Hay (London 1938) besides putting a good case for James, quotes from contemporary correspondence in the Blairs Archives and other sources. Hay elucidates the misunderstandings of James's religious policy which have been derived from Ambassador Barillon's reports to Louis XIV, and tracks his reputation in Scotland, etc.

Nathaniel, Lord Crewe, Bishop of Durham by C. E. Whiting (1940) is a detailed biography of the Anglican bishop who supported James till 1688, quoting diaries and letters of others, which I have used.

Lord Chancellor Jeffreys and the Stuart Cause by G. W. Keeton (1965) is a study by a lawyer expert in legal history and state trials which quotes much contemporary material on the issues of the day.

The Letters of Queen Anne, edited by Beatrice Curtis Brown (2nd edition 1968). Spelling, etc has been modernized.

The Diary of John Evelyn edited by E. S. de Beer (1959). This is the one-volume edition compressed from six of this modern scholar's work, which I also consulted for his notes, etc.

The Diary of Samuel Pepys edited by Robert Lathom and William Matthews. This massive modern edition has also been consulted but some of the quotations are taken from earlier editions in my possession. Quotations from Pepys's letters after the period of the diary are taken from Arthur Bryant's detailed three-volume biography: *The Man in the Making*, *The Years of Peril*, and *The Saviour of the Navy*.

The Journal of James Yonge, Plymouth Surgeon (1647–1721) edited by F. N. L. Poynter (1963) from which is quoted his account of King James's reception of the Papal Nuncio. Yonge also provides a lot of background information on naval and medical life.

William and Mary by Henri and Barbara van der Zee, Dutch husband and English wife, (1973). I found this useful for William's activities, as Dutch archives are quoted. Also useful were the relevant chapters of *The Bentincks: The History of a European Family* by Paul-Emile Schazmann, translated by Steve Cox, (1976).

Mary II Queen of England by Hester W. Chapman (1953) gives quotations from Mary's letters and memoirs. Her book on the second Duke of Buckingham, *Great Villiers* (1949), gives a sympathetic portrait of this flamboyant character.

Enigmas of History by Hugh Ross Williamson (1957) contains an account of Sir John Fenwick with quotations from his letters to his wife from the Tower, useful for the 1696 Jacobite Plot. Entirely devoted to that plot is *The Triumphs of Providence* by Jane Garrett (1980). *Impostor at the Bar* by George Campbell (1961) traces the career of William Fuller, an informer who produced pamphlets on the substitute Prince in *1696*; the Williamites were still flogging this old story as late as this.

[303]

The Killing of Justice Godfrey by Stephen Knight (1984) concerns the murder of Sir Edmond Bury Godfrey in 1678.

The Marshal Duke of Berwick by Sir Charles Petrie (1953) is a life of James's illegitimate son by Arabella Churchill, which quotes his memoirs. His book *The Great Tyrconnel* (1972) is a life of Richard Talbot, Earl, later Duke of Tyrconnel; James's letter to him in 1689 is quoted from this book.

Charles Middleton: the Life and Times of a Restoration Politician by George Hilton Jones (1967) uses State Papers which clarified for me what the Regency Council was doing in December 1688, as well as the activities of the secretaries of state of the period.

The History of the Popes by Ludwig von Pastor, translated by Dom Ernest Graf, Vol XXXII (translation published in 1940) has a small section on James II (and his 'imprudence' etc).

Claude de la Colombière by Margaret Yeo (1940). Life of the French Jesuit, confessor to St Margaret Mary (Sacred Heart visionary) who was chaplain to Maria in 1678.

The Lords of Cobham Hall by Esme Wingfield-Stratford (1959) contains information about Frances Stuart who married Charles Stuart, Duke of Richmond; also about Edward Hyde, Viscount Cornbury (who led the desertions from the army in 1688) the son of Henry Hyde, second Earl of Clarendon, brother of James's first wife Anne Hyde.

The King's Friend by Cyril Hughes Hartmann (1951) is a life of Charles Berkeley, Viscount Fitzhardinge and Earl of Falmouth; he was James's friend too and was killed beside him in the sea battle of 1665.

Sacharissa (Dorothy Sidney, Countess of Sunderland) by Julia Cartwright (n.d) contains the letters during the Exclusion crisis from which I have quoted.

The Life and Loyalties of Thomas Bruce, Earl of Ailesbury by the Earl of Cardigan (1951).

Guglielma: Wife of William Penn by L. V. Hodgkin (1947).

Edmond Halley by Angus Armitage (1966).

Sir Christopher Wren by Bryan Little (1975)

The Monmouth Episode by Bryan Little (1956). I have quoted facts and figures from this carefully researched account.

Cold Caleb by Cecil Price (1956) (*The scandalous Life of Ford Grey,*

First Earl of Tankerville 1655–1701) – Monmouth's friend who made confessions about Rye House and the Rebellion of 1685 and became a prominent Whig peer under William.

In this list I have not included works of modern historians, only books from which I have taken facts or quotations. But I must make mention of *James II, Soldier and Sailor* by Jock Haswell (1972) because he has so successfully illuminated the subject of seventeenth-century warfare on land and sea, which was certainly of central concern to James II.

Index